ETHICS AND MANIPULATION IN ADVERTISING

ETHICS AND MANIPULATION IN ADVERTISING

Answering a Flawed Indictment

Michael J. Phillips

Q

QUORUM BOOKS
Westport, Connecticut • London

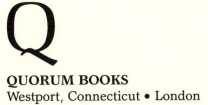

Library of Congress Cataloging-in-Publication Data

Phillips, Michael J.
   Ethics and manipulation in advertising : answering a flawed
indictment / Michael J. Phillips.
         p.   cm.
   Includes bibliographical references and index.
   ISBN 1-56720-063-X (alk. paper)
   1. Advertising—Psychological aspects. 2. Advertising—Moral and
ethical aspects. 3. Manipulative behavior. 4. Consumer behavior.
I. Title.
HF5822.P49   1997
659.1'01'9—dc21   96-40911

British Library Cataloguing in Publication Data is available.

Library of Congress Catalog Card Number: 96-40911
ISBN: 1-56720-063-X

First published in 1997

Quorum Books, 88 Post Road West, Westport, CT 06881
An imprint of Greenwood Publishing Group, Inc.

Printed in the United States of America

The paper used in this book complies with the
Permanent Paper Standard issued by the National
Information Standards Organization (Z39.48-1984).

10 9 8 7 6 5 4 3 2 1

CONTENTS

PREFACE

This book discusses and critically analyzes an attack on advertising that has been a permanent feature of American intellectual life since at least the 1930s. Briefly put, the attack says that advertising manipulates consumers, and that this manipulation justifies corrective political action. This attack's influence waxes and wanes, but it is never without adherents. It finds support because it is initially plausible, and because many people find its political conclusions congenial. By and large, however, there is little to support this assault on advertising. Advertising almost certainly does not manipulate as well as its critics believe.

This book's aim, then, is to undermine a critique of advertising that emphasizes its manipulativeness. Chapter 1 opens by developing that critique and the political agenda it has inspired. This agenda ranges from modest recommendations for increased regulation of certain ads, through proposals to limit the volume of advertising, to John Kenneth Galbraith's ambitious program for a less consumerist America. After developing this book's conception of the term "manipulative advertising," the chapter observes that because advertising's manipulativeness might be a good thing—by hypothesis it keeps the economy humming, after all—its critics badly need a moral argument to justify their political agenda. Without such an argument, that agenda is a complete non sequitur even if advertising's powers are enormous. Advertising's traditional critics, many of whom were economists and implicit utilitarians, usually were not too articulate about the moral underpinnings of their work. But with the emergence of the business ethics movement in the 1970s and 1980s, moral arguments for manipulative advertising's badness finally became available.

Chapters 2 and 3 examine the ethicists' arguments on the assumption that advertising manipulates as well as its critics believe. These chapters consider how manipulative advertising fares under three well-known ethical theories (utilitarianism, Kant's categorical imperative, and virtue ethics) and one widely accepted ethical value (autonomy). Chapters 2 and 3 conclude that, although the utilitarian arguments against manipulative advertising are inconclusive, there are other moral grounds for adjudging it wrong if it works. But does manipulative advertising really manipulate? Employing empirical work and informed speculation of various kinds, chapters 4 and 5 maintain that manipulative advertising does not work especially well. (This of course does not mean that it is powerless or useless to business.) Chapter 4 reaches this conclusion about manipulative advertising's ability to dictate consumer choice among products and services, and chapter 5 reaches the same conclusion about advertising's stimulation of the propensity to consume.

As one might expect, chapters 4 and 5 have implications for the ethical conclusions reached in chapters 2 and 3. They vitiate all the earlier moral arguments against manipulative advertising except one argument based on Kant's categorical imperative. In chapter 6, I try to dispose of that last ethical argument. Its elimination also eliminates the last advertising-related rationale for the more ambitious portions of the critics' agenda. I say "advertising-related" because the failure of the critics' assault on manipulative advertising does not necessarily doom these far-reaching proposals. But it *does* preclude using advertising's manipulativeness to justify them. On the other hand, nothing in the book necessarily argues against the piecemeal regulation of particular manipulative ads.

This book does not consider whether advertising's other allegedly noxious attributes—for example, its tastelessness, its omnipresence, or its effect on the mass media—might justify its regulation. In addition, the book examines only the ethical theories or values employed in the business ethics literature on manipulative advertising. Despite my legal training, moreover, the book does not consider whether the regulation of manipulative advertising might offend the First Amendment. My concern is with the *ethical* implications of advertising's asserted manipulativeness. (And if enough influential Americans become convinced that advertising's manipulativeness justifies political controls of one kind or another, American constitutional law most likely will follow their lead.) Furthermore, the book makes only scattered references to a conception of advertising residing 180 degrees away from the vision propounded by advertising's critics. This, briefly, is the view that advertising is information; that consumers respond to it rationally; and that it therefore is a powerful force for competition, efficiency, and abundance. I give this view relatively short shrift because my concerns lie elsewhere and because I am unpersuaded by it. I differ from this advertising-as-information view in thinking that there are forms of advertising to which the label "manipulative" fairly applies. I differ from critics of this manipulative advertising in denying that it manipulates very well.

Although I am not an expert in the philosophical, economic, and marketing matters this book considers, I doubt whether this lack matters much. My presentation of the various ethical theories is, and need only be, rudimentary. The theories' application to manipulative advertising does not require philosophical abilities of a high order. Because I conclude that manipulative advertising does not work very well, I largely am spared the philosophers' problem of adjudicating among the theories. As for the economic and marketing literature on advertising, I do not perform or critique such studies, but merely report them. Due to the vast amount of relevant work, of course, that report is not exhaustive.

This book tries to tie together several distinct branches of knowledge as they apply to advertising. If such books require professional training in all the relevant disciplines, few will ever be written. Such integrative efforts are needed not only to offset the one-sidedness of single-discipline books, but also to avoid their tendency to make casual assumptions about matters that are contentious outside the discipline. Although economists frequently praise or condemn advertising, for example, the utilitarian assumptions that usually underlie their evaluations rarely are developed or even made articulate. This means that those utilitarian evaluations do not consider or confront evaluations of advertising from other ethical perspectives. Worse yet, as chapters 2 and 4 suggest, it sometimes appears as if economists' economic/utilitarian arguments are influenced by those other perspectives. As for business ethicists, their pronouncements about advertising often make factual assumptions about the very issues disputed by economists and other social scientists. The usual assumption, of course, is that manipulative advertising works quite well in one or both of the senses described earlier.

The failure of this assumption has a further implication. Critics of consumerism who urge a transformation of American society should stop relying on advertising's manipulativeness to justify their position. Too often, I think, that assumption is both an implicit substitute for moral argument (as if consumerism's illegitimacy and the new society's superiority follow from it), and a tacit justification for the critics' paternalism (as if manipulation by business validates manipulation for supposedly better ends). As I suggest in chapter 1, neither conclusion follows even if advertising manipulates as well as its critics believe. And while there are moral arguments for each conclusion, it turns out that manipulative advertising does not manipulate too well. This is not, of course, to say either that a consumerist life is the best life and no alternatives are conceivable, or that paternalism is always wrong. But it is to say that advertising's asserted manipulativeness cannot aid those who would argue the contrary.

Chapter 1

THE INDICTMENT OF
MANIPULATIVE ADVERTISING

Early in the first Reagan administration, Robert Heilbroner critiqued supply-side economics in the *New York Review of Books*.[1] One of his themes was capitalism's moral instability. According to Heilbroner, capitalism displaces traditional values and instills commercial ones in their stead. The main culprit in this unhealthy process, he thought, is advertising.

> If I were asked to name the deadliest subversive force within capitalism—the single greatest source of its waning morality—I should without hesitation name advertising. How else should one identify a force that debases language, drains thought, and undoes dignity? If the barrage of advertising, unchanged in its tone and texture, were devoted to some other purpose—say the exaltation of the public sector—it would be recognized in a moment for the corrosive element that it is. But as the voice of the private sector it escapes this startled notice.[2]

To Heilbroner, in sum, advertising erodes the virtues and habits of mind on which capitalism depends.

Some months later, the *Business and Society Review* asked some advertising industry leaders and other assorted observers to comment on Heilbroner's remarks.[3] For the most part, these people did not address Heilbroner's specific moral indictment of advertising.

Instead, they made some familiar defenses and criticisms of the institution. Thus, the industry people maintained that advertising makes our economic system work more effectively by giving consumers the information they need to make informed product choices, thereby promoting competition and innovation and opening up concentrated industries. Advertising has these effects, they felt, because consumers evaluate it rationally and act on that evaluation.

Other commentators, however, dissented on the last point. Representative Millicent Fenwick remarked, "I have heard [advertising] criticized for overpromoting consumer appetites and for a consequent materialism, and perhaps there is a grain of truth in these criticisms."[4] George Gerbner, a communications professor at the University of Pennsylvania, went further. "Advertising," he said, is "one of the . . . principal socializing forces of our species. Ads mobilize publics on behalf of the institutions using them."[5] Preeminent among those institutions, of course, are business firms of all kinds. According to International Association of Machinists and Aerospace Workers president William Winpisinger, therefore, advertising's "major function and purpose has been to feed already bloated corporate beasts. They've discovered that the only way they can keep their revenues up is by paying exorbitant sums to advertising professionals who combine art and psychology to exploit and manipulate the vast range of human fears and needs."[6]

This book critically analyzes the familiar indictment of advertising that springs from Fenwick's, Gerbner's, and (especially) Winpisinger's remarks. Stated simply, the indictment is that advertising *manipulates* the people exposed to it, that this manipulation is a bad thing, and that the political system should do something about it. In this chapter, I set out the main elements of the indictment, developing two important ways in which advertising is said to manipulate the public, sketching the wide range of political steps such manipulation has been asserted to justify, and identifying and describing the kinds of advertising that might plausibly be regarded as manipulative. I conclude by asking why this manipulative advertising should be considered a problem. This query raises a question considered at length in chapters 2 and 3: assuming that it works, why is manipulative advertising wrong?

THE INDICTMENT

In post–World War II America, John Kenneth Galbraith reigns as *the* critic of manipulative advertising. His most important and wide-ranging attack on that institution came in 1958 with publication of *The Affluent Society*. In that book, Galbraith described advertising as one element within a process he called the dependence effect.[7] The dependence effect is the creation of consumer wants by the productive process that also satisfies those wants. According to Galbraith, this can occur through emulation, in which *A*'s desire to keep abreast or ahead of *B* makes *A* desire goods produced and sold to *B*. But the most direct link between production and consumer wants is created by advertising, whose main function is to create desires that did not previously exist.

In a footnote to his chapter on the dependence effect, Galbraith remarked that advertising also is important in competitive strategy.[8] Ten years later, this hint was developed in his *The New Industrial State*.[9] Like *The Affluent Society*, *The New Industrial State* rejected the orthodox notion of consumer sovereignty, in which instruction flows from the individual to the market to the producer. In the portions of the economy dominated by large corporations, Galbraith maintained, this accepted sequence is being replaced by the revised sequence.[10] In the revised sequence, producing firms control their markets and also manage the market behavior and shape the social attitudes of those they ostensibly serve. One way in which large corporations control their markets is through the management of specific demand, which includes the quantity of the firm's products bought by consumers. Firms manage specific demand through processes such as product design, sales strategy, packaging, model change, and (apparently most important) advertising. Although some of this advertising is informative, much of it builds brand loyalties and attracts new customers through nonrational appeals. Because all competitors within an industry must play this game and many possess the resources to play it successfully, a rough equilibrium eventually results among the survivors.

Despite its new emphasis on advertising's competitive impact, *The New Industrial State* did not slight its ability to stimulate consumption as such. The management of demand, Galbraith said, creates "a relentless propaganda on behalf of goods in general."[11] The result is that "while goods become ever more abundant they do not seem to be any less important. On the contrary it requires an act of will to imagine that anything else is so important."[12] Were things different—were the techniques of persuasion not so pervasive and so strong—increasing abundance might have made people less interested in acquiring more goods. But "[t]he consequence—a lower and less reliable propensity to consume—would have been awkward for the industrial system."[13]

According to Galbraith, therefore, advertising manipulates people in two distinguishable ways. First, it effectively makes people consumers by creating a propensity to consume. Second, it helps direct the product and brand choices those consumers make. He evidently regarded each as central to the perpetuation of mass-consumption capitalism. Of course, neither view of advertising's power originated with Galbraith.[14] But he gave them vivid expression and, more important, he disseminated them to the educated public.

Galbraith's views about advertising's impact probably have typified liberal-to-left economists from the 1950s onward. Even Galbraith's critics among that group have tended to echo him on this particular issue. For example, consider the extended debate about Galbraith's *The New Industrial State* which appeared in the journal *The Public Interest* in 1967 and 1968.[15] The participants were the economists Robert M. Solow and Robin Marris, plus Galbraith himself. Solow led off the exchange by summarizing the main points in *The New Industrial State*'s argument: (1) the social and economic preeminence of the large corporation, (2) management's dominance over the shareholders and the directors within such firms, (3) the large corporation's ability to avoid risk by controlling both its supply of materials and capital and its sales, (4) the primacy of sales over profits within big enterprises, (5) the widespread conviction that increasing material abundance is the main goal of national life, and (6) the power and moral authority of the "scientific and educational estate" within American society. Advertising's two main assumed effects—determining product choices and stimulating the propensity to consume—are relevant to points three and five, respectively. That is, advertising not only helps firms control their sales, but also helps create the American preoccupation with material things.

Apparently addressing the first effect, Solow guessed that, rather than dictating consumer purchases, advertising messages tend to cancel each other out. He seemed not to consider the second specifically, except to make the familiar observation that Galbraith's views on advertising complement his essentially paternalistic aims. Solow also claimed that Galbraith offered no evidence for firms' ability to stabilize specific demand through advertising, which "perhaps . . . is why he states his conclusion so confidently and so often."[16] There was virtually nothing in Galbraith's lengthy response to rebut this charge. However, Galbraith did emphasize that corporations have only partial control over the demand for their products.

Marris agreed with Solow that Galbraith's case against advertising depended largely on assertion. His own views on the subject, however, resembled Galbraith's. To Marris, conventional economic assumptions fail to explain much consumer behavior, which makes it reasonable to assert that advertising influences that behavior. Then, after admitting that economists had not really tested the matter, he invoked the aid of sociologists and market researchers to sketch his own theory. This, briefly, was that consumer tastes are influenced to roughly equal degrees by (1) other consumers and (2) advertising and marketing efforts.

In the debate's concluding essay, Solow arguably reversed the positions he had taken in his opening statement. He began that last essay by invoking a most familiar argument for advertising's effectiveness: "the fact that profit-seeking corporations regularly spend billions of dollars on advertising."[17] Then he reiterated his view that much advertising merely cancels out other advertising, but he did so only by assuming that the persuasive powers of *unchecked* ads are great indeed. Advertising must cancel other advertising, Solow maintained, or "otherwise there would be nothing to stop both the cigarette industry and the detergent industry from expanding their sales to their hearts' desire and to the limits of consumers' capacity to carry debt."[18] After this, Solow tried to argue that his first essay's criticisms of Galbraith involved only advertising's ability to stimulate consumption in general, and not its power to affect individual purchases. In that article, Solow claimed, he really wanted "to show how shaky the foundations are for the naive belief that not only the fortunes of individual companies, but also the viability of capitalism, rests on the success of the Madison Avenue shock troops, because without them the flow of consumer spending would dry up."[19]

To Galbraith advertising is only one instance of a more general phenomenon: corporate domination of American society. This perception naturally has generated demands that business behave ethically. One manifestation of these demands is the emergence of business ethics as an academic discipline. Like the economists just discussed, business ethicists who have written about advertising generally assume that it works in one or both of the senses we have been considering. Some of them emphasize advertising's presumed ability to distort competition,[20] while others stress its power to stimulate consumption. Of the ethicists, Richard Lippke has provided what is probably the most fully developed statement of the latter view.[21]

To Lippke, the problem with advertising is not that it makes people choose the wrong products, but rather that it makes them consumers in the first place. In the process, advertising helps undermine human autonomy. Most people, Lippke averred, can resist an ad's explicit content: its entreaty to buy a particular product or service. But this is not true of advertising's implicit content, which "consists of messages about, broadly speaking, the consumer lifestyle."[22] Those messages—some of which are better described as effects—include (1) encouragement to accept emotional appeals, oversimplification, superficiality, and shoddy standards of proof for claims; (2) an emphasis on ease and gratification rather than on austerity and restraint; (3) the notion that people should let advertisers show them how to live the good life; (4) a constant encouragement to consume lest one miss out on something new; (5) the false belief that products will deliver the non-market goods with which they are associated; and (6) the idea that political and economic institutions should be judged by their ability to deliver consumer products. According to Lippke, advertising succeeds in implanting these beliefs for two sets of reasons. The first is the existence of background social conditions that are not conducive to autonomy; these include the political, social, and economic power of corporations; their hierarchical, authoritarian management structures; unequal access to quality education; and the mass media's insipid program content. In such an environment, second, advertising's implicit content triumphs because it is pervasive, it is not effectively challenged, and it begins to influence people very early in their lives.

It is only a short step from Lippke's position—or from Galbraith's picture of the U.S. economy—to holistic views of American society which view it as an organism (or maybe a machine) devoted almost entirely to the production of material things. If this system is to work properly, its human parts must be motivated and enabled to assist the productive process. This is accomplished by implanting in people a strong desire for consumer goods, and by making them do productive work to get the money to buy those goods. Advertising naturally helps accomplish the first task, and once the desire to consume is created, the second follows naturally. Galbraith's dependence effect, which says that consumer wants are created by the productive process which satisfies them, suggests that he is basically of this view.[23] In a 1976 book, Stuart Ewen tried to explain how we arrived at this condition.[24]

Until the early twentieth century, Ewen asserted, working-class culture had largely resisted capitalism and capitalist attitudes. But this changed when the advertising industry began to assume modern proportions and a mass consumer market came into being. This was part of a process whereby businessmen "looked to move beyond their nineteenth-century characterization as captains of industry toward a position in which they could control the entire social realm. They aspired to become captains of consciousness."[25] However, it might be more accurate to say that the *industrial system required* businessmen to think in this way, for Ewen rooted advertising's rise in the excess productive capacity created by modern capitalism.

> With a burgeoning productive capacity, industry now required an equivalent increase in potential consumers of its goods. . . . The mechanism of mass production could not function unless markets became more dynamic, growing horizontally (nationally), vertically (into social classes not previously among the consumers), and ideologically. Now men and women had to be habituated to respond to the demands of the productive machinery.[26]

Thus, "[b]y the twenties, the ideological vanguard of the business community saw the need to endow the masses with . . . the money, commodity, and psychic wages (satisfactions) correlative and responsive to the route of industrial capitalism."[27] This required the higher wages and shorter working hours needed to make mass consumption feasible. But mass consumption also required new attitudes, and modern mass advertising emerged to create them. Thus, "[m]odern advertising must be seen as a direct response to the needs of mass industrial capitalism."[28] To fulfill its role, moreover, this advertising had to be manipulative in nature.

> While agreeing that human nature is more difficult to control than material nature, ad men spoke in specific terms of human instincts which if properly understood could induce people to buy a given product if it was scientifically presented. If advertising copy appealed to the right instincts, the urge to buy would surely be excited. The utilitarian value of a product or the traditional notion of mechanical quality were no longer sufficient inducements to move merchandise at the necessary rate and volume required by mass production.[29]

Thus, "the creation of 'fancied need' was crucial to the modern advertiser."[30]

THE CRITICS' POLITICAL AGENDA

To its critics, advertising's manipulativeness is a bad thing. Thus, they urge political action to restrain it or to counteract its effects. Of course, section 5 of the Federal Trade Commission Act now empowers the FTC to regulate advertising that is deceptive or unfair.[31] But many of advertising's critics do not regard advertising's deceptiveness—its express or implied provision of false or misleading factual information—as its main sin. And it seems safe to say that the FTC has not aggressively used its "unfairness" jurisdiction to attack advertising that manipulates without necessarily deceiving.

For some time, therefore, there has been relatively little government regulation of advertising that allegedly manipulates rather than deceives. But proposals for increased regulation of such ads are common political events. For example, commercial messages aimed at young people often are candidates for greater controls. This is especially true for ads that tout harmful products such as cigarettes and alcohol. Indeed, actual and proposed bans, limits, or warnings on such ads are not uncommon even when such ads are directed only at adults. The same tactics might be applied to ads that are very manipulative even though the products they aim to sell are not especially harmful or dangerous.

Some critics of advertising, however, think that its bad effects justify stronger medicine than these targeted regulations. Although some of the tougher measures they propose are aimed mainly at deceptive advertising and the advertising of harmful or dangerous products, they suggest the sorts of controls that might be applied to manipulative advertising. In a 1994 book devoted mainly to deception, Ivan Preston recommended a rule under which advertisers would be required to "have a reasonable basis for *using* their claims."[32] This means that advertisers would imply to consumers that their own personnel would "rely on those claims for making *their own* purchasing decisions."[33] It is difficult to see how the typical manipulative ad could survive this rule. What rational advertiser would rely on such an ad in his or her own life?

A British proposal from the 1960s displays different approaches to the control of advertising, approaches that arguably go farther than Preston's. In 1964 Paul Baran and Paul Sweezy recommended (1) legislation imposing severe penalties on "mendacious and misleading" advertisements, (2) the creation of a government board empowered to ban false advertisements unless the advertiser can prove their accuracy, and (3) a direct ban on the advertising of tobacco, liquor, and other harmful products.[34] Baran and Sweezy also proposed a system of noncommercial radio and television that is free from commercial advertising.

So far we have been considering proposals aimed mainly at advertising's assumed distortion of consumer choice. Recommendations to curb its other asserted effect—the stimulation of consumption itself—necessarily are more radical because here the problem is systemic. Some proposals of this kind apparently operate on the theory that advertising's stimulation of the propensity to consume is a function of its ubiquitousness. Their aim, therefore, is to limit the volume of advertising. For example, another 1960s British writer considered limitations on the space and time that the mass media could devote to advertising and limits on advertising expenditure as a percentage of a firm's sales, before finally recommending a carefully crafted tax on advertising expenditures.[35] Such a tax, the author said, "is little different in objective from discriminating taxes against alcoholic drinks, tobacco or petrol."[36]

    As we saw earlier, Lippke believes that one reason for advertising's stimulation of the propensity to consume is that background social forces predispose people to accept its message. Thus, his main proposals to control advertising and increase human autonomy attacked those background forces. These proposals included worker participation mechanisms, more and higher-quality education, a reduction in the political influence exerted by wealth and economic power, and the media's liberation from commercial support and commercial influence.[37] Interestingly, though, Lippke was skeptical about regulating or eliminating noninformative advertising because of the definitional problems, the massive bureaucracy, and the corporate evasive maneuvers such measures would create.[38] He also considered limitations on the quantity of all forms of advertising, while wondering about their effectiveness and their enforceability.[39]

    Sometimes these proponents of stronger medicine seem to wonder whether they have gone far enough. Toward the end of their article, for example, Baran and Sweezy noted that the structural changes in the social and economic order needed to counteract advertising's negative impact on society's moral and cultural standards were beyond the scope of their study. Before making the less ambitious recommendations described above, however, they observed that because it is so central to modern business, "the elimination of advertising as we know it today would require the elimination of capitalism."[40] "This," they immediately added, "is a conclusion which socialists should find neither surprising nor disturbing."[41] Prior to his proposals, Lippke sounded a similar note. After suggesting that the main threat to autonomy in "advanced capitalist countries like the United States" is the "dominance of corporate interests," he remarked that, to some people, the only way to counteract those interests "is to abandon capitalism altogether."[42]

    If their authors' general views about advertising's power are correct, the preceding remarks make some sense. If advertising's malign influence is part and parcel of modern capitalism, and if suppressing the former requires eliminating the latter, then maybe capitalism really should go. On the critics' assumptions, it seems to have little intrinsic value. In other words, if the critique of advertising we have been considering is correct, modern consumer capitalism loses much of its justification. That critique necessarily undermines consumer sovereignty, and consumer sovereignty seems crucial to capitalism's legitimacy. If consumers' choices are not genuinely their own but instead are dictated by advertising, how can capitalism claim that it enables people to choose the products and services that best satisfy their needs? Even more deadly to consumer capitalism is the critics' claim that advertising stimulates the propensity to consume—that it makes people consumers in the first place. If *that* claim is true, what can justify capitalist consumerism itself? And how can that system's defenders resist political control of consumption choices and, indeed, of the choice whether or not to consume?

If advertising's manipulativeness delegitimizes consumer capitalism, it may justify measures even more sweeping than any we have considered thus far. Unlike Lippke's proposals, the measures in question need not have human autonomy as their goal. As Marris once observed without apparent disapproval, if Galbraith is correct about advertising's power, "the notion of 'consumers' sovereignty' becomes vague, to say the least, and we are provided with a virtually complete justification for a wide range of political action to impose social value judgments in the direction of consumption patterns."[43] In other words, once the critique of advertising exposes capitalism as an expression of business power, the door is opened for a different elite to direct American life. And that is exactly what Galbraith advocated in *The New Industrial State*.[44] After recommending certain reforms of the industrial system, he said that "[o]ther steps—the expansion of public services that are not sponsored by the industrial system, the assertion of the aesthetic dimension of life, widened choice as between income and leisure, the emancipation of education—require that the monopoly of the industrial system on social purpose be broken."[45] The means to this end was increased political activity by intellectuals, mainly those lodged in the educational and scientific estate. "[I]t is safe to say that the future of what is called modern society depends on how willingly and effectively the intellectual community in general, and the educational and scientific estate in particular, assume responsibilities for political action and leadership."[46] "For the goals that are now important," Galbraith later urged, "there are no other saviors."[47]

Galbraith's practical political agenda envisioned a more or less statist, though formally democratic, order in which his scientific and educational saviors would have considerable influence, and public policy would reflect their vision of the good life.[48] Of course, Galbraith's views about advertising are not the only justifications for his agenda, but those views at least clear a path for that agenda. Evidently, Galbraith did not invariably favor giving greater power to the chief executive or the federal bureaucracy, but instead wanted to revitalize Congress and give it greater supervisory powers over the agencies. One component in Congress's revitalization was the elimination of the seniority system. Another, more important, component was the creation of a new radical party, which apparently would arise out of the Democratic party after its conservative elements had been expelled. To invigorate this party and to hold all politicians' feet to the fire, Galbraith also advocated greater public involvement in politics. Naturally he envisioned that this would come from his educational-scientific estate rather than from, say, the Perotistas.

What, in Galbraith's view, was this revitalized, congressionally led political structure supposed to *do*? As one might expect, much of its energy would be devoted to regulation. The objects of such regulation included national economic planning, the nationalization of certain industries, wage and price controls, environmental protection, and the protection of minorities and women. But the state also would promote certain activities. These included the creative arts, as well as more prosaic activities such as education, slum clearance, recreation, parks, and income maintenance. As part of the economic plan, large business entities would get guaranteed markets, the necessary physical infrastructure (e.g., roads), trained personnel (through an expanded educational system), and other forms of assistance. For small businesses, which would continue to exist in Galbraith's new order, he mainly proposed various devices to protect these firms from competition: state-assisted cartels and mergers, restrictions on entry, regulated prices, and guaranteed markets.

As we have just seen, the suggested political responses to manipulative advertising range from increased regulation at the relatively innocuous extreme, through efforts to suppress advertising's volume, to plans for suppressing the preconditions of advertising's effectiveness or for counteracting its influence. In schemes of the last kind, political action is directed, not toward advertising itself, but toward society in general. By the time we reach Galbraith's ambitious agenda, moreover, manipulative advertising becomes less a problem to be addressed than the partial justification for a thoroughgoing transformation of American life.

Of course, few critics of advertising have been willing to go so far as Galbraith. And his political program was not justified solely by his views about advertising. By making his views part of the critics' political agenda, therefore, I might be accused of setting up an unrepresentative straw man. But advertising's manipulativeness—especially its asserted stimulation of the propensity to consume—goes some way toward justifying Galbraith's position. If advertising really manipulates, consumer capitalism loses important justifications. On that assumption, the consumerist lifestyle is not freely chosen, but rather is imposed from without. If this thesis is correct, it becomes easy to regard modern mass-consumption capitalism as a monstrous imposition on the American people. And if that perception is accurate, is not social change justified, indeed obligatory? In sum, my point is that if people who share Galbraith's views about advertising do not share his agenda or something like it, they at least have reason to think about it.

The previous argument, however, requires a significant qualifier. One cannot reason directly from the fact that business dominates American society through advertising, to the claim that Galbraith's scientific-academic saviors should rule instead. For that, advertising's critics need a moral argument. Presumably, such an argument would stress the wrongfulness of manipulative advertising and the society it produces, but it would also require a demonstration that the critics' new order would be better. But even if advertising's manipulativeness does not take the critics everywhere they want to go, it at least seems to get them part way there. In fact, some critics might say that maybe we do not need a moral argument after all. If advertising has the force we believe it has, people may be highly manipulable and everything may be up for grabs. If so, and if *someone* must call the tune, why should we not rule? The only practical alternative is business dominance, and they are already manipulating people. So why can't we? Recently, Ralph Nader made an argument that combined a frank paternalism with the claim that business is doing it too. The subject was the public's increased acceptance of automobile seat belts, and on this matter Nader said, "People learned. You have to teach people what they want. Corporations understand this—they create wants all the time. But we need to create other wants."[49]

WHAT IS MANIPULATIVE ADVERTISING?

At this point, attention shifts to some questions that arguably have been too long held in abeyance. How is the term manipulative advertising defined in this book? How is it distinguished from other kinds of advertising? What are some specific examples of manipulative advertising? What percentage of all ads might fairly be regarded as manipulative? This section and the following one consider such questions.

Informative and Manipulative Advertising

Is advertising as potent a force as its critics assert? Chapters 4 and 5 devote considerable attention to this question. As an initial matter, though, one obvious objection to strong claims for advertising's power is that not all of it can plausibly be regarded as manipulative. Everyday experience suggests that many commercial advertisements are *informative* to a greater or lesser extent. Examples include the Yellow Pages, classified ads, many mail-order ads, and much supermarket and department store advertising. Even though they may try to manipulate, magazine and television ads often contain information as well. To all appearances, these ads operate on the premise that consumers rationally evaluate the information presented by the ads and make their purchase decisions on that basis. Such ads, in short, seem consistent with consumer sovereignty and inconsistent with the claims made by advertising's critics.

Within the universe of commercial advertisements, can we identify the proportion that qualifies as predominantly informative? The main technique used by researchers addressing this question is content analysis of actual ads. Of course, such studies present difficulties, and for that reason their findings are manipulable. Some advertisements contain both rational and emotional appeals. Should such ads be judged informative if they contain *any* solid information about the product, or must informational messages preponderate over emotional ones? The line between information and emotion, moreover, is hardly clear cut. For example, how should one characterize a statement that "this car makes you feel like you're in command"?

Despite the problems they present, content analyses of existing ads still are useful to our inquiry. The many such studies usually show a fairly high percentage of "persuasive" or "emotional" advertisements, and a lower percentage of "informative" ads or ads that make "rational" appeals. Only infrequently, in fact, does the latter's share exceed 50 percent.[50] A common explanation for the preponderance of noninformational ads is that much consumer advertising involves "homogeneous package goods" (or HPGs), such as soft drinks, gum, candy, soaps, cleaners, tobacco, beer, wine, gasoline, liquor, nonprescription drugs, perfumes, cosmetics, and other toilet preparations. These products, it is said, differ relatively little from brand to brand and thus are difficult to advertise informatively.[51]

Despite the apparent predominance of nonrational appeals, however, it still appears that a significant proportion of American advertising is basically informative.[52] But advertising's critics can cheerfully concede the point, for the concession hardly seems damaging to their position. Even if only a majority of consumer ads are predominantly manipulative, consumers' choices of goods and services still will be significantly affected. Also, it is possible that, due to its pervasiveness and its implicit endorsement of a consumerist lifestyle, even informative advertising might stimulate consumption to some degree.

The Characteristics of Manipulative Advertising

What exactly is a manipulative advertisement? Sometimes such ads are called *persuasive* rather than manipulative.[53] But persuasion is too broad a term to capture the traits that make advertising objectionable. In ordinary usage, persuasion includes situations in which desired behavior is produced be means of rational argument. According to Tom Beauchamp, for example, persuasion occupies one end of a continuum of influences, with coercion at the other end and manipulation in between.[54] He defines the former as "a deliberate and successful attempt by one person to get another person by appeals to reason to freely accept beliefs, attitudes, values, intentions, or actions."[55] As this definition suggests, Beauchamp equates persuasion with rational persuasion and regards nonrational persuasion as a form of manipulation. To

Beauchamp, "the essence of rational persuasion is that it induces change by convincing a person through the merit of the reasons put forward."[56] Of course, this is exactly what purely informational advertising endeavors to do. For example, consider an ad for a new computer that bombards the reader with technical data demonstrating the computer's superiority over other existing designs. It would be hard for most people to condemn this ad as long as it was accurate or reasonably so and did not omit too many significant facts. Indeed, most people probably would regard it as beneficial.

In a sense, of course, even this informative ad manipulates. The ad, after all, at least was a necessary condition of the purchase. But critics of advertising who attack it for its manipulativeness have other situations in mind. In the previous example, let us assume, the computer buyer rationally determined that the computer met the buyer's needs, needs that came from inside himself or herself and from nowhere else. Critics of advertising who attack it for its manipulativeness focus on situations in which this model short-circuits because the seller's advertising has exerted some untoward influence over the buyer. How might we define this kind of manipulation? Beauchamp describes it as including "any deliberate attempt by a person P to elicit a response desired by P from another person Q by noncoercively altering the structure of actual choices available to Q or by nonpersuasively altering Q's perceptions of those choices."[57] As applied to advertising, at least, Beauchamp's definition presents two problems. First, it is unclear how advertising might noncoercively alter the structure of choices available to consumers. Second, the latter portion of Beauchamp's definition includes *deceptive advertising*; indeed, virtually all his examples of manipulative advertising involve deception.[58] Deceptive advertisements nonpersuasively alter consumers' perceptions of their choices by misstating or omitting significant facts about advertised products or services. Although deceptive advertising arguably is manipulation, this book does not discuss it. For one thing, deception probably does little to stimulate the propensity to consume. For example, Galbraith seems to have been relatively unconcerned with it. In addition, deceptive advertising is a different phenomenon than manipulative advertising. Deception still treats consumers as rational actors. It "manipulates" not by undermining the *capacity* for reasoned evaluation of products and services, but simply by presenting false or misleading information about their nature. Even when consumers are deceived, they still may be making a hard-headed evaluation of the product and its ability to serve their needs; the problem is that the information used in this evaluation is false or misleading. For example, suppose that after a lengthy, dispassionate examination of the advertisements in *Computer Shopper*, I buy the wrong mail-order computer simply because I relied on false technical data in a particular ad.

So what is the specific kind of manipulation with which this book is concerned? Following Beauchamp's scheme, we might first describe it as advertising involving efforts to nonpersuasively alter consumers' perceptions of products by means other than deception. Speaking very generally, at least two such means seem conceivable. The first is the nonpersuasive alteration of consumers' desires or tastes. "To say that advertising changes tastes," Vincent Norris explains, "is to say that it causes consumers to change their minds about what qualities they prefer, or dislike, in the goods they consume."[59] For example, suppose that an automobile ad somehow causes Sue Consumer to value size, power, and luxury over safety, practicality, and good gas mileage. If so, Sue's perceptions of certain cars should become more favorable, and her perceptions of others less so. In addition to changing consumers' minds about desirable product qualities, advertising might also alter more basic or more general desires. For example, it might make people more (or less) health conscious, or more obsessed with sex. Such attitudinal changes could have implications for the marketing of certain products. As we have seen, finally, advertising might be a powerful stimulus toward consumption itself. Here, advertising would cause people to form more favorable perceptions of consumer goods and services in general. This would make them tend to devote more of their incomes to consumption, and less to savings. As I noted earlier, even informative advertising might have this effect. Perhaps, for example, it makes people consumers by drowning out other messages offering competing conceptions of the good life.

Some readers may wonder just how advertising, in effect, manipulatively injects new desires into consumers.[60] At first glance, it seems that these new wants must at least be latent, for how could advertising create them out of nothing? Nonetheless, I include the possibility because some accounts of manipulative advertising—Norris's, for example—seem to assume that this happens. As we will see later, moreover, subliminal advertising's assumed efficacy may depend on some process of this kind. In any event, this problem seems not to affect the second way in which advertising might manipulate. This involves efforts to associate the advertised product with things consumers *presently* desire. In Norris's words, advertising might induce in consumers "a *mental set* to perceive, in the advertised product, the qualities they *already* prefer. That is, it induces consumers to perceive ('experience') mellowness in the advertised brand of beer, and 'masculinity' in Marlboros."[61] Here, advertising does not induce purchases by changing basic desires or tastes. Instead, it foils the rational evaluation of a product by creating the illusion that it will satisfy conscious or unconscious desires that it may not, in fact, satisfy.

Purchase decisions caused by this second form of manipulation might conceivably be described as instances of deception.[62] According to this view, Marlboro ads associating the product with masculine themes simply present false or misleading information about that product's qualities and effects, and Marlboro purchasers rationally act on that misinformation. But because they make appeals to reason, we normally think of deceptive utterances as having some degree of plausibility, and many of the associations created by our second form of manipulation are very implausible. In our rational moments, for example, we all know that men are unlikely to become more manly by smoking Marlboros. (Nonetheless, Marlboro smokers may get satisfaction because Marlboro's advertising makes them *feel* more manly; chapter 2 pursues this possibility.) Where deception occurs, in other words, the victim may be fooled, but he or she is still capable of rationally scrutinizing the false representation. Because many manipulative associations are so implausible that they would not survive such scrutiny, we cannot attribute their successes to deception.

But why might manipulative associations work? Why do some consumers apparently fail to rationally scrutinize the ads containing them? One possible reason is that unlike many deceptive advertisements, manipulative ads of this kind do not highlight the association's implausibility by making the connection between product and desire explicit. For example, Marlboro sales probably would be lower were its ads to state expressly: "Want to be a real man? Smoke Marlboros." Another possible explanation is that the desires tapped by this form of manipulation are not always present to consciousness. If consumers were more self-aware about their wants, needs, and fears, they might be better equipped to spot ads that play on those drives. Perhaps the most important reason for consumers' assumed failure to exercise rational scrutiny, however, is the strength of the desires our second form of manipulation tries to tap. Someone once remarked that in relations between the sexes, our passions often are grander than their objects. The strength of those passions, in other words, tends to defeat rational evaluation of the people toward whom they are directed. Similarly, the powerful drives our second form of manipulation often tries to exploit (e.g., sex, love, status, fear) could undermine rational examination of the products with which those drives are associated.

TWO EXAMPLES OF MANIPULATIVE ADVERTISING

Conventions and Limitations

In line with the preceding discussion, this book treats the term manipulative advertising as including all advertisements that attempt to either (1) nonrationally change consumers' desires or tastes or (2) associate the product or service with the satisfaction of conscious or unconscious desires that it is unlikely, in fact, to satisfy. (I add the qualifier "attempt to" because, as chapters 4 and 5 reveal, it is unclear how well such ads actually manipulate.) Within that universe of advertisements, this book evaluates two: (1) subliminal advertising and (2) so-called associative advertising. Each is discussed in some detail below. Although it is unclear how subliminal advertising is supposed to work, it probably involves either or both of the forms of manipulation just noted. (Indeed, subliminal advertising's inclusion is one reason for my considering the first form at all.) As its name suggests, associative advertising involves only the second form of manipulation. For the most part, this book does not consider another form of advertising that may be manipulative either under my definition or other plausible definitions of manipulative advertising: ads aimed at susceptible groups such as the young and the sick. It also pays little attention to tobacco and alcohol advertising as such. Separate treatment of these ads would unduly lengthen and complicate the book. Also, some ads within each category may be primarily informative or deceptive rather than manipulative. Of course, the book's general conclusions about manipulative advertising obviously are relevant to the evaluation of the ads I do not consider, even if they are not dispositive.

In addition to the previous omissions, this book does not emphasize another way in which advertising might manipulate. This involves the possibility, noted earlier, that *all* advertising (including purely informative advertising) might increase the propensity to consume by continually making implicit suggestions that the purchase of goods and services is life's most important activity. I have several reasons for downplaying this possibility. One is the terminological problems it creates. (These arise because manipulative advertising comes to mean one thing when the propensity to consume is at issue, and another when our concern is advertising's effect on competition.) Another is that, if the studies on the incidence of manipulative ads are accurate, they constitute well over half of all advertising in any event. Furthermore, it matters little whether I explicitly consider this possibility of "inadvertent manipulation" or not. One reason is that, as we will see in chapter 5, manipulative advertising's impact on the propensity to consume is not profound. Another is that the sources I use when considering this question, which refer to advertising in general rather than just manipulative advertising, take the possibility of "inadvertent manipulation" into account anyway. For this reason, the book often uses the term "advertising" in such discussions. Technically, though, the book is concerned only with manipulative advertising as defined here (basically, the associative and subliminal advertising described in more detail below). When advertising in general is discussed instead, it serves as a proxy for manipulative advertising; I use it in this way because it is all that I have.

Subliminal Advertising

On September 12, 1957, a man named James Vicary announced that his company had perfected a means for flashing high-speed commercial messages during movies and television broadcasts.[63] The messages, he claimed, could not be perceived consciously but could be detected by the subconscious—and with dramatic results. According to Vicary, the unannounced transmission of the messages "Hungry? Eat Popcorn" and "Drink Coca-Cola" to movie audiences increased popcorn sales by 57.7 percent and Coke sales by 18.1 percent. Vicary's announcement triggered outraged editorials and other expressions of indignation, but the outcry eventually faded.

Vicary's ploy is one example of a marketing technique known as subliminal advertising. Subliminal advertising exposes people to commercial messages of which they are subconsciously, but not consciously, aware. Evidently such messages can be detected, for the phenomenon of subliminal communication is well established.[64] In other words, people have been shown to respond to stimuli even though they were unable to report on the existence of those stimuli. However, the intensity thresholds below which a signal cannot be consciously detected, and above which it can be knowingly perceived, vary both for one person and among different people.

It seems that three forms of subliminal communication might find utilization in advertising.[65] The first, exemplified by Vicary's experiment, is to present visual stimuli of very brief duration. Television appears to be the most likely medium for this particular technique. The second is the use of accelerated, high-frequency, or low-volume speech in auditory messages. Presumably radio would be the preferred medium for this form of subliminal communication, although it could find application elsewhere. The third form of subliminal communication with advertising applications, one described at length in a series of books by Wilson Bryan Key,[66] is to embed images or words in pictorial advertisements. These images or words are apt to involve sex, and their preferred means of transmission is the magazine ad. Perhaps the best-known example is Key's claim to have discovered the word "sex," partially erect male organs, seminal fluid, female genitals, and onlooking male and female faces in an ad for Gilbey's London Dry Gin.[67]

Are we really being exposed to these subliminal techniques? Except for several regulations issued by the Bureau of Alcohol, Tobacco, and Firearms, there appear to be few, if any, explicit legal restrictions on *advertisers* who employ subliminal advertising.[68] However, the Federal Communications Commission has declared that *broadcasters'* transmission of subliminal messages is inconsistent with its licensees' obligations and contrary to the public interest.[69] Turning to nonlegal sanctions, the National Association of Broadcasters' Television Code forbids broadcasters from transmitting any information below the threshold of conscious perception.[70] These restrictions, however, do not extend to printed advertising.

Thus, the incidence of subliminal advertising probably is determined less by public and private checks than by advertisers' judgments about its effectiveness, its risks, and its morality. High-level advertising industry spokesmen routinely deny that subliminal techniques are used in commercial advertising.[71] "I don't like to destroy cherished illusions," John O'Toole has declared, "but I must state unequivocally that there is no such thing as subliminal advertising. I have never seen an example of it, nor have I ever heard it seriously discussed as a technique by advertising people."[72] Referring to Vicary's technique, David Ogilvy states that "no advertiser has ever used it."[73] Some critics of advertising, however, take a contrary view. On the first page of Key's *Subliminal Seduction*, for example, we learn that "[e]very person reading this book has been victimized and manipulated by the use of subliminal stimuli directed into his unconscious mind by the mass merchandisers of media."[74] Without any apparent documentation, Key later asserts that a large proportion of advertisers' budgets is dedicated to the research, development, and application of subliminal stimuli; that every major advertising agency's art department has at least one technician skilled in embedding; and that most national advertising contains embeds.[75]

The claim that visual and auditory broadcasts contain subliminal messages is difficult to disprove because only rarely are those messages consciously perceived. Key's main concern, however, is the embedding of subliminal messages in print advertisements, and here he tries to prove his case by providing readers with examples. But the detection of embeds is very much an individual matter. As Timothy Moore has observed, "[a] diligent search for a phallic symbol will probably be successful. . . . The amount of information available from a purposeful scrutiny of a display is limited only by the viewer's imagination. Holding advertisers responsible for one's erotic musings is analogous to accusing Rorschach of insinuating particular themes into the inkblots."[76] Because people do detect embeds in advertisements, however, it is difficult to disprove Key's assertion that advertisers have put them there.[77]

The general public apparently is more inclined to side with Key than with O'Toole and Ogilvy. For example, a 1983 article reporting on a survey of Washington, D.C. area suburbanites reported that 81 percent of the respondents had heard of subliminal advertising.[78] (Indeed, subliminal advertising is becoming so well known that ads spoofing it have appeared.[79]) Of this 81 percent, a second 81 percent thought that subliminal techniques are being used in advertising, almost 51 percent believed that advertisers employ subliminal advertising "always" or "often," 12 percent were uncertain whether subliminal advertising is used, and over 68 percent believed that it is effective in selling products.[80] Other studies have produced roughly similar results.[81] Unlike ad industry leaders such as O'Toole and Ogilvy, lower-level ad industry employees apparently share the general public's views. In a recent survey of advertising and media personnel, 66 percent believed that advertisers place subliminal messages or imagery in advertisements, and about 50 percent thought that such tactics are effective.[82]

Lending some support to these perceptions are several reported instances in which subliminal messages have been employed outside the context of commercial advertising. These include subliminal words and images in horror films, subliminal statements in rock songs, subliminal self-help tapes, subliminal anti-theft messages by retailers, subliminal messages in stress-management seminars, subliminal write-in campaigns by radio stations, and subliminal public service messages on television.[83] Lending considerably more support to those perceptions are occasional reports of subliminal advertising itself. During the Christmas season of 1973, for example, several people complained to the Federal Trade Commission and the Federal Communications Commission that a national television commercial for a children's game contained a subliminal command to "get it."[84] In addition, three academic advertising researchers claim to have spotted sexual embeds in ads for Marlboro Lights cigarettes and Chivas Regal whiskey.[85] In all likelihood, such reports are merely the tip of an iceberg of uncertain size. As Moore observes, due to its covert nature and the ethical objections it raises, the prevalence of subliminal advertising most likely is underestimated by published reports.[86]

Also likely to underestimate subliminal advertising's prevalence are published surveys of advertising practitioners and people in related jobs regarding their own direct experiences with subliminal advertising. One such survey of 100 randomly selected art directors at advertising agencies produced 47 usable responses.[87] Two (4 percent) of the respondents admitted that they had embedded a subliminal message in artwork for a client, two admitted to having supervised embedding in such work, and three (6 percent) claimed personal knowledge of embedding by others. One of the self-identified embedders, however, may have confused subliminal advertising with the associative advertising discussed below.[88] In a more recent study, a survey of 750 personnel from advertising agencies, their clients, the media, and media production companies generated 256 responses.[89] Of the 256, 24 (9.4 percent) claimed that either their present employer, a past employer, or both had used subliminal advertising.[90] However, half of the 18 respondents stating that their *present* employers used subliminals gave responses suggesting an uncertain grasp of the nature of subliminal advertising. Within the total sample of 256, moreover, about 30 percent seemed unclear on this point. But while such confusions suggest that the reported incidence of subliminal advertising in our two studies may be high, they hardly negate all the reports of its use. In addition, these studies may understate the frequency with which advertisers employ subliminal techniques. Despite promises of anonymity from the researchers, respondents who use or witness those techniques have little apparent motivation to disclose what they know. This seems especially true when the offender is the respondent's current employer.

All things considered, therefore, it seems likely that U.S. advertisers make some use of subliminal advertising. However, the extent of that use is anyone's guess. Whether this situation is a cause for alarm should depend heavily on the effectiveness of subliminal appeals. As chapter 4 reveals, the limited evidence on subliminal advertising's efficacy suggests that it is not especially useful to advertisers. As chapter 4 also reveals, there are certain theoretical reasons for suspecting that subliminal advertising's impact is weak. Some of these reasons involve a problem whose omission may not have escaped readers skeptical about subliminal advertising's alleged powers. The subliminal advertising literature I have consulted is most unclear on a critical point: how that tactic is supposed to work. Subliminal advertising obviously uses both of the general techniques discussed in the preceding section—attempting to inject new desires into consumers (e.g., Vicary's "drink Coca-Cola" and the command to "get it") and associating the product with desires consumers already have (e.g., sexual embeds). Key believes that the subliminal presentation of such messages makes them vastly more effective than they would be if they were presented supraliminally. Indeed, he maintains that "the more subliminal or deeply buried a stimulus, the greater the probable effect."[91] But why should this be true? Why should a subliminal command to drink Coca-Cola or a subliminal association between sex and product be more effective than their supraliminal counterparts?

As best I can determine, two factors underlie the widespread belief that subliminal advertising is a potent marketing tool. The first is that subliminal messages are not perceived by consumers; the second is the notion that human behavior is largely determined by a subconscious with impressive powers of information assimilation and information retention. Key's apparent rationale for subliminal advertising's effectiveness combines these two notions.[92] The basic idea is that while the conscious mind filters and rejects much of the content of advertisements, the subconscious takes in and retains virtually all of it. This includes an ad's subliminal content, which apparently influences the subconscious in profound ways. The subconscious, in turn, profoundly affects our conscious desires and behavior. In this way, subliminal advertising messages induce consumers to purchase the advertised product. Although the conscious mind might be able to foil this process were it aware of the process, that awareness is lacking because the original appeal was subliminal. Chapter 4 examines this argument in more detail; as readers might suspect, that discussion suggests some difficulties with the claim that subliminal advertising powerfully influences consumer behavior.

Associative Advertising

As just observed, subliminal advertising might utilize either of the two manipulative techniques discussed earlier in the chapter. The form of manipulative advertising described here as associative uses only the second. Because subliminal advertising also employs associations, this second kind of manipulative advertising might better be described as "overtly associative." For simplicity's sake, however, I simply refer to it as associative advertising. As the term overt suggests, here the association usually is more or less visible to conscious perception.

Business ethicists concerned about advertising and its alleged power often emphasize associative ads.[93] An article written by one of those ethicists, John Waide, is my point of departure for describing this form of advertising.[94] According to Waide, associative advertising is a marketing technique with six characteristics. The first, which seems trivial, is that advertisers using this tactic do so in order to get people to buy products, and not because they desire to improve or enrich people's lives. The second is the advertiser's identification of a deep-seated nonmarket good for which the targeted consumers feel a strong desire. By a nonmarket good, Waide means something that cannot normally be bought or sold in market transactions; his examples include friendship, esteem, sex, and power. Michael Schudson provides some additional examples in the following description of advertising messages: "The ads say, typically, 'buy me and you will overcome the anxieties I have just reminded you about' or 'buy me and you will enjoy life' or 'buy me and be recognized as a successful person' or 'buy me and everything will be easier for you.' "[95] The third characteristic of associative advertising is that the advertised product has little or no connection with this nonmarket good.[96] Waide's example is a soft drink's usual failure to give its buyers friends, sex, or excitement. Associative advertising's fourth—and critical—characteristic is that through such advertising "the marketed product is associated with the non-market desire."[97] However, Waide does not assume that the association necessarily causes consumers to buy the product. Waide's fifth point is that because we can clearly spot the association between product and nonmarket good if we bother, associative advertising is not deceptive in the usual sense of the term. Finally, Waide maintains that even though associatively advertised products generally do not satisfy the nonmarket desires with which they are linked, the advertising may nonetheless give consumers some psychic benefits. His example is a mouthwash whose use reduces consumers' anxiety over bad breath even though it actually does little to allay that condition.

With some qualifications that expand the concept's scope, this book adopts Waide's description of associative advertising. The first qualification involves his assumption that in such advertising the advertised product does little to satisfy the desire with which it is linked. If manipulation is the concern, this assumption seems unnecessarily restrictive. Consider for example the seemingly endless series of televised Michelin tire ads associating Michelin tires with the safety and security of infant children (and the adults who are the ad's targets). If we assume, as is highly likely, that Michelins are safe tires, it is difficult to argue that they fail to deliver the safety and security with which they have been associated. But the ad's blatant fear appeal is the antithesis of rational persuasion. For all that we know, it may prevent safety-conscious buyers from finding and purchasing even better tires or cheaper tires of equivalent quality. Where ads undermine the critical evaluation of products through visible associations with strong human desires, therefore, this book treats them as associative even if they actually satisfy the relevant desire.

My second qualification to Waide's definition concerns his assumption that we can spot associative advertising techniques if we bother. Sometimes associations are difficult to detect because they appeal to subconscious drives or to desires that we try to hide from ourselves. Vance Packard's *The Hidden Persuaders* is replete with examples; one of the best known is the association between baking a cake and having a baby.[98] Thus, I include in my definition of associative advertising ads that associate the product with subconscious or half-hidden desires. I do so even though such associations arguably straddle the line between associative ads and associative subliminal ads.

In their attempts to manipulate consumers through association, advertisers employ all kinds of marketing, psychological, and survey research techniques. These have included general approaches such as Motivation Research, attitudinal surveys such as VALS (Values and Life Styles), and specific techniques such as copy testing, focus groups, depth interviews, and brain-wave measurement.[99] The associative ads that result from these and other efforts play upon a wide range of human desires. Perhaps the most common example, one specifically discussed in chapter 4, is sex. As my Michelin tire example suggests, fear appeals linking the product to drives for safety and reassurance also are common. Attempts to link certain products with the possession of social status are almost too numerous and too obvious to mention. Another frequently used ploy is to play upon guilt feelings that the product supposedly will alleviate.[100] Still another involves appeals to particularistic drives such as patriotism, nationalism, the desire for community, and familial ties.[101] A somewhat less well-known

example is the association of the product with feelings of self-esteem ("You've come a long way, baby"; "This Bud's for all you
do").[102] Ads targeting groups such as blacks, Hispanics, and gays
might qualify as associative if they try to link the product to group
pride, group solidarity, or personal traits group members perceive
as desirable.[103] Cutting across some of the previous categories,
finally, is the ill-defined phenomenon known as emotional advertising.[104] This brief listing obviously is far from exhaustive.

WHAT IS SO BAD ABOUT MANIPULATIVE ADVERTISING?

By now, this chapter has gone some way toward developing a
familiar attack on advertising: the critique that emphasizes its
asserted manipulativeness. It has identified two ways in which
advertising might manipulate: by stimulating the propensity to
consume and by dictating consumers' choice of particular products
and services. It also has isolated the forms of advertising that are
most likely to have these effects. In the process, the chapter has
distinguished manipulative advertising from its informative and
deceptive counterparts. Furthermore, the chapter has sketched the
political agenda that flows from these perceptions about advertising's impact.

For that agenda to seem compelling, however, at least two and
perhaps three further requirements are necessary. The first, discussed at length in chapters 4 and 5, is that manipulative advertising actually does manipulate people in the two senses discussed.
The second requirement probably is even more basic to the critics'
case. Even if manipulative advertising works as advertised, one is
unlikely to urge its regulation or suppression without some reason
for believing that it is *wrong*, indeed profoundly wrong. A third
requirement, one that applies only the most ambitious components
of the critics' agenda, is that the transformed society they propose
actually is superior to the one we have.

The second question—the question of manipulative advertising's
immorality—is not an idle or frivolous one. Some people evidently
believe that advertising's manipulativeness is a good thing. Business people and advertising executives regularly extol advertising's
ability to keep the economy humming. In a *Business and Society
Review* exchange on fast-food advertising, for example, one business

participant described advertising expenditures as "healthy and necessary stimulation of the consumption that makes our economy the most dynamic and productive in the world," and "the driving force behind consumption, job creation, and prosperity."[105] To be sure, this observer might have believed that advertising can achieve these results without manipulating anyone, but this hardly seems likely. If consumption, job creation, and prosperity are the desiderata, moreover, maybe advertising *ought to be* as manipulative as we can make it. This is especially true when we consider the economic collapse that might attend its abolition.

As chapter 2 observes, some critics of manipulative advertising do not buy the assumption that it maximizes economic well-being. Many more, however, reject the idea that economic abundance is the principal criterion by which advertising should be judged. What are their alternative criteria? The answers have varied from critic to critic. In the quotation that opened this chapter, for instance, Heilbroner condemned advertising because it undermines certain traditional virtues. As we will see throughout this book, Galbraith probably would agree, and also would maintain that a life devoted to consumption is a relatively infelicitous one. To Lippke, on the other hand, manipulative advertising is bad not because it leads to bad character or unhappiness, but because it undermines personal autonomy. Packard made a related objection when he concluded that the manipulators' most serious offense "is that they try to invade the privacy of our minds," the "privacy to be either rational or irrational."[106] To some, finally, there is something intrinsically wrong with manipulation itself—with the effort to *use* other people through means that do not respect their rationality.

Some of the preceding criteria, of course, are more or less incommensurable. Traditional virtue and autonomy, for example, may not always be inconsistent, but they coexist uneasily. What if, due to my autonomous choice, I decide to pursue vice? But the critics' moral problems do not end here. Assuming that they all could agree on why manipulative advertising is bad, how could they *justify* the criterion on which that judgment is based? Suppose you believe, as some critics of advertising apparently do believe, that advertising is wrong because it promotes consumerism and because consumerism is a low, vulgar, and superficial way of life. When confronted with a defender of advertising who insists that the accumulation of material things is life's ultimate good, what can you say in reply? Is it just a question of which party can yell more loudly or with more feeling?

For the most part, advertising's traditional critics have not overcome, or even addressed, problems of these kinds. Beginning in the 1970s and 1980s, however, business ethicists have tried to remedy the deficiency. Because many of these people are philosophers, they usually approach the evaluation in a characteristic fashion. As one philosopher has observed:

> Most people think that the study of ethics is the concrete investigation and critique of certain modes of conduct; business ethics is an investigation of what kinds of professional behavior are right and wrong for corporation executives; medical ethics has to do with determining what is proper and improper action for doctors and nurses; and so forth. Philosophers, on the other hand, conceive ethics as the abstract and theoretical determination of the principles that underlie modes of conduct, along with the examination of the concepts and arguments alleged to justify or undermine those principles.[107]

This author might have added that when philosophically oriented business ethicists examine business practices such as advertising, they often pursue the first inquiry by means of the second. In other words, they determine "what kinds of professional behavior are right and wrong for corporation executives" by evaluating business conduct under "the principles that underlie modes of conduct." Various sets of such principles exist, and they sometimes are called ethical theories.

Chapters 2 and 3 consider manipulative advertising in much this fashion. Drawing upon the published business ethics literature on advertising and upon other materials, they evaluate that practice under four different ethical theories or values. Chapter 2 considers several utilitarian arguments for and against manipulative advertising. Chapter 3 considers the practice's fate under three other well-known ethical criteria: Kant's categorical imperative, the value of autonomy, and the ethical style now called virtue ethics. As these chapters should make abundantly clear, many everyday moral evaluations of advertising are expressible in the concepts and vocabulary of ethical theory.

Chapters 2 and 3 proceed on the assumption that advertising has much of the manipulative power its critics say it has. Based on that assumption, the practice seems wrong under many of the moral criteria applied in those chapters. If these chapters are the final word on the subject, therefore, the critics' agenda or something like it may be justified. But are the critics' assumptions about advertising's efficacy correct? As chapters 4 and 5 argue in detail, those assumptions considerably overstate the power of advertising. While advertising is far from impotent, it is not nearly so strong a force as its critics believe. In those chapters, and in chapter 6, I reconsider the ethical conclusions reached in chapters 2 and 3. The result, stated fully in chapter 6, is that manipulation in advertising is not sufficiently unethical to justify most aspects of the critics' political agenda.

Of course, one might wonder whether my theory-by-theory approach captures every ethical objection to advertising that manipulates or tries to manipulate consumers. As I briefly suggest in chapter 6, one also might wonder whether any of the theories is adequate by itself, or whether they are anything more than abstracted strands from a moral tradition in which they uneasily coexist. However, because the ethical debate over manipulative advertising has largely invoked these theories, and because they at least impose some organization on this book's ethical discussion, I employ them here. Due principally to my conclusion that advertising does not manipulate especially well, I largely am spared the difficult task of adjudicating among the theories. And whatever the limits of a theory-based approach to the evaluation of manipulative advertising, by proceeding in that fashion I can eliminate the most important moral objections to it. The claims each theory makes, I believe, resonate to a greater or lesser extent with most morally reflective people.

NOTES

1. Robert L. Heilbroner, "The Demand for the Supply Side," *New York Review of Books*, 11 June 1981, 37–41.
2. Ibid., 40.
3. "Advertising and the Corrupting of America," *Business and Society Review* 41 (Spring 1982): 64–69.
4. Ibid., 67.
5. Ibid., 68.
6. Ibid., 65.

7. John Kenneth Galbraith, *The Affluent Society* (Boston: Houghton Mifflin, 1957), chap. 11.

8. Ibid., 155, note 3.

9. John Kenneth Galbraith, *The New Industrial State* (Boston: Houghton Mifflin, 1967), chaps. 18, 19.

10. Galbraith conceded that in areas of the economy not dominated by large corporations, the "accepted sequence" (in which instruction flows from consumers to producers) still rules. He also conceded that even where large firms dominate, the accepted sequence has not been completely superseded by the revised sequence. See *The New Industrial State*, 212–13.

11. Ibid., 209.

12. Ibid.

13. Ibid.

14. For example, they appear in various forms throughout Neil H. Borden, *The Economic Effects of Advertising* (Chicago: Richard D. Irwin, 1942).

15. Robert M. Solow, "The New Industrial State *or* Son of Affluence," *Public Interest* 9 (Fall 1967): 100–108; John Kenneth Galbraith, "A Review of a Review," *Public Interest* 9 (Fall 1967): 109–18; Robert M. Solow, "A Rejoinder," *Public Interest* 9 (Fall 1967): 118–19; Robin Marris, "Galbraith, Solow, and the Truth about Corporations," *Public Interest* 11 (Spring 1968): 37–46; Robert M. Solow, "The Truth Further Refined: A Comment on Marris," *Public Interest* 11 (Spring 1968): 47–52.

16. Solow, "The New Industrial State," 105.

17. Solow, "The Truth Further Refined," 48.

18. Ibid.

19. Ibid.

20. For example, both participants in a 1980s *Journal of Business Ethics* exchange on advertising and autonomy seemed to believe that advertising manipulates consumers' choices of products and services. Robert L. Arrington, "Advertising and Behavior Control," *Journal of Business Ethics* 1 (1982): 3–4; Roger Crisp, "Persuasive Advertising, Autonomy, and the Creation of Desire," *Journal of Business Ethics* 6 (1987): 413.

21. Richard L. Lippke, "Advertising and the Social Conditions of Autonomy," *Business and Professional Ethics Journal* 8, no. 4 (1990): 37–39, 41–48. Much the same arguments appear in Richard L. Lippke, *Radical Business Ethics* (Lanham, Md.: Rowman & Littlefield, 1995), chap. 5.

22. Lippke, "Advertising and the Social Conditions of Autonomy," 38.

23. For a discussion of Galbraith's work that emphasizes this point, see David A. Reisman, *Galbraith and Market Capitalism* (New York: New York University Press, 1980), 75–77.

24. Stuart Ewen, *Captains of Consciousness: Advertising and the Social Roots of the Consumer Culture* (New York: McGraw-Hill, 1977), preface and pt. 1. For another statement of this general view, see Joseph Wood Krutch, *Human Nature and the Human Condition* (New York: Random House, 1959), chap. 2. Krutch's position is discussed in Chapter 3 of this book.

25. Ewen, 19.

26. Ibid., 24–25.

27. Ibid., 28.

28. Ibid., 31.

29. Ibid., 34 (quotations and footnote omitted).

30. Ibid., 35.

31. 15 U.S.C. § 45 (1988). Specifically, an advertisement is deceptive under section 5 if it (1) involves a material (significant) misrepresentation or omission, (2) that is likely to mislead a consumer, who (3) acts reasonably under the circumstances. See FTC v. Patriot Alcohol Testers, Inc., 798 F. Supp. 851, 855 (D. Mass. 1992). For an ad to be adjudged unfair, it must (1) create a serious consumer injury, (2) which exceeds any offsetting benefits it produces for consumers, and (3) which consumers could not reasonably have avoided. In the Matter of International Harvester Co., 104 F.T.C. 949 (1984). For more on how the FTC handles deception cases, see Ivan L. Preston, *The Tangled Web They Weave: Truth, Falsity, and Advertisers* (Madison: University of Wisconsin Press, 1994), chap. 1.

32. Preston, 186 (emphasis in original); see also ibid., 186–95.

33. Ibid. (emphasis added).

34. Paul A. Baran and Paul M. Sweezy, "Theses on Advertising," *Science and Society* 28 (Winter 1964): 29–30.

35. Peter Doyle, "Economic Aspects of Advertising: A Survey," *Economic Journal* 78 (1968): 597–98.

36. Ibid., 598.

37. Lippke, "Advertising and the Social Conditions of Autonomy," 53. Five years later, however, Lippke evidently came to believe that even these measures might be insufficient to restrain advertising's impact. Lippke, *Radical Business Ethics*, 118.

38. Lippke, *Radical Business Ethics*, 118–19; Lippke, "Advertising and the Social Conditions of Autonomy," 54.

39. Lippke, "Advertising and the Social Conditions of Autonomy," 55. See also Lippke, *Radical Business Ethics*, 119.

40. Baran and Sweezy, "Theses on Advertising," 29.

41. Ibid.

42. Lippke, "Advertising and the Social Conditions of Autonomy," 53.

43. Marris, "Galbraith, Solow, and the Truth about Corporations," 40.

44. See Galbraith, *The New Industrial State*, chap. 34.

45. Ibid., 379–80.

46. Ibid., 381.

47. Ibid., 385.

48. This paragraph and the following paragraph are based on Reisman, *Galbraith and Market Capitalism*, chap. 6.

49. Michael Lewis, "The Normal Person of Tomorrow," *New Republic* 214, no. 21, 20 May 1966, 20.

50. See the discussions of content analyses in Mark S. Albion and Paul W. Faris, *The Advertising Controversy: Evidence on the Economic Effects of Advertising* (Boston: Auburn House, 1981), 39–40; Borden, *Economic Effects of Advertising*, 662–63; and Vincent P. Norris, "The Economic Effects of Advertising: A Review of the Literature," *Current Issues and Research in Advertising* 2 (1984): 49–51.

51. On such products and their advertising, see Julian L. Simon, *Issues in the Economics of Advertising* (Urbana: University of Illinois Press, 1970), 270–84.

52. Another view of advertising, one I dub the advertising-as-information school, asserts that all or virtually all advertising is, or should be viewed as, informational. For descriptions and statements of this view, see for example Albion and Faris, *The Advertising Controversy*, 35–38, 47; Robert B. Ekelund, Jr, and David S. Saurman, *Advertising and the Market Process: A Modern Economic View* (San Francisco: Pacific Research Institute for Public Policy, 1988), chaps. 3, 4; Franklin G. Mixon, Jr., "The Role of Advertising in the Market Process: A Survey," *International Journal of Advertising* 13 (1994): 15–23.

How does the advertising-as-information school try to overcome the everyday observation that much advertising seems to lack significant informational content? One strategy is to find some irreducible minimum of information that every ad must contain; virtually all ads, for example, at least identify the product advertised and inform consumers that it is being advertised. Phillip Nelson, "Advertising as Information," *Journal of Political Economy* 82 (July-August 1974): 732. Another is to define information so broadly as to embrace manipulative appeals. An example is the definition of information as "any stimulus that is relevant to the decision to buy or consume a product or service." Albion and Faris, *The Advertising Controversy*, 39 (quoting but not endorsing this definition). Yet another possibility is suggested by the following comment: "Today, advertising *is* the product. What people are buying, whether it's drink, jeans, medicines, or electronic gadgets, is the perception of the product they have absorbed from advertising." Eric Clark, *The Want Makers. The World of Advertising: How They Make You Buy* (New York: Viking Penguin, 1988), 23–24. By associating the product with some desired state, that is, advertising might both provide consumers "information" (a favorable perception of the product) and enhance their welfare (the satisfaction they get from that favorable perception). Finally, the assumption that advertising is informative might be justified by its ability to facilitate the prediction and explanation of economic phenomena. According to this view, which sometimes is called instrumentalism, it does not matter whether an economic theory's assumptions are "realistic" in the sense that they can be validated by everyday experience. Because this last position raises so many enduring problems in the philosophies of science and social science, I cannot begin to evaluate it here.

It should go without saying that the advertising-as-information view opposes virtually every significant assertion made by advertising's critics. Despite the aid this school might provide this book's overall argument, I do not rely on it. The principal reason is my skepticism about the advertising-as-information view's ability to overcome the problem discussed in the previous paragraph. In other words, I am unimpressed by the alchemy through which the school attempts to render plainly noninformational ads informational. However, I cannot pretend to justify that position here. This book's position, by contrast, is that while manipulative advertising exists, it does not manipulate especially well.

53. See, for example, Crisp, "Persuasive Advertising," 413–18 passim.

54. Tom L. Beauchamp, "Manipulative Advertising," *Business and Professional Ethics Journal* 3 (1984): 3–6.

55. Ibid., 5.

56. Ibid., 6.

57. Ibid., 8.

58. Ibid., 10–16.

59. Norris, "The Economic Effects of Advertising," 65.

60. As Geoffrey Lantos has observed, the (real or alleged) problem is not that advertising puts false needs in people, but that it appeals to genuine needs in unscrupulous ways. Geoffrey P. Lantos, "Advertising: Looking Glass or Molder of the Masses?," *Journal of Public Policy and Marketing* 6 (1987): 125.

61. Norris, "The Economic Effects of Advertising," 65 (emphasis in original).

62. Ivan Preston, I think, sometimes does this at one point in his recent book on deceptive advertising. See Preston, *The Tangled Web They Weave*, 79–100 (discussing deception by means of "nonfacts").

63. On Vicary and his experiment, see Clark, *The Want Makers*, 118–19; Philip Gold, *Advertising, Politics, and American Culture: From Salesmanship to Therapy* (New York: Paragon House, 1987), 35–37; Scot Silverglate, "Subliminal Perception and the First Amendment: Yelling Fire in a Crowded Mind?," *University of Miami Law Review* 44 (1990): 1244–45, 1254.

64. Timothy E. Moore, "Subliminal Advertising: What You See Is What You Get," *Journal of Marketing* 46 (Spring 1982): 39–40; Alvin W. Rose, "Motivation Research and Subliminal Advertising," *Social Research* 25 (Fall 1958): 278–80; Silverglate, "Subliminal Perception and the First Amendment," 1253–55.

65. Moore, "Subliminal Advertising," 39; Sid C. Dudley, "Subliminal Advertising: What Is the Controversy About?," *Akron Business and Economic Review* 18, no. 2 (Summer 1987): 6 (mentioning a fourth possible means).

66. Wilson Bryan Key, *Subliminal Seduction: Ad Media's Manipulation of a Not So Innocent America* (New York: Penguin, 1981). Key's other titles include *Media Sexploitation* (Englewood Cliffs, N.J.: Prentice-Hall, 1976); *The Clamplate Orgy* (Englewood Cliffs, N.J.: Prentice-Hall, 1980); and *The Age of Manipulation: The Con in Confidence, the Sin in Sincere* (Lanham, Md.: Madison Books, 1989).

67. Key, *Subliminal Seduction*, 3–7, and figure 1 following p. 102.

68. 27 C.F.R. §§ 4.64(k), 5.65(h), 7.54(h) (1996) prohibit the use of subliminal techniques for wine, distilled spirits, and malt beverages, respectively. They define subliminal stimuli as images or sounds of a very brief nature that cannot be perceived at normal levels of awareness. They make no specific reference to subliminal embeds.

Following the flap over Vicary's disclosure, two bills restricting subliminal advertising were introduced in Congress, but both died in committee. Silverglate, "Subliminal Perception and the First Amendment," 1266–67. Various state bills also have failed to pass. Pamela Marsden Capps, "Rock on Trial: Subliminal Message Liability," *Columbia Business Law Review* 1 (1991): 31. However, the Federal Communications Commission has declared that subliminal communication is contrary to the public interest and inconsistent with the obligations of its licensees. FCC Public Notice, FCC 74–78 (Jan. 24, 1974), reprinted at 39 Fed. Reg. 3714 (1974). But the FCC's authority extends only to broadcasters, and sanctions may be imposed only if the broadcaster has knowledge of the subliminal message. Silverglate, "Subliminal Perception and the First Amendment," 1267–68.

Regulatory authority over *advertisers* rests mainly with the Federal Trade Commission. Section 5 of the FTC Act, 15 U.S.C. § 45 (1988), forbids unfair or deceptive acts or practices. If it actually affects consumers, subliminal advertising might conceivably run afoul of either restriction. Diane Kiesel, "Subliminal Seduction: Old Ideas, New Worries," *American Bar Association Journal* 70 (July 1984): 27 (quoting an FTC official). Even if the FTC were to act against an advertiser, however, that action might conceivably be checked by the First Amendment's protection of commercial speech. On that protection, see Silverglate, "Subliminal Perception and the First Amendment," 1261–66. Indeed, the same might be true of the Bureau of Alcohol, Tobacco, and Firearms regulations cited at the beginning of this note. Because First Amendment protection does not extend to advertising that deceives or misinforms, however, a successful constitutional challenge to the regulation of subliminal advertising seems unlikely. Ibid., 1264–65.

69. FCC Public Notice, FCC 74–78 (Jan. 24, 1974), reprinted at 39 Fed. Reg. 3714 (1974). But the FCC may impose sanctions only if the broadcaster has knowledge of the subliminal message. Silverglate, "Subliminal Perception and the First Amendment," 1267–68.

70. Silverglate, "Subliminal Perception and the First Amendment," 1268.

71. In addition to the quotations below, some examples can be found in Clark, *The Want Makers*, 118.

72. John O'Toole, *The Trouble with Advertising* (New York: Times Books, 1985), 16.

73. David Ogilvy, *Ogilvy on Advertising* (New York: Vintage Books, 1985), 209.

74. Key, *Subliminal Seduction*, 1.

75. Ibid., 8, 108.

76. Moore, "Subliminal Advertising," 45.

77. J. Steven Kelly, "Subliminal Embeds in Print Advertising: A Challenge to Advertising Ethics," *Journal of Advertising* 8 (1979): 20 (making and developing this point).

78. Eric J. Zanot, J. David Pincus, and E. Joseph Lamp, "Public Perceptions of Subliminal Advertising," *Journal of Advertising* 12, no. 1 (1983): 41. On the other hand, a 1959 study found that only 41 percent of the respondents had heard of subliminal advertising. Ralph Norman Haber, "Public Attitudes regarding Subliminal Advertising," *Public Opinion Quarterly* 23 (Summer 1959): 292. This study did not question respondents about subliminal advertising's incidence or effectiveness.

79. Cleveland Horton, "Toyota Double Talk; Ads with 'Hidden' Messages Tout New Paseo," *Advertising Age*, 10 June 1991, 53. As a later *Advertising Age* editorial describes this phenomenon, "Seagram's Extra

Dry gin puts easily spotted 'hidden' figures in ice cubes in its print ads; Toyota TV spots flash words like 'sexy' and 'wild' on screen while the announcer drones on about the practicality of the new Paseo; and Miller Lite's new ads feature Kevin Nealon, in his 'Saturday Night Live' role as 'subliminal man,' who may be responsible for the sudden fad." "Hot Trend," *Advertising Age*, 17 June 1991, 18.

80. Zanot, Pincus, and Lamp, "Public Perceptions of Subliminal Advertising," 41.

81. Martha Rogers and Christine A. Seiler, "The Answer Is No: A National Survey of Advertising Industry Practitioners and Their Clients about Whether They Use Subliminal Advertising," *Journal of Advertising Research* 34, no. 2 (March-April 1994): 36 (summarizing those other studies).

82. Ibid., 41. However, some 30 percent of those polled gave responses indicating confusion about the concept of subliminal advertising.

83. Capps, "Rock on Trial," 31–32; Dudley, "Subliminal Advertising," 7, 9; Kiesel, "Subliminal Seduction," 25, 26; Silverglate, "Subliminal Perception and the First Amendment," 1248–49.

84. Capps, "Rock on Trial," 30; Kiesel, "Subliminal Seduction," 27. This apparently led to the FCC statement discussed earlier.

85. William E. Kilbourne, Scott Painton, and Danny Ridley, "The Effect of Sexual Embedding on Responses to Magazine Advertisements," *Journal of Advertising* 14, no. 2 (1985): 50. These ads and the study based upon them are discussed in chapter 4.

86. Moore, "Subliminal Advertising," 38–39.

87. Jack Haberstroh, "Can't Ignore Subliminal Ad Charges: Adfolk Laugh, but Students Listen," *Advertising Age*, 17 September 1984, 42.

88. This respondent stated: "All advertising is a mixture of product and subliminal messages, i.e., a product with an attractive person means if you use the product, subliminally you can look like this, feel like this or receive a positive response from people." Ibid.

89. Rogers and Seiler, "The Answer Is No," 39–44.

90. Ibid., 40, table 1.

91. Key, *Subliminal Seduction*, 27.

92. See ibid., 50–55, 61.

93. See, for example, Arrington, "Advertising and Behavior or Control," 3; Crisp, "Persuasive Advertising," 414; Lippke, "Advertising and the Social Conditions of Autonomy," 36; John Waide, "The Making of Self and World in Advertising," *Journal of Business Ethics* 6 (1987): 73–74.

94. See Waide, "The Making of Self and World," 73–74.

95. Michael Schudson, *Advertising, the Uneasy Persuasion: Its Dubious Impact on American Society* (n.p.: Basic Books, 1986), p. 6.

96. If Eric Clark's descriptions are at all representative, Japanese ads go much farther than their American counterparts in this respect. One of his examples involves an ad for whiskey. In the ad, "a puppy is shown having various small adventures as it wanders around the city in the rain. The commercial switches to a closing scene of one hand passing a tumbler of whiskey on ice to another hand. The voice-over says, 'There are all kinds of ways of living. Take care. Anyhow, take care. Everyone take care.'" Clark, *The Want Makers*, 48. For a similar discussion, see David Kilburn, "Japan's Sun Rises: Emotional Ads Gain Global Support as Japanese Avoid Westernization," *Advertising Age*, 3 August 1987, 42.

97. Waide, "The Making of Self and World," 73.

98. See Vance Packard, *The Hidden Persuaders* (New York: David McKay, 1957), chaps. 5–14. The association between cake baking and bearing a child is found on page 77.

99. For discussions of these and other approaches, methods, and techniques, see Clark, *The Want Makers*, chaps. 2, 3, and pp. 164–67 (motivation research, VALS, and a host of specific techniques); Gold, *Advertising, Politics, and American Culture*, 39–53, 109–16 (motivation research and VALS); Packard, *The Hidden Persuaders*, chap. 3 (motivation research).

100. See, for example, Mary Beth Pinto and Susan Priest, "Guilt Appeals in Advertising: An Exploratory Study," *Psychological Reports* 69 (1991): 375–85.

101. Clark, *The Want Makers*, 184 (providing an example of an ad appealing to familial ties); Kate Fitzgerald, "Patriotic Ads Sway Few," *Advertising Age*, 27 May 1991, 38; Fadil Pedic, "Persuasiveness of Nationalistic Advertisements," *Journal of Applied Social Psychology* 20, no. 9 (1990): 724–38. Certain General Motors "Heartbeat of America" ads, especially those in rural settings, strike me as appealing to the quest for community.

102. See Jeffrey F. Durgee, "Self-Esteem Advertising," *Journal of Advertising* 15, no. 4 (1986): 21–27, 42.

103. For some possible examples, see Clark, *The Want Makers*, 181–85.

104. One source defines emotional advertising as involving "the 'touchy-feely' mode." Merle Kingman, "Emotion Imbues TV's Best Spots," *Advertising Age*, 23 March 1987, 35 (containing numerous examples). For some other examples, see Kate Fitzgerald, "Changing Course: Emotional Ads Steer to Younger Boaters," *Advertising Age*, 2 April 1990, 51 (father finally communicates with son after buying a boat); Patricia Strand, "Back to Emotion: Goodyear Rolls New Effort from JWT," *Advertising Age*, 19 February 1990, 71 (a fear appeal for Goodyear tires

Utilitarian Arguments

As we saw in chapter 1, businesspeople sometimes praise advertising because it keeps the economy growing. But why is economic growth a good thing? Unless money is desirable in itself, the answer cannot be simply that growth makes people wealthier. As Ronald Dworkin once maintained, "Money or its equivalent is useful so far as it enables someone to lead a more valuable, successful, happier, or more moral life. Anyone who counts it for more than that is a fetishist of little green paper."[1] If someone replies that wealth is good because it enables people to buy things, we might ask why material things are good. The answer, presumably, is that they make people happier or more satisfied—that they give people utility. As the business ethicists would be quick to point out, this is a *utilitarian* argument. According to a moral theory known as utilitarianism, utility is the sole standard for judging the rightness or wrongness of an action. Thus, if the theory is valid, utility is the sole criterion for determining the rightness or wrongness of manipulative advertising.

A BRIEF SKETCH OF UTILITARIANISM

Utilitarianism comes in several forms.[2] Here, it enjoins that we ought to act—and ought only to act—so as to maximize the total amount of utility in the world.[3] This need not mean a positive balance of utility over disutility, but merely the best balance obtainable under the circumstances. Because its criterion for the morality of actions is whether they maximize utility, utilitarianism is a *teleological* or *consequentialist* ethical theory: one that judges the morality of actions by their consequences alone. To a strict utilitarian, an action's innate nature and the motives underlying it are ethically irrelevant unless they have implications for utility.

What is utility? According to Jeremy Bentham, utility and disutility were pleasure and pain, respectively.[4] In Bentham's scheme, the value of a pleasure or pain depended on certain more or less quantifiable factors. These included its intensity, duration, certainty or uncertainty, propinquity or remoteness, fecundity (the chance of being followed by a sensation of the same kind), purity (the chance of not being followed by a sensation of the opposite kind), and extent (the number of people experiencing it). This emphasis on quantity gave Benthamite utilitarianism a certain antielitist thrust: if each yields equal aggregate utility, a Beethoven symphony is no better than a Black Sabbath concert. In objecting to this feature of Bentham's theory, John Stuart Mill affirmed that some pleasures are *qualitatively* more valuable than others.[5] But while this broadened the definition of utility and brought it more into line with ordinary moral sentiments, it also gave up utilitarianism's apparent promise of providing definite quantitative answers to moral questions. Of course, there have been other approaches to the definition of utility.[6] This book defines it as *happiness* or *satisfaction* broadly conceived. It also assumes, for the sake of argument, that quantitative comparisons of the satisfaction resulting from particular actions are possible in principle.

Why is utilitarianism supposed to be true? Mill's answer was that because each person desires his own happiness, we can conclude "that happiness is a good: that each person's happiness is a good to that person, and the general happiness, therefore, a good to the aggregate of all persons."[7] This justification provoked a famous rebuke from G. E. Moore, who maintained that by arguing from the fact that happiness is desired to the conclusion that it is desirable, Mill had committed the "naturalistic fallacy."[8] Utilitarianism might also be justified on intuitionistic grounds,[9] but moral intuitions obviously differ. For example, Moore was an intuitionist, but he did not think that pleasure, happiness, and satisfaction are the only—or even the main—good things in the world.[10] Due to the heterogeneity of our moral perceptions, some philosophers maintain that while we have a duty to maximize utility, that duty exists in tension with various other duties we have.[11] However much it might appeal to common sense, though, this last position is not a genuinely utilitarian one.

In addition to questions about its justification, utilitarianism's claim to preempt the moral universe is weakened by other objections it has attracted over time. Some of these are prosaic—for example, the difficulty of making the utility calculations utilitarianism requires and the question of whether (or to what extent) the utility of animals counts in those calculations. Another is utilitarianism's preoccupation with consequences to the exclusion of everything else. Still other objections concern utilitarianism's apparent implications if it is taken seriously. Because utilitarianism enjoins us to maximize aggregate utility (and not merely our own), it might create obligations to humanity that clash with the common moral perception that, within certain bounds, we are entitled to favor our own projects over the general good as measured by utility.[12] More important, it seems that so long as total utility is maximized, utilitarianism is indifferent to the means through which this occurs. Such means might include the satisfaction of desires that ordinary morality would regard as perverse and the violation of rights that ordinary morality would regard as sacred.[13] Suppose that 10,000 depraved Romans enjoy themselves by watching a lion devour a Christian at the Coliseum. Each Roman gains one unit of utility from the event while the Christian loses 9,999. (If it matters, assume that the lion also enjoyed himself.) Could a committed utilitarian object?[14]

A form of utilitarianism known as *rule-utilitarianism* might avoid some of the problems just raised. So far, we have been considering a view called *act-utilitarianism*, which judges the rightness of an action by *that action's* consequences for utility. But act-utilitarianism may not maximize utility in the real world. Because continually calculating the consequences of our actions is an onerous business, the whole act-utilitarian project involves a certain amount of disutility. Worse yet, the inherent difficulty of those calculations suggests that additional utility will be lost as people calculate incorrectly. Still worse, people may consciously or subconsciously "cook" the calculations when their self-interest is involved.

("Wouldn't Dad really be better off dead than suffering the way he is now? And wouldn't I get more utility from the $5.2 million in his estate than he can? All it would take is an overdose of his medication. He wouldn't feel a thing.") Because act-utilitarianism is highly discretionary, finally, it may reduce the utility society derives from the existence of stable moral and legal rules. Due to considerations such as these, some philosophers maintain that the test for an action's rightness is its conformity to the *rule* that would maximize utility if consistently followed in like cases.[15] Many traditional moral rules might find justification under this rule-utilitarian test. Consider, for example, telling the truth and keeping one's promises. Respect for human rights and human life is another possibility. As these examples suggest, however, a consistent rule-utilitarianism is difficult to maintain. Experience and reflection suggest that, in some cases, utility is likely to be maximized by, for instance, lying, breaking a promise, or taking a human life. Making exceptions in such cases, however, brings us back to the dilemmas facing act-utilitarians.

This chapter's evaluation of manipulative advertising follows something like a rule-utilitarian approach. In other words, it mainly considers the following question: Would utility be maximized by following a rule permitting manipulative advertising or by one forbidding it? One reason the chapter proceeds in this way is that the sources it discusses stress advertising's overall implications for utility, and not the individual circumstances when advertising may or may not maximize it. Another, more important, reason springs from the nature of our inquiry. As chapter 1 maintained, critics of advertising who condemn it for its manipulativeness need a moral argument for their position. Here, the argument is that a world without manipulative advertising would possess more utility than a world in which the practice is allowed to exist. This seems equivalent to saying that a rule forbidding such advertising, if followed, would generate more utility than a rule permitting it. As we will see, however, manipulative advertising almost certainly increases total utility in some cases—perhaps in many cases. Thus, it might seem that utility would best be maximized by an act-utilitarian analysis identifying those situations. This would enable the government to permit manipulative advertising in cases where it increases utility and to forbid it in the others. But there is little reason to think that any regulator could make these determinations reliably. As Chapter 4 maintains, it is very difficult to determine the effectiveness of particular advertising appeals. And as the present chapter suggests, it is even more difficult to isolate the exact situations in which effective manipulative ads might make consumers happier or unhappier. Finally, the effort to make these determinations would itself consume a certain amount of utility.

The chapter's next three sections examine three important utilitarian arguments against manipulative advertising. They consider three general ways in which manipulative advertising might reduce total utility; their implicit reference point is a regime in which such advertising does not exist. The first argument, which comes from John Kenneth Galbraith, concerns advertising's presumed ability to make people consumers. Essentially, it maintains that advertising yields relatively little utility when it stimulates consumption and, worse yet, that it deflects human energies away from alternative activities which would produce greater happiness. The other two arguments involve manipulative advertising's asserted power to distort competition. They tacitly assume that consumerism increases utility, but urge that consumers would get more satisfaction from their purchases if manipulative advertising were forbidden. The first of these arguments is that, by making consumers buy products and services relatively unsuited to their needs, manipulative advertising robs them of the utility they would get from superior alternatives. The second argument is that manipulative advertising causes additional utility losses by helping business keep prices above free market levels. Relying on the arguments developed in its three predecessors, the chapter concludes by attempting a crude cost-benefit analysis of manipulative advertising. In that section, and throughout the chapter, I assume for purposes of argument that manipulative advertising is very effective in making people consumers and in dictating their particular consumption choices.

CONSUMERISM AND UTILITY

Arguments that advertising stimulates the propensity to consume usually refer to advertising as a whole rather than to manipulative advertising alone. Hence, this section unavoidably uses advertising-as-a-whole as a proxy for the manipulative advertising defined in chapter 1. If advertising stimulates consumption, one would think, it almost certainly increases total utility. On that assumption, people acquire more goods and services than would otherwise be the case, and thus get more satisfaction as well. To argue otherwise, one would have to assume that all Americans are so jaded that they get no satisfaction from their marginal purchases. Advertising's ability to stimulate mass consumption might also increase utility by making economies of scale possible.[16]

To Galbraith, however, economic efficiency is relatively unimportant if the extra commodities it generates produce little extra utility.[17] And, contrary to the argument just made, he thought that in fact they do not give consumers much, if any, additional satisfaction. *The Affluent Society* contains his main argument to this effect, and that argument sets the larger context within which chapter 1's discussion of the dependence effect resides.[18]

Galbraith's Argument

Why should additional consumption mean little or no additional utility? In chapter 9 of *The Affluent Society*, Galbraith noted the great emphasis Americans place on the production of goods and services. But, he continued, the American people are irrational in the types of production they value, foolishly favoring privately produced items over public services. Thus, for example, we stress automobiles over good roads, telephones over postal services, and vacuum cleaners over clean streets. According to Galbraith, the conventional economic wisdom justifies this misemphasis by maintaining that it results from free consumer choice. Specifically, the justification rests on a theory of consumer demand with two main propositions: (1) the urgency of wants does not diminish appreciably as more of them are satisfied, and (2) wants originate in the personality of the consumer. If the second proposition is accurate, America has an abundance of cars, telephones, and vacuum cleaners because those products reflect genuine wants. And if the intensity of those wants does not decline as material abundance increases, critics of consumerism cannot dismiss them as unimportant just because America has become an affluent society.

After discussing economic debates on the first proposition and apparently finding them inconclusive, Galbraith tried to refute it by showing that the second proposition is invalid. His vehicle was the dependence effect. As we saw in chapter 1, the dependence effect is the productive process's ability to generate consumer wants through emulation and (more important) through advertising. As we also saw, to Galbraith much advertising is manipulative. For this reason, it subverts the second claim made by conventional economists: wants originate in the personality of the consumer. Thus, the first proposition—that the urgency of wants does not decline as more of them are satisfied—cannot stand either. To be genuinely urgent, Galbraith thought, wants must originate from within and must not be contrived from without. Thus, "[t]he fact that wants can be synthesized by advertising, catalyzed by salesmanship, and shaped by the discreet manipulations of the persuaders shows that they are not very urgent. A man who is hungry need never be told of his need for food."[19] If the demand for most privately produced consumption goods is not urgent, Galbraith continued, their purchase cannot generate much utility. Because this demand "would not exist, were it not contrived, its utility or urgency, ex contrivance, is zero. If we regard this production as marginal, we may say that the marginal utility of present aggregate output, ex advertising and salesmanship, is zero."[20]

Not only does advertising yield us relatively little utility, Galbraith added, but it also prevents us from pursuing activities that would make our lives happier. It does so by consuming resources and lessening the demand for public services that could give people greater satisfaction. "Presumably a community can be as well rewarded by buying better schools or better parks as by buying bigger automobiles. By concentrating on the latter rather than the former it is failing to maximize its satisfactions."[21] Also reducing aggregate satisfaction, according to Galbraith, are the exertions advertising forces consumers to undergo. As increasing production generates increasing wants, increasing efforts to make the money to satisfy those wants, and still more production, the consumer comes to resemble a squirrel who struggles "to keep abreast of the wheel that is propelled by his own efforts."[22]

The Costs of Getting from Here to There

For all these reasons, Galbraith evidently believed that total utility would be higher if modern consumer advertising did not exist. Any serious effort to produce that blessed state, however, could involve serious transition costs. In Galbraith's view, advertising is one of the central ordering forces in contemporary society. What would happen to the economy were it to be severely curtailed?

Unlike some other critics of consumerism, Galbraith recognized this problem.[23] Imagine, he said, what would happen if by chance advertising becomes so loud, shrill, and pervasive that people finally tune it out completely. One consequence would be a decline in consumption and a corresponding increase in consumer saving. Unless these savings were quickly offset by increased spending elsewhere, total spending and total economic output would decline. In a time of weak demand and even weaker business confidence, that increased spending would be unlikely to come from the private sector. Thus, the most probable consequence of advertising's diminished influence would be increased unemployment, decreased national income, and a general diminution of economic security.

Of course, Galbraith believed that restructuring American society to achieve a better balance between public and private goods would increase utility. Presumably, he thought that these gains would outweigh the short-run transition costs, and that the problem of unemployment could be addressed through proper planning. For his restructured America, he envisioned an expanded system of unemployment compensation and a concomitant increase in leisure time.[24] To the British economists Paul Baran and Paul Sweezy, on the other hand, the answer was "comprehensive and effective planning for full and socially desirable employment."[25]

We might address the relative merits of these and other solutions from a utilitarian perspective. Here, I emphasize only that the transition period preceding their implementation is likely to involve significant disutility. More important, Galbraith may have underestimated the problems advertising's termination would create. The reason is the radical nature of his assumption that advertising is largely responsible for the propensity to consume. On this assumption, again, advertising is one of the major—perhaps *the* major—ordering forces in American society. Thus its elimination would strip people of what had previously been the central focus of their lives. This might not matter if, as Galbraith apparently believed, people really desire his preferred mix of private and public production. But as we will see, there is no particular reason to assume that they do. Thus, advertising's reduced influence—and the resulting disappearance of consumerism—could create a void that different people would fill in different ways. This could mean either a degree of social disintegration, and/or a more authoritarian government to check that disintegration. In either case, the prospects for utility could well be worse than its prospects under current conditions.

Hayek's Rejoinder

Although the costs of getting from here to there cannot be ignored, they hardly provide decisive utilitarian reasons for rejecting Galbraith's position. For one thing, those arguments obviously are speculative. Even if the problems they pose are real ones, moreover, skillful political leadership could go some way toward reducing them. And if such leadership succeeds in bringing us to Galbraith's promised land, the transitional costs might be well worth bearing.

But even assuming that the transition is an easy one, is Galbraith's argument valid? Stripped to its essentials, the argument was that because manipulated product wants have low urgency, their satisfaction generates little additional utility. The "urgency" of which Galbraith spoke, however, might mean: (1) low subjective urgency at the time of the sale, or (2) low innate urgency. Because the first interpretation makes it difficult to see why advertising makes consumers buy things, presumably Galbraith had innate urgency in mind. Presented schematically, therefore, his argument seems to run like this:

Want's contrivance from outside ⟶ Want's low innate
urgency ⟶ Little utility from want's satisfaction.

This chapter assumes that advertising creates the propensity to consume; on that assumption, the desire for consumer goods and services is not innate. Here, therefore, criticism of Galbraith's argument is limited to its second leg: the assertion that a desire's low innate urgency implies low utility from its satisfaction.

In a 1961 article, Friedrich Hayek called this assertion "a complete *non sequitur*."[26] Because Hayek thought that innate human wants probably are confined to food, shelter, and sex, he evidently agreed with Galbraith that our desire for products and services comes from outside ourselves. But he denied that this makes consumer desires unimportant. What is true of our desire for goods, he maintained, also is true of most of civilized life's other amenities. Therefore, if Galbraith's argument is valid, it forces us to conclude that those amenities also have little value. "To say that a desire is not important because it is not innate," Hayek observed, "is to say that the whole cultural achievement of man is not important."[27] Although Hayek could have been clearer on the point, he seemed to equate "importance" with utility. For instance, he observed that some students acquire a taste for poetry and continue to demand it only because their teachers have instilled that taste. But is this supposed to mean that that demand's "utility or urgency, ex contrivance, is zero?"[28]

So far as it goes, Hayek's argument seems difficult to counter. (And if Galbraith ever refuted it, that refutation has escaped me.) Upon reflection, there is little apparent reason to assume that a desire's origin outside the individual means low utility from the desire's satisfaction. Even if that assumption somehow is correct, moreover, it may doom Galbraith's claim that people get significant utility from public services. Suppose that Hayek is correct when he argues that the only innate desires are those for food, shelter, and sex. Or at least suppose that the desire for Galbraith's public goods is not innate. If so, and if only innate desires generate significant utility when satisfied, people should get as little utility from better schools and parks as from consumer goods. As with consumer goods, moreover, manipulation would be needed to make people desire public production.

Despite Hayek's apparent success in attacking Galbraith, however, it is important to recognize that attack's limited scope. Hayek merely undercut Galbraith's claim that a want's origin outside the individual means low utility from the want's satisfaction. He did not show that by increasing the propensity to consume, manipulative advertising actually produces more utility than would be produced through different human activities. In particular, he did not show that a consumer society generates more utility than the Galbraithian alternative. That showing would be fairly easy if consumerism is innate and the marginal utility derived from each new consumer purchase does not decline despite increasing abundance. But Galbraith and Hayek both rejected the first position, and the second is not obviously true. Therefore, it is difficult to say whether manipulative advertising's assumed ability to promote consumption means more aggregate utility than would be produced under alternative social arrangements.

Nonetheless, it is possible that modern consumerism generates more utility than any alternative way of life. On this chapter's assumptions, however, this probably means that manipulation would be necessary for utility to be maximized. Readers who find this morally repugnant probably are quarreling with utilitarianism as much as they are quarreling with the factual claim that manipulative advertising is the key to happiness. Utilitarianism, after all, is routinely criticized precisely for being indifferent to the means or the activities through which happiness is maximized. Were the technology available, in fact, it might logically compel that we all be permanently wired to devices that stimulate the brain's pleasure centers.[29] As suggested earlier, Mill's effort to surmount such problems by emphasizing qualitatively higher satisfactions took him part way outside the utilitarian camp. One might say that he was motivated by moral sentiments that were not utilitarian at all. The same may be true of people who affirm utilitarianism but recoil from the notion that manipulated consumerism maximizes utility. Chapter 3 suggests a few examples; among them is Galbraith himself.

THE PROBLEM OF SUBOPTIMUM CONSUMER CHOICE

The previous section opened with the assumption that because advertising stimulates consumption, it also increases aggregate utility. As we have seen, Galbraith did little to dislodge that assumption. Although it is possible that a world without advertising would create even more utility, moreover, Galbraith hardly established that contention either. Thus, this section and the following section assume that people derive some utility from their consumer purchases. They also assume that some products or services give them more utility than others.

On these assumptions, manipulative advertising obviously can cost consumers utility. As R. M. Hare has observed,

> [T]he market economy is only defensible if it really does . . . lead to the maximum satisfaction of the preferences of the public. And it will not do this if it is distorted by various

well-known undesirable practices. . . . By bringing it about that
people decide on their purchases . . . after being deceived or
in other ways manipulated, fraudulent advertisers impair the
wisdom of the choices that the public makes and so distort the
market in such a way that it does not function to maximize
preference-satisfactions.[30]

For example, suppose that Charlie Consumer's preferences would
find their greatest satisfaction in a Honda. However, Charlie buys
a Chevrolet instead because the car's advertising successfully
associates it with patriotism and traditional American values. If
Charlie would have bought the Honda absent the advertising, and
if it would have satisfied his original preferences better than the
Chevy, presumably that advertising cost him some utility. The same
should be true if, rather than affecting brand choices, manipulative
advertising causes a consumer to buy the wrong *product*. Thus, if
the sexual embeds in a magazine ad for a particular boat cause
Charlie to buy a boat rather than a car, and if the car would have
better satisfied his original desires, then the ad robbed him of
utility.

Homogeneous Package Goods

So far, then, it seems that manipulative advertising prevents
consumers from maximizing the utility they derive from their
purchases. Chapter 1, however, observed that manipulative advertising frequently is used to promote so-called homogeneous package goods (HPGs) such as soft drinks, gum, candy, soap, cleaning
products, tobacco, beer, wine, gasoline, liquor, nonprescription
drugs, perfumes, cosmetics, and other toilet preparations.[31] As their
name suggests, the physical characteristics of HPGs often do not
differ significantly from brand to brand. To the extent that this is
so, the previous argument against manipulative advertising col-
lapses. In such cases, the brand a consumer is induced to buy has
the same objective properties as the brand he or she would have
bought absent the manipulation. Thus, if Charlie buys Blitz Beer
rather than its competitor Blotz because Blitz's advertising successfully associates it with beach parties, good times, and semiclad
women, and if Blitz and Blotz are objectively indistinguishable, the
advertising has not cost Charlie any utility.

However, this conclusion requires at least two qualifications. First, experience suggests that different beers sometimes do differ in taste and other relevant properties, and the same may be true for some other HPGs in the previous list. (The researchers, however, say that "blind" tests usually prove me wrong.[32]) If so, Charlie still may lose utility if Blitz and Blotz differ and he really would have preferred the latter. Even where the products are identical, consumers still may lose utility because they are paying for advertising from which they derive no apparent benefit. This possibility is discussed in the last section of this chapter.

Added Value from Manipulative Advertising

Our discussion thus far suggests that manipulative advertising costs consumers utility in non-HPG cases. In true HPG situations (those in which brands really are identical or nearly so) those losses should not occur. However, these considerations must be balanced against the possibility that manipulative advertising of the associative variety also *generates* consumer utility in both HPG and non-HPG situations.[33] For true HPGs, this possibility, if realized, should mean that associative manipulative advertising is utility enhancing. For other products and services, this raises the possibility that the utility lost as associative advertising steers consumers away from rationally preferable purchases might be outweighed by the utility gained from the advertising. But how could associative advertising give consumers utility?

When consumers buy associatively advertised products, some say, they effectively buy both the physical product and the qualitative mental states associated with it. "Today," Eric Clark once remarked, "advertising *is* the product. What people are buying, whether it's drink, jeans, medicines, or electronic gadgets, is the perception of the product they have absorbed from advertising."[34] When this happens, consumers may gain utility from the pleasing ideas with which the product has been associated. If an ad linking sex and alcohol really does its job, for example, "you pop a cap off a beer and you are a superman."[35] As Stuart Ewen has observed, in such cases "the notion of value is extended beyond the question of how a given commodity is to be *used* by people in their daily lives."[36] Now, he continues, it includes economic elements such as fashion, taste, status, sensuality, and a broad range of aesthetic values.

According to Neil Borden, a long list of specific examples might be cited. They include the belief that romance will be attained through use of cosmetics, the belief that manly dominance might come from drinking milk or eating cereals or swallowing vitamins, and the belief that gifts of sterling silverware or chocolates or of a diamond ring mark the giver as a discriminating person.[37] Such processes, it should be noted, are distinguishable from situations in which consumers buy high-status products or products with a particular image in the conscious hope that those products will favorably impress other people. For example, I might buy a Lexus LS 400 not because that car's advertising makes me associate it with high social status, but because I rationally believe that it will give me more status. Sometimes such beliefs are justified.

According to the theory we are considering, when associative advertising is successful, we do not simply buy a physical product, but also a set of positive feelings created by that advertising. Those feelings should give us extra utility or added value in addition to the satisfaction we get from the product's performance of its functions. For true homogeneous package goods, where by definition products are physically and functionally equivalent, this evidently means that associative advertising increases utility. (Again, I am deferring until later the utility lost when noninformative advertising is included in the product's price.) In non-HPG situations, the extra utility we gain from such advertising could outweigh the utility we lose because it has made us buy a suboptimum product. Thus, it seems difficult to conclude that manipulative advertising necessarily costs consumers utility. Indeed, it might even increase their utility.

But is this "extra utility" or "added value" theory valid? Although experience and observation suggest that it has some truth, one cannot be certain. As Borden remarked in 1942, the matter often cannot be put to objective test or experimental check.[38] According to Julian Simon's 1970 book, our knowledge on this question had not improved twenty-eight years later.[39] Simon also dismissed as "tautologous" the argument that when consumers pay extra for associatively advertised goods, they must be getting extra utility for the additional expenditure.[40] His apparent point was that the additional expenditure might be explained on other grounds—for example, by the assumption that consumers have been manipulated. As Simon further observed, even if associative advertising does give consumers extra utility, they may also lose utility when its false hopes fail to be realized.[41] Maybe this factor could create utility losses even in HPG cases.

Summary

This section assumes that advertising increases utility by stimulating the propensity to consume. (Of course, this is not to deny that a nonconsumerist lifestyle might generate even more utility.) But manipulative advertising may also prevent consumers from maximizing the satisfaction they derive from their purchases. It could do so primarily by leading them to buy suboptimum products and services. When the products are true HPGs, however, no utility loss should occur. In addition, associative advertising may give consumers extra utility or added value through the pleasing mental states it induces. The extent and magnitude of this effect, however, are most uncertain. In true HPG situations, the possibility of added value should mean that associative ads are utility neutral at worst and utility enhancing at best. In non-HPG cases, it is unclear whether the added value produced by the associations outweighs the utility consumers lose from the purchase of inappropriate products. In both HPG and non-HPG situations, finally, another factor comes into play: the possibility that consumers may also lose utility when associative advertising raises false hopes that later are dashed. This conceivably could mean that manipulative advertising costs consumers utility even in HPG cases.

THE TRADITIONAL ECONOMIC CRITIQUE OF ADVERTISING

So far, it is unclear whether manipulative advertising reduces the total utility consumers derive from their purchases. However, a well-known economic critique of advertising provides additional reasons for believing that such losses occur. My summary of this critique combines the views of many economists into a brief composite sketch.[42] The main thrust of the argument is that manipulative advertising helps promote and sustain certain anticompetitive pricing practices and market structures and the losses in welfare that often accompany them. These losses arise mainly from higher prices, and perhaps also from reduced product quality and innovation. Thus, they are over and above whatever losses consumers suffer because such advertising has diverted them from products or services that would have better satisfied their desires.

For example, suppose that manipulative advertising makes Jill Consumer buy Brand X widgets when she really would have preferred Brand Y widgets. Jill loses utility because she has purchased suboptimum widgets. And if that advertising enables X to sell its widgets at a higher-than-free-market price, Jill loses additional utility for this reason. If the price is high enough, moreover, Jill may lose out on balance even if the widgets are HPGs whose advertising creates pleasurable product associations. On that assumption, Jill also should lose out even if she sees through X's manipulative ads and is totally unaffected by them. In that case, all the previous section's potential gains and losses drop out of consideration, but Jill still would be compelled to pay an excessively high price for her widgets.

The Critique

The traditional economic critique of advertising assumes that much advertising is manipulative. This means that consumer purchases often are dictated more by advertising than by the rational evaluation of products. The result is a considerable degree of advertising-induced brand or product differentiation in consumers' minds. One example is the growth of strong brand loyalties. This causes a lower elasticity of demand than would exist in purely "rational" markets: in other words, the quantity demanded is relatively unresponsive to changes in price because consumers are emotionally attached to particular brands. In such an environment, price competition tends to be subdued. Thus, firms can raise prices without suffering inordinate losses in sales and thus can obtain higher revenues than they would obtain under perfect competition. As a result, consumers pay more for products than they would pay if advertising were nonmanipulative, and thus they suffer losses in economic welfare. All things being equal, this means that they have less utility.

So far, the traditional critique of advertising illustrates another dimension of a point made earlier: in addition to steering consumers toward suboptimum products, manipulative advertising may cause them to pay higher prices for those products. Still, rational consumers like Jill would not be affected in either way. But in addition to reducing consumer welfare through irrational brand identifications, the argument continues, manipulative advertising causes additional welfare losses—losses not even Jill could avoid—by promoting economic concentration. Apparently concentration causes these losses because anticompetitive practices such as collusive prices are easier to implement when a few large firms dominate an industry.[43] One way in which manipulative advertising promotes concentration is by helping to create economies of scale in production. The idea is that some firms are the first to make large advertising outlays—perhaps because they already are bigger than their immediate competitors. For this reason, they steal sales from those competitors. The resulting higher output means that unit costs go down, which in turn means extra profits. Those profits, combined with the increased revenues resulting from higher sales, enable the firm to invest in more efficient plant and equipment, thereby increasing its scale economies and its profit edge. Once this occurs, the process may feed on itself, as the firm uses some of its new wealth to buy still more advertising, which may further increase sales, and leave its competitors even farther behind. As well as drowning competitors in advertising, the higher revenues and profits may also permit temporary predatory pricing in selected markets.[44] The likely result is that some competitors will go out of business, thus increasing concentration and the opportunity to increase profits through oligopolistic pricing.

Economic opportunities like those just described, one imagines, should attract new entrants to the industry, thereby increasing competition and driving prices down. However, manipulative advertising also can assist in creating barriers to the entry of new firms. For one thing, potential competitors may have to make disproportionately high advertising expenditures to overcome entrenched brand loyalties. This deterrent effect is especially likely when the would-be entrant is a small firm with insufficient access to capital. More important, the argument continues, there are economies of scale in *advertising* as well as in production. That is, once advertising expenditures reach a certain level and so long as they remain below a still higher level, those expenditures maximize the sales gains from advertising. Presumably, existing firms within the industry are sufficiently big to afford advertising outlays within the proper range. Unless the potential entrants have similar resources, they should be at a competitive disadvantage and thus may decline the challenge.

The result of all the foregoing processes, the traditional critique concludes, is a loss in total economic welfare. The main reason for this loss is the higher prices made possible by manipulative advertising. As we have seen, manipulative advertising creates these results both directly (through brand loyalties) and indirectly (by helping promote and sustain oligopoly). (Of course, *nonmanipulative* advertising may also produce the "indirect" effects, but manipulative advertising should do a better job in this respect.) Due to the relative absence of competition in oligopolistic industries, moreover, product quality and product innovation may suffer as well. All these consequences should mean losses in aggregate utility.

Again, these losses are in addition to the possible utility losses described in the previous section. On the negative side of our utility ledger, therefore, we now have (1) the economic losses just described, (2) the utility consumers lose by purchasing suboptimum products, and (3) the emotional suffering consumers may undergo when associative advertising's false hopes are dashed. As we have seen, though, the second sort of loss should not occur in HPG cases. However, our first and third categories of loss should exist no matter what the nature of the product. On the positive side of the ledger, we have the pleasing product-related associations manipulative advertising might produce. Because they are somewhat speculative, however, it is questionable whether these utility gains could outweigh the various losses just summarized—even in HPG cases. On the other hand, the emotional suffering resulting from frustrated expectations obviously is speculative as well.

The Critique Examined

Clearly, there is vast room for disagreement about the frequency and magnitude of the various utility gains and losses we have been considering. So far, though, it at least is evident that the negative considerations outnumber the positive factors. For that reason, and because the utility derived from product associations is uncertain, it now appears that manipulative advertising costs consumers utility when it distorts competition. But this tentative conclusion depends heavily on the validity of the traditional economic critique of advertising. Is the critique valid? Over the past twenty or thirty years, it has undergone a significant challenge.

The New Defense of Advertising. In a 1981 article, Robert Jacobson and Franco Nicosia identified four research traditions in advertising: (1) research on the effects of advertisements for specific brands, products, and company images; (2) efforts by trade associations and government bodies to determine whether advertising contributes to the sale of a product or a product class; (3) studies on the economic effects of advertising at the industry level; and (4) research on the macroeconomic effects of advertising.[45] The traditional economic critique of advertising fits within the third tradition. Much of the work constituting that critique appeared before the 1970s. Galbraith's *The Affluent Society* and *The New Industrial State* are obvious, if not completely representative, examples. Since the 1970s, however, a contending position has emerged.[46] This new view of advertising challenges the traditional critique on almost all points. The following description of this view is a brief composite sketch that blends the work of several scholars.[47]

Unlike the traditional view, the new defense of advertising views it as primarily *informative* rather than manipulative. It assumes that consumers are rational, self-interested actors whose product preferences are determined by factors other than advertising. Thus, advertising does not create tastes, artificially differentiate products, or generate brand loyalties. Instead, it provides information that rational consumers evaluate for themselves. For all these reasons, advertising also does not reduce elasticity of demand. Indeed, it tends to make demand more elastic. Perhaps the most important information advertising provides consumers concerns alternative products and services. Because this includes information about prices, and because consumers respond to such information rationally and self-interestedly, demand for products of equivalent value varies with their price. This naturally tends to force prices down, thereby maximizing consumers' utility per dollar spent.

The new defense of advertising also rejects the notion that advertising helps sustain oligopoly. In particular, it rejects the claim that advertising creates barriers to entry. As we have seen, one traditional argument for this claim is that new entrants would have to make disproportionately high advertising expenditures to overcome existing brand loyalties. But this obstacle disappears if advertising cannot create such loyalties. In addition, some defenders say, it is doubtful whether there are economies of scale in advertising.[48] If such economies do not occur, large existing firms lose another asserted advantage over potential competitors. Finally, the new defense of advertising stresses how advertising can actively assist new entrants. If such firms offer superior products and/or low prices, advertising enables them to make this information known with some assurance that rational consumers will respond to it.

In sum, the new defense of advertising regards it as a force for competition. As such, it tends to lower prices and to give consumers more utility per dollar spent. Advertising also increases consumer utility by providing information about higher value alternative products and services and thus facilitating their purchase. In the process, it reduces the cost of searching for such products and services, thereby further increasing consumer utility. By enabling them to trumpet the fact, finally, advertising rewards firms that market cheaper and/or better products and services, and penalizes those that do not. Thus, it is a powerful stimulus to further efficiency and innovation.

The Empirical Evidence

In theory, the debate between the traditional view of advertising and the new advertising-as-information view seems amenable to empirical examination. The research on that question has focused primarily on two issues: (1) the relationship between advertising and industry concentration, and (2) the relationship between advertising and price. More specific issues that affect these general concerns have been examined as well. For at least four reasons, this body of research presents significant problems. The first is its bulk: articles on advertising and competition have clogged the economics journals for at least twenty-five years. The second is the highly technical nature of those articles. Because several authors have summarized the relevant research in a fairly accessible fashion, these two problems are not fatal to our inquiry.[49] The other two difficulties, however, are more intractable. For one thing, the debate over advertising's power unsurprisingly has a high ideological component. While suggesting that researchers' positions in that debate tend to correlate with their political views, for example, Vincent Norris asserts that economics "is still ultimately a branch of moral philosophy."[50] Or maybe it would be more accurate to say that the debate over advertising's power is moral argument carried on by other means. For this reason, some suggest, the empirical research on that question is conducted in something less than a scientific spirit. After claiming that the debate over advertising resembles an ideological war, Mark Albion and Paul Farris observe that "[a]s a result, the body of research on this proposition is immense, with many biased reviews of the literature, flagrant subjectivity, and little appreciation of the pertinent marketing literature."[51] This third problem naturally suggests a fourth: researchers' failure to reach agreement on many key questions. Indeed, researchers may not even agree on the issues that separate them. As Albion and Farris also observe, "[O]ften terminology and issues are confused, as is apparent after any review of the seemingly endless number of 'comments' and 'replies' in the economic journals on this subject."[52]

Advertising and Concentration. Of the several scenarios through which manipulative advertising might rob consumers of utility, one goes something like this:

> High advertising expenditures ⟶ Consumers manipu-
> lated ⟶ More sales ⟶ Economies of scale in produc-
> tion ⟶ More profits ⟶ Purchase of more efficient
> plant and equipment ⟶ Still more scale economies
> and profits ⟶ More advertising purchased ⟶
> Weaker competitors fail ⟶ More concentration ⟶
> More opportunities for remaining firms to collude to raise
> prices ⟶ Consumers lose wealth and utility.

A solid correlation between advertising expenditure and industry concentration might help support this chain of causation. To those for whom advertising is information, on the other hand, advertising promotes competition, assists new entrants to an industry, and does not create scale economies. For those reasons, it tends to defeat the emergence of oligopoly. If the relationship between advertising and concentration is weak or nonexistent, we might have some reason to accept these claims. We might also have some reason to believe that rather than taking utility from consumers, advertising assists them in getting maximum value for their dollars.

The studies on the relationship between advertising intensity and concentration usually try to establish the correlation between these two variables, to determine causation between them through regression analysis, and to use still other methods to determine whether the first two relationships are significant.[53] Summaries of such research often regard it as inconclusive.[54] Writing in 1970, Simon claimed that no test yet performed adequately measured the causal effect of advertising on concentration.[55] By the 1980s, much more research on the advertising-concentration relationship was available, but solid conclusions on the question still were not within reach. After summarizing a number of articles, Albion and Farris concluded that most of these studies had established some relationship between advertising intensity and concentration.[56] But, they immediately added, "[q]uestions still remain concerning its form, its importance, the direction of causation, and the conditions under which it is found."[57] Albion and Farris also introduced evidence suggesting that television advertising creates barriers to entry, the principal reason being that there is only so much "prime time" available and that large existing firms apparently preempt much of it.[58]

However, Robert Ekelund and David Saurman were more skeptical about the claim that advertising causes concentration. After listing or discussing over ten studies on the question, they concluded as follows: "The notion that heavy advertising causes industries to be highly concentrated has very little logical or empirical support in relation to the evidence that states this relationship not to be the case. There are no data or evidence that consistently show that advertising, however measured, causes concentration."[59] Critics of advertising who recognize the highly ideological character of the debate over advertising's power might try to discount this statement because Ekelund and Saurman are open proponents of the view that advertising is informative and a force for competition. But the same argument might be used against studies supporting their position.

Advertising and Profits. According to the traditional critique, advertising might also reduce consumer utility through something like the following scenario:

> High advertising expenditures ——→ Consumers manipulated ——→ More product or brand differentiation ——→ Demand less elastic ——→ Firms can raise prices above competitive levels ——→ Firms reap greater profits and consumers lose money and utility.

A strong correlation between advertising expenditures and profits at the firm or industry level might support this scenario. A weak or nonexistent relationship between advertising and profits, on the other hand, might well suggest that advertising makes demand *more* elastic, as increased advertising provides rational consumers with more information about prices, product quality, and the like. On this assumption, firms would be unable to raise prices above competitive levels. Consumers, on the other hand, would maximize the utility they get from their expenditures.

Unfortunately, it seems that the research on the advertising-profits relationship is inconclusive. This is true despite Albion and Farris's statement that a majority of the relevant empirical studies find a positive relationship between advertising and profitability.[60] One problem arises from the familiar observation that a correlation between x and y does not show that x causes y (or that y causes x). As we will see in chapter 5, for example, firms tend to reduce their advertising expenditures when business turns bad. This tendency could go some way toward explaining any correlation between advertising and profits.[61] As Albion and Farris also report, moreover, some of the studies find little or no correlation between advertising and profits.[62] The main reason, apparently, is that they define profitability differently than do many of the studies that find a correlation. The details of this particular issue are beyond the scope of this book.[63]

Other Inquiries. If measuring profitability creates so many problems, why not test the traditional critique by determining the relationship between advertising and *price*?[64] The prices consumers pay, after all, cause the utility losses they assertedly suffer, and firm profits depend on many factors other than the prices the firm charges. Similarly, why bother with the advertising–concentration relationship when a more direct measure of that relationship's ill effects is available? Because so many considerations affect a product's price, however, researchers apparently have had difficulty isolating advertising's impact upon it. Thus, few efforts have been made to directly examine the relationship between advertising and elasticity of demand (which is measured by changes in price). Instead, profits and industry concentration have been used as surrogates for the market power whose presence might better be captured by elasticity of demand.[65]

However, another measure of market power has attracted some research attention. According to the traditional critique, advertising's ability to reduce elasticity of demand and raise prices depends on its manipulative powers. These, in turn, are said to manifest themselves primarily in the creation of brand loyalties. If we have some reason to believe that advertising creates brand loyalties, therefore, we might also have some reason to believe that it enables competitors to raise prices. Apparently, however, the necessary evidence is lacking. Albion and Farris conclude that "[t]here is no convincing body of evidence that advertising always, or even usually, increases the amount of brand loyalty in industries."[66] One reason for this conclusion is some scattered evidence that product quality and consumers' experience with a product are the main generators of brand loyalty.[67] The other is the existence of several studies concluding that advertising intensity tends to be associated with unstable market shares.[68] If advertising were a source of enduring brand loyalties, one would expect market shares to be more stable in industries where advertising intensities are high.

A Brief Summary. This section's discussion hardly exhausts the vast literature evaluating advertising's impact on competition. Nor does it attempt to make any firm conclusions on the issues addressed by that literature. Nevertheless, the section casts some doubt on the traditional economic critique of advertising. First, it is unclear whether or to what extent advertising increases industry concentration. For that reason, it also is unclear whether or to what extent advertising facilitates the anticompetitive pricing often found in concentrated industries. Second, advertising's relationship with profitability may depend as much on the definition of profitability as on anything else. Also, a positive correlation between advertising intensity and profits might be explained by the way firms typically budget their advertising. Thus, it is uncertain whether advertising helps create the higher prices for which increased profitability is a surrogate. Worse yet, it is difficult to measure the relationship between advertising expenditures and those prices themselves. The same is true of the relationship between advertising and elasticity of demand. Finally, although the relevant evidence seems sketchy, it appears that advertising does not significantly influence brand loyalties.

For all these reasons, it also is unclear whether advertising costs consumers utility. To be sure, the available evidence hardly supports the claims made by those who view advertising as informative. If anything, in fact, it strikes me as lending somewhat more support to the traditional critique. That support, however, is limited. As observant readers no doubt have already noted, the same is true of an assumption on which this chapter proceeds: that advertising manipulates consumers by dictating their product and service choices. The traditional critique depends to a considerable degree on just that assumption, and if the critique's validity is uncertain, the same is true of the assumption that advertising manipulates. In particular, how do we square advertising's supposed manipulativeness with its apparent weakness in creating brand loyalties? Chapter 4 pursues these and related questions.

TRYING TO PUT IT ALL TOGETHER

The preceding remarks notwithstanding, this chapter assumes that advertising manipulates in both the senses described in chapter 1: (1) it stimulates consumption and (2) it directs the consumption choices consumers make when it tries to manipulate. Even on those assumptions, does the chapter justify the political agenda propounded by critics of advertising? Specifically, does it give their proposals moral underpinnings by showing that advertising reduces aggregate utility by manipulating consumers? As stated earlier, I consider that question primarily from a rule-utilitarian perspective rather than an act-utilitarian one. One way to frame this rule-utilitarian inquiry is to ask whether a rule forbidding all manipulative ads would generate more utility than a rule permitting them. This would seem to be the case if manipulative advertising takes away more utility than it generates. In effect, then, this chapter attempts a big, crude cost-benefit analysis of manipulative advertising. Its implicit comparison is with an environment from which such advertising is absent.

Our aim, then, is to determine the costs and benefits of advertising that manipulates consumers. This requires that we consider some factors not addressed earlier. One of these is the money spent on advertising. According to John O'Toole, for example, American businesses devoted over $84 billion to advertising in 1984, which was approximately 2.3 percent of the American gross national product for that year.[69] (In all likelihood, much of this expenditure was passed on to consumers in the form of higher prices.) If chapter

1's content analyses of advertising are at all representative, a significant portion of this expenditure went for manipulative, as opposed to informative, ads. Apparently pulling in the other direction, however, is the claim that advertising helps provide free—or at least cheap—mass media by subsidizing those media.[70] But many of the same people who obtain this benefit pay for it through the higher prices just discussed.[71] Thus, it seems that we must balance advertising's costs against whatever utility people derive from free—or relatively cheap—communications media. Although I wonder whether the latter outweigh the former, at least they blunt the utility losses associated with advertising's costs.

These inconclusive preliminaries bring us to the main arguments considered in this chapter. The chapter began with the provisional assumption that advertising increases utility by stimulating the propensity to consume, thus helping ensure a steady flow of consumer goods and the economy's continued functioning. As I briefly noted, moreover, maybe the mass consumption generated by advertising also generates some incremental utility by increasing economies of scale and lowering prices.[72] Galbraith attacked these assumptions by maintaining that the satisfaction of artificially created consumer desires generates little utility. This argument gave important support to a major item in his political agenda: the shift toward a society with a different balance between public and private goods. But as Hayek asserted in reply to Galbraith's argument, a desire's genesis outside the individual does not imply low utility from the desire's satisfaction. Of course, this does not necessarily mean that people get more utility from consumer goods and services than they would get from alternatives such as Galbraith's public production. Then again, we have no particular reason to regard Galbraith's alternative as superior either. Thus, our initial assumption that consumerism generates some utility remains undisturbed. That assumption, by the way, is indirectly corroborated by the concern some critics of advertising have expressed about the economic consequences of curtailing it too radically.[73] If advertising did not generate utility, would they be so worried? And as that concern suggests, even if some alternative arrangement would generate more utility than today's consumer society, we must consider the transition costs of moving to that better state. Conceivably, they could outweigh the long-term gains from the move.

Even though Galbraith possibly may have offered a superior alternative, therefore, our opening assumption that advertising increases utility remains largely undisturbed. But Galbraith's argument depended on only one of advertising's assumed effects: its stimulation of the propensity to consume. Now, we shift our focus to manipulative advertising's asserted ability to distort competition by dictating consumer purchase decisions. Does this significantly reduce the utility consumers derive from their purchases of goods and services? If so, advertising's critics at least have a case for increased government regulation of manipulative advertising. And if the utility losses are sufficiently severe, maybe the more stringent proposals discussed in chapter 1 begin to look more attractive.

Advertising's assumed power to shape consumer choice, we initially observed, had three consequences: (1) utility losses resulting from the purchase of suboptimum products, (2) the possibility of added value or extra utility caused by the pleasing product associations manipulative advertising creates, and (3) the possibility of lost utility as the expectations created by those associations fail to come true. The first factor, however, should not apply where the product is an HPG. After putting these three factors together, it was unclear whether manipulative advertising caused significant utility losses by distorting competition. Apparently changing that picture for the worse, however, was the argument that manipulative advertising costs consumers additional money by enabling firms to charge higher-than-free-market prices. But this traditional economic critique of advertising has been vigorously challenged in recent years. My tentative conclusion was that the utility losses identified by the traditional critique probably are modest at best.

All things considered, manipulative advertising probably costs consumers some utility when it dictates product choices. The previous analysis has identified four ways in which manipulative advertising might reduce utility when it has this effect: (1) its cost, (2) losses through the purchase of suboptimum products, (3) losses identified by the traditional economic critique of advertising, and (4) losses resulting from the dashed hopes created by associative advertising. On the positive side of the ledger, we have (1) the added value or extra utility produced by manipulative advertising's pleasing associations and (2) the gains resulting from free or cheap mass media. Even if advertising's cost is balanced by the benefits of inexpensive media, the potential sources of loss still outnumber the potential sources of gain. In addition, the remaining argument of the latter kind (the added-value argument) seems conjectural. Among the negative factors, the dashed-expectations argument obviously is highly conjectural. Except in HPG cases, however, utility losses from the purchase of suboptimum products are a fairly predictable consequence of manipulative advertising's effectiveness. And while I do not find the traditional economic critique of advertising especially persuasive, it probably identifies some genuine utility losses attributable to manipulative advertising.

In the aggregate, therefore, manipulative advertising probably costs consumers some utility through its assumed ability to dictate the choice of products and services. If that assumed ability is real, maybe these losses could justify some targeted regulation of particular kinds of manipulative ads. But the losses in question hardly seem sizable enough to outweigh the economic abundance, scale economies, and resulting utility gains that flow from advertising's stimulation of the propensity to consume. That being the case, it is difficult to mount a utilitarian argument for efforts to suppress the volume of advertising, such as taxes or other limitations. It is even more difficult to justify radical changes in modern consumer capitalism on utilitarian grounds. Relatively speaking, the utility we gain from consumption is a known quantity. Any utilitarian argument for a different social order must show that it is likely to produce more utility, and just how is that demonstration to be made? Even if the demonstration were possible, it also is possible that the costs of realizing the new regime would negate the gains from its realization.

NOTES

1. Ronald Dworkin, *A Matter of Principle* (Cambridge, Mass.: Harvard University Press, 1985), 245–46.

2. This book's brief account of utilitarianism is based primarily on William K. Frankena, *Ethics*, 2d ed. (Englewood Cliffs, N.J.: Prentice-Hall, 1973), chap. 3; Richard A. Posner, *The Economics of Justice* (Cambridge, Mass.: Harvard University Press, 1983), chap. 3; James Rachels, *The Elements of Moral Philosophy*, 2d ed. (New York: McGraw-Hill, 1993), chaps. 7, 8; J.J.C. Smart and Bernard Williams, *Utilitarianism: For and Against* (Cambridge, England: Cambridge University Press, 1976), pp. 3–74.

3. Thus, I exclude versions of utilitarianism whose criterion is *average per capita utility*. I do so on the simple assumption that, if utility is a good thing, more of it is better than less of it.

4. Jeremy Bentham, *An Introduction to the Principles of Morals and Legislation*, in *A Bentham Reader*, ed. Mary Peter Mack (New York: Western Publishing, Pegasus paperback, 1969), 85-89, 96-100 (chaps. 1, 4, 5).

5. John Stuart Mill, *Utilitarianism*, in *J. S. Mill, Utilitarianism, On Liberty, and Considerations on Representative Government*, ed. H. B. Acton (London: J. M. Dent & Sons, Everyman's Library paperback reprint, 1988), 6-12 (chap. 2).

6. One such approach assumes that "in talking of happiness or utility one is talking about people's desires or preferences and their getting what they want or prefer, rather than about some sensation of pleasure or happiness." Bernard Williams, "A Critique of Utilitarianism," in Smart and Williams, *Utilitarianism*, 80. Here, however, I define utility in the latter sense—as involving psychic states of happiness or satisfaction. Manipulative advertising raises many questions about the true nature of our desires and preferences. If we are uncertain on that score, it is difficult to determine when or whether people get what they desire or prefer.

7. Mill, *Utilitarianism*, 36 (chap 4).

8. G. E. Moore, *Principia Ethica* (1903; Cambridge, England: Cambridge University Press, 1962), 66-67 (chap. 3, sec. 40).

9. According to Moore, for example, Henry Sidgwick justified utilitarianism in this way. Ibid., 59, 92-95 (secs. 36, 55-56). See, for example, Henry Sidgwick, *The Methods of Ethics*, 7th ed. (1907; Indianapolis: Hackett Publishing, 1981), 388-89, 406-7.

10. See, for example, Moore, *Principia Ethica*, chap. 6. To be sure, Moore's position is sometimes described as utilitarian, specifically, as "ideal utilitarianism." According to J.J.C. Smart: "Moore, who believed that some states of mind, such as those of acquiring knowledge, had intrinsic value quite independent of their pleasantness, can be called an ideal utilitarian." Smart, "An Outline of a System of Utilitarian Ethics," in Smart and Williams, *Utilitarianism*, pp. 12-13. As this quotation suggests, however, Moore was not a utilitarian as the term is defined in this book.

11. Frankena, *Ethics*, 43-56; W. D. Ross, *The Right and the Good* (1930; Indianapolis: Hackett Publishing, 1988), chap. 2, especially pp. 20-26.

12. I take Bernard Williams, "A Critique of Utilitarianism," in Smart and Williams, *Utilitarianism*, 108-18, to be making an argument of this general sort.

13. See, for example, Posner, *The Economics of Justice*, 56–57 (pulling wings off flies and painlessly murdering one's malicious, old, and unhappy grandfather).

14. This example closely resembles one found in Michael Sandel, ed., *Liberalism and Its Critics* (New York: New York University Press, 1987), 2 (editor's introduction).

15. For example, J.J.C. Smart (who rejects rule-utilitarianism) defines it as "the view that the rightness or wrongness of an action is to be judged by the goodness and badness of the consequences of a rule that everyone should perform the action in like circumstances." Smart, "An Outline of a System of Utilitarian Ethics," in Smart and Williams, *Utilitarianism*, 9.

16. Peter Doyle, "Economic Aspects of Advertising: A Survey," *Economic Journal* 78 (1968): 578, 582–85 (describing the argument).

17. John Kenneth Galbraith, *The Affluent Society* (Boston: Houghton Mifflin, 1958), 285–89.

18. Ibid., chaps. 9–11. This argument, however, did not originate with Galbraith. Vincent P. Norris, "The Economic Effects of Advertising: A Review of the Literature," *Current Issues and Research in Advertising* 2 (1984): 67–68. A closely related argument, which I do not explicitly consider, is that manipulative advertising reduces utility by undermining our cognitive faculties and thus our ability to determine what our real needs are. Paul C. Santilli, "The Informative and Persuasive Functions of Advertising: A Moral Appraisal," *Journal of Business Ethics* 2 (1983): 27, 29.

19. Galbraith, *The Affluent Society*, 158.

20. Ibid., 160.

21. Ibid., 259.

22. Ibid., 154. A related but distinguishable argument is that, as advertising makes people more consumeristic, ever-greater pleasures are needed to maintain a constant level of satisfaction. Russell W. Belk and Richard W. Pollay, "Images of Ourselves: The Good Life in Twentieth Century Advertising," *Journal of Consumer Research* 11 (March 1985): 889.

23. Galbraith, *The Affluent Society*, 203. Also recognizing it were Paul Baran and Paul Sweezy, who remarked that "attempts to abolish or curtail advertising could have seriously adverse effects unless accompanied by comprehensive and effective planning for full and socially desirable employment." "This is a point," they add, "which critics of advertising consistently neglect." Paul A. Baran and Paul M. Sweezy, "Theses on Advertising," *Science and Society* 28 (Winter 1964): 23–24 (italics omitted). A few business ethicists have noted the problem as well. See Richard L. Lippke, *Radical Business Ethics* (Lanham, Md.: Rowman &

Littlefield, 1995), 116–17; John Waide, "The Making of Self and World in Advertising," *Journal of Business Ethics* 6 (1987): 77.

24. Galbraith, *The Affluent Society*, chaps. 21, 24.

25. Baran and Sweezy, "Theses on Advertising," 23 (italics omitted).

26. F. A. Hayek, "The *Non Sequitur* of the 'Dependence Effect,'" *Southern Economic Journal* 27 (1961): 346.

27. Ibid.

28. Ibid., 347.

29. For a discussion of this standard criticism by a defender of utilitarianism, see Smart, "An Outline of a System of Utilitarian Ethics," 18–21.

30. R. M. Hare, "Commentary," *Business and Professional Ethics Journal* 3 (1984): 27–28.

31. Julian L. Simon, *Issues in the Economics of Advertising* (Urbana: University of Illinois Press, 1970): 270–71; see also 272–85. See also Norris, "The Economic Effects of Advertising," 55–56.

32. See, for example, Ivan L. Preston, *The Tangled Web They Weave: Truth, Falsity, and Advertisers* (Madison: University of Wisconsin Press, 1994), 81.

33. This should be true both for the normal associative ad (in which the association is more or less present to consciousness) and for associative subliminal ads. As we saw in chapter 1, subliminal ads might also manipulate by changing consumers' tastes. Because this possibility is so speculative, I ignore it here. Chapter 4 casts additional doubt on the idea that subliminal advertising can change consumers' tastes.

34. Eric Clark, *The Want Makers. The World of Advertising: How They Make You Buy* (New York: Viking Penguin, 1988), 23–24. Another possibility, which I ignore for purposes of simplicity, is that people get utility simply from viewing a manipulative ad. Richard W. Pollay and Banwari Mittal, "Here's the Beef: Factors, Determinants, and Segments in Consumer Criticism of Advertising," *Journal of Marketing* 57 (July 1993): 102 (noting this possibility).

The idea that associative advertising gives consumers extra utility or added value received its ultimate formulation in a 1970 article written by Theodore Levitt. Theodore Levitt, "The Morality (?) of Advertising," *Harvard Business Review* (July-August 1970): 84–92. Levitt's main thesis was that "embellishment and distortion are among advertising's legitimate and socially desirable purposes" (p. 85.) (However, Levitt did condemn falsification with larcenous intent—that is, the *deceptive* advertising discussed in chapter 1.) The reason is that advertising enables us to escape our dismal and depressing natural existence. When viewed without illusions, Levitt maintained, human life is a poor thing. Natural reality, he claimed, is "crudely fashioned"; "crude, drab, and generally

oppressive"; and "drab, dull, [and] anguished" (pp. 86, 90). Thus, "[e]ve-
rybody everywhere wants to modify, transform, embellish, enrich, and
reconstruct the world around him—to introduce into an otherwise harsh
or bland existence some sort of purposeful and distorting alleviation" (p.
87). People accomplish this mainly though art, but also through advertising. "[W]e use art, architecture, literature, and the rest, and advertising
as well, to shield ourselves, in advance of experience, from the stark and
plain reality in which we are fated to live" (p. 90). For these reasons,
consumers want more than simple operating functionality from the
products they buy. As Charles Revson of Revlon, Inc. once said, "In the
factory we make cosmetics; in the store we sell hope" (p. 85). Thus "[i]t
is not cosmetic chemicals women want, but the seductive charm promised by the alluring symbols with which these chemicals have been
surrounded—hence the rich and exotic packages in which they are sold,
and the suggestive advertising with which they are promoted" (p. 85). In
other words, consumers demand an expanded notion of functionality
which includes " 'nonmechanical' utilities," and do so to "help . . . solve
a problem of life" (p. 89.) Therefore, the "products" they buy include not
only narrowly functional attributes, but also the emotional or affective
content produced by their advertising. From this, it follows that advertisements are not supposed to be literal representations of the products
they tout. "[D]eep down inside," moreover, "the consumer understands
this perfectly well" (p. 90). Indeed, the consumer gives industry a "fiat . . .
to 'distort' its messages" (p. 89). While he wants "'truth,'" "he also wants
and needs the alleviating imagery and tantalizing promises of the advertiser and designer" (p. 92).

35. Ira Teinowitz, "This Bud's for Her: Women to Get 'Equal Roles'
in New A-B Campaign," *Advertising Age*, 28 October 1991, 1.

36. Stuart Ewen, *Captains of Consciousness: Advertising and the Social
Roots of the Consumer Culture* (New York: McGraw-Hill, 1977), 89–90.

37. Neil H. Borden, *The Economic Effects of Advertising* (Chicago:
Richard D. Irwin, 1942), 662.

38. Ibid., 661.

39. Simon, *Issues in the Economics of Advertising*, 273.

40. Ibid., 273–74.

41. Ibid., 274.

42. Most of the points made in the following paragraphs come from
Mark S. Albion and Paul W. Faris, *The Advertising Controversy: Evidence
on the Economic Effects of Advertising* (Boston: Auburn House, 1981),
30–35; and Robert B. Ekelund, Jr., and David S. Saurman, *Advertising and
the Market Process: A Modern Economic View* (San Francisco: Pacific
Research Institute for Public Policy, 1988), 20–33. Each work describes
views it later tries to evaluate. The proponents of those views include

Edward Chamberlin, Joan Robinson, Nicholas Kaldor, Joe S. Bain, William S. Comanor, Thomas S. Wilson, and John Kenneth Galbraith. For an early statement that makes some similar points, see Borden, *The Economic Effects of Advertising*, 850–51, 871–74.

43. Albion and Faris, *The Advertising Controversy*, 56–57.

44. Norris, "The Economic Effects of Advertising," 91.

45. Robert Jacobson and Franco M. Nicosia, "Advertising and Public Policy: The Macroeconomic Effects of Advertising," *Journal of Marketing Research* 18 (February 1981): 29–30.

46. Actually, there may be a second contender as well: a view of advertising based on the "Austrian school" of economics associated with such names as Ludwig von Mises and Friedrich Hayek. It differs from both the traditional critique of advertising and its new defense by not regarding perfect competition as the correct description of properly functioning markets. See Jerry Kirkpatrick, *In Defense of Advertising: Arguments from Reason, Ethical Egoism, and Laissez-Faire Capitalism* (Westport, Conn.: Quorum Books, 1994), chap. 5.

47. Most of the positions stated below come from Albion and Faris, *The Advertising Controversy*, 30, 35–38, 47; and Ekelund and Saurman, *Advertising and the Market Process*, chap. 3.

48. Albion and Faris, *The Advertising Controversy*, 103–14 (mild skepticism about economies of scale); Simon, *Issues in the Economics of Advertising*, chap. 1 (little evidence for increasing marginal returns to advertising).

49. These sources include Albion and Faris, *The Advertising Controversy*, chaps. 3, 5; Ekelund and Saurman, *Advertising and the Market Process*, chaps. 5, 6; Norris, "The Economic Effects of Advertising," 79–106; Simon, *Issues in the Economics of Advertising*, chap. 9.

50. Norris, "The Economic Effects of Advertising," 117.

51. Albion and Faris, *The Advertising Controversy*, 45.

52. Ibid.

53. Ekelund and Saurman, *Advertising and the Market Process*, 100.

54. While relying on a variety of miscellaneous studies employing different research methods, Vincent Norris seemed more inclined than the following commentators to find a relationship between advertising and concentration. See Norris, "The Economic Effects of Advertising," 88–92.

55. Simon, *Issues in the Economics of Advertising*, 230–31; see 226–31.

56. Albion and Faris, *The Advertising Controversy*, 66; see 62–66.

57. Ibid.

58. Ibid., 66–67.

59. Ekelund and Saurman, *Advertising and the Market Process*, 102–3.

60. Albion and Farris, *The Advertising Controversy*, 55; see 53–55 (summarizing several studies).

61. Ibid., 56. For some other possible explanations of the correlation, explanations that do not involve the assumption that advertising causes profits, see pp. 51–52; see also Norris, "The Economic Effects of Advertising," 83.

62. Albion and Farris, *The Advertising Controversy*, 52, 55.

63. Nonetheless, I will try to provide a few of those details. Most observers seem to agree that raw dollar profits are a poor measure of a firm's ability to extract extra money from advertising and that rate of return on capital is a more appropriate measure. The studies finding little correlation between advertising and profitability further maintain that because advertising's effects often persist well into the future, it should be treated as a capital expenditure rather than as a current expense. This increases the denominator (the value of capital assets) in the equation by which profitability (rate of return) is calculated. The change in denominator, in turn, drives profitability down and reduces the correlation between it and advertising expenditure. (This effect should be most pronounced when advertising expenditures are large.) Furthermore, because advertising expenditures are firm capital, they must be depreciated over time. This means that the current year's capital includes varying percentages of past years' advertising expenditures, which further enlarges the denominator. It also makes the depreciation rate another critical variable in the determination of profitability, and the experts naturally have disagreed on the appropriate percentage. On this whole subject, see Ekelund and Saurman, *Advertising and the Market Process*, 104–11; and Norris, "The Economic Effects of Advertising," 83–84.

64. Another subject that has attracted some research attention is the question of whether there are economies of scale in advertising. As we have seen, the traditional critique assumes that such economies exist and that they create a barrier to entry. Economists who defend advertising, on the other hand, tend to deny both propositions. For example, Julian Simon has vigorously maintained that increasing returns to advertising do not exist (Simon, *Issues in the Economics of Advertising*, chap. 1). For other discussions of the subject, see Albion and Farris, *The Advertising Controversy* 103–13; Ekelund and Saurman, *Advertising and the Market Process*, 43–46.

65. Albion and Farris, *The Advertising Controversy*, 46–48.

66. Ibid., 97.

67. Ibid., 95.

68. Ibid., 96–97; see also Ekelund and Saurman, *Advertising and the Market Process*, 86–87. Here, however, there also are studies to the contrary; see Albion and Farris, *The Advertising Controversy*, 97.

69. John O'Toole, *The Trouble with Advertising* (New York: Times Books, 1985), 23, 213. For some statistics for various years between 1935 and 1982, see Michael Schudson, *Advertising, the Uneasy Persuasion: Its Dubious Impact on American Society* (n.p.: Basic Books, 1986), 67. As Schudson's statistics indicate, something over 40 percent of the yearly total usually represents local, as opposed to national, advertising expenditure.

70. See, for example, Doyle, "Economic Aspects of Advertising," 590 (stating the argument).

71. Norris, "The Economic Effects of Advertising," 113. Actually, advertising's subsidization of the media probably redistributes income. For example, lower income groups with low consumer expenditures may spend more time watching television than higher income groups with larger consumer expenditures. Because the latter groups probably read more newspapers and magazines than the former, however, those media may redistribute income in the other direction. Doyle, "Economic Aspects of Advertising," 590–91.

72. See, Doyle, "Economic Aspects of Advertising," 583. A related claim is that by spurring the propensity to consume, advertising stimulates technological progress and the production of higher-quality goods in various ways. See 588–90, where Doyle seems skeptical about advertising's contributions in these areas.

73. See, for example, Baran and Sweezy, "Theses on Advertising," 23–24; Galbraith, *The Affluent Society*, 203; Lippke, *Radical Business Ethics*, 116–17; Waide, "The Making of Self and World," 77.

Chapter 3

THREE OTHER ETHICAL CRITICISMS

As chapter 1 suggested, business ethicists have been of great service in the assault on manipulative advertising. Many of advertising's traditional critics were economists, and their arguments against advertising were explicitly or implicitly utilitarian. If chapter 2 was at all on the mark, however, those arguments are inconclusive. But while it might derail the economists, chapter 2 is of little use against many business ethicists who are critical of advertising because they can bring other, nonutilitarian, moral arguments to bear.

In fact, some business ethicists who are critics of manipulative advertising might not be particularly bothered by chapter 2's inconclusions about the practice's implications for utility. The reason is that to them utilitarianism is a flawed criterion in the first place. In their view, manipulative advertising would be wrong—and political action to control it would be justified—even if by chance it does increase the total amount of happiness in the universe. Some of these people might say that it simply is unethical to manipulate or *use* another person for one's own ends. Others might stress a related point: that manipulative advertising is wrong because it violates personal *autonomy*. Another group of critics pursue a different line of attack. To them, manipulative advertising is wrong because it undermines traditional *virtues* and prevents people from living the best life of which they are capable. This chapter examines these three criticisms, two of which rely upon well-known ethical theories and one of which invokes a widely praised moral value. Like chapter 2, it assumes that all advertising socializes people to a life of consumption and that manipulative advertising distorts the choices consumers make.

A KANTIAN CRITIQUE OF MANIPULATIVE ADVERTISING

One of utilitarianism's most striking features is its command that the morality of actions be judged solely by their consequences (in this case, their consequences for utility). This uncompromising consequentialism is bound to offend some sensibilities. It collides with the widespread view that the morality of actions is determined not only by their consequences, but also by their own nature and the motives underlying them. This view expresses a *deontological* approach to ethics.[1] To contrast it with utilitarianism, consider the following example from W. D. Ross:

> Suppose . . . that the fulfillment of a promise to *A* would produce 1,000 units of good for him, but that by doing some other act I could produce 1,001 units of good for *B*, to whom I have made no promise, the other consequences of the two acts being of equal value; should we really think it self-evident that it was our duty to do the second act and not the first?[2]

Ross answered his rhetorical question in the negative. "We should, I fancy, hold that only a much greater disparity of value between the total consequences would justify us in failing to discharge our *prima facie* duty to *A*. After all, a promise is a promise, and is not to be treated so lightly as the theory we are examining would imply."[3]

Because Ross thought that a sufficiently large benefit to B would justify breaking the promise to A, he did not hold that consequences are irrelevant in determining the rightness of actions. Instead, he argued that we have a set of "prima facie duties," each of which is absolutely binding unless it collides with a prima facie duty that is more compelling under the circumstances.[4] Ross apparently believed that we must adjudicate conflicts among these duties by intuition.[5] One of the prima facie duties, the duty of beneficence, can be read as a duty to maximize utility.[6] Thus, if manipulative advertising increases utility but violates one of the other prima facie duties, Ross's approach requires that we weigh the duty of beneficence against the other duty as each applies to manipulative advertising.

The messiness and uncertainty of Ross's intuitionistic weighing process might make some foes of advertising wish for absolute moral rules that apply irrespective of consequences—and that definitively condemn manipulative advertising. Such a strict deontology also would rid us of all the troublesome questions about consequences that pervaded chapter 2. Immanuel Kant's ethical philosophy seems to fill the bill on all counts. The following brief sketch of Kantian ethics limits itself to the well-known presentation contained in his *Groundwork of the Metaphysic of Morals.*[7]

The Categorical Imperative

In the first sentence of his opening chapter, Kant tells us that "[i]t is impossible to conceive anything at all in the world, or even out of it, which can be taken as good without qualification, except a *good will.*"[8] His reason was that all other human excellences and advantages might be evil and hurtful when employed by a bad will. After this apparent concession to consequences, Kant almost immediately reverted to a strongly deontological position. The good will's goodness, he said, does not depend on its ability to produce good results. Even if it accomplishes nothing, "it would still shine like a jewel for its own sake as something which has its full value in itself."[9] Kant's extreme anticonsequentialism also is evident in his discussion of the good will's content, which essentially is duty for duty's sake. Thus, good actions motivated by self-interest have little or no moral value. The same is true even of good actions motivated by warm, generous sentiments. Only when a good act is performed *from duty* does it have genuine moral worth.

What is the content of this duty? As the preceding remarks suggest, it does not depend on our inclinations. Instead, it is *"the necessity to act out of reverence for the law."*[10] By law, Kant meant rationally derived moral principles, not the legal system's rules.[11] He called these principles or commands of reason *imperatives.*[12] Imperatives may be *hypothetical*, in which case they merely describe the means necessary to achieve whatever aim we happen to desire. Thus, the moral quality of a hypothetical imperative is relative to the moral quality of the end (or inclination) it seeks to advance. But an imperative may also be *categorical*—one that is "objectively necessary in itself apart from its relation to a further end."[13] The categorical imperative "is concerned, not with the matter of the action and its presumed results, but with its form and with the principle from which it follows; and what is essentially good in the action consists in the mental disposition, let the consequences be what they may."[14]

What does the categorical imperative command us to do? As the previous discussion suggests, it cannot get content either from our inclinations or from the consequences of actions taken to advance those inclinations. In their absence, Kant said, all that remains to motivate the good will is the idea of universality that inheres in the notion of a moral law or principle.[15] This led him to the first major formulation of the categorical imperative, which comes in several roughly similar versions. One rendition tells us to "*[a]ct only on that maxim through which you can at the same time will that it should become a universal law*."[16] This statement of the imperative might justify many customary moral rules, judgments, or intuitions. To take one of Kant's clearer examples, suppose that someone is considering whether, in order to get a much-needed loan, she can justifiably make a false promise to repay it. According to Kant, the maxim justifying this action would go as follows: "'Whenever I believe myself short of money, I will borrow money and promise to pay it back, though I know that this will never be done.' "[17] But, he maintained, no one would will this maxim's universalization. If the maxim were universally accepted, it would be useless to make a false promise to repay money because no one would believe *any* such promise.

The categorical imperative has a second major formulation, one Kant evidently regarded as equivalent to the first.[18] It says: "*Act in such a way that you always treat humanity, whether in your own person or in the person of any other, never simply as a means, but always at the same time as an end*."[19] A debtor's false promise to repay money fares no better under this version of the imperative than under its predecessor. Someone who intends to make a false promise will immediately see that he aims to make use of another person merely as a means to an end that person does not share.[20]

As might be expected from the preceding sketch, Kant's ethical theory is vulnerable to any number of criticisms. Utilitarians naturally will balk at his assertion that morality has nothing to do with the satisfaction of our inclinations. And one need not be a utilitarian to wonder about Kant's extreme anticonsequentialism.[21] A related objection is the Kantian system's apparent inability to handle situations in which moral rules conflict; how do we adjudicate among deontological absolutes? Another difficulty with Kant's ethics is why he thought that his two major formulations of the imperative are equivalent.[22] One also might wonder why they pack the moral weight Kant thought they do.

Perhaps the most prominent criticism of Kantian ethics, however, is that the imperative's first formulation is vacuous. Here, it is important to emphasize that this version of the imperative goes beyond the trivial command that we apply our principles consistently in different cases; rather, it is supposed to be a criterion for choosing correct principles. One version of the argument that the imperative lacks content says that universality is an empty formalism that cannot generate any substantive moral results.[23] To this, a Kantian might respond that while we cannot *deduce* rules from this version of the imperative, it still can—and does—determine the worth of the moral maxims that come before its tribunal.[24] But, as Alasdair MacIntyre has observed, this means that rather than setting universal standards that all societies ought to follow, in its practical application the imperative "is parasitic upon some already existing morality, within which it allows us to sift."[25] But actually, MacIntyre immediately adds, the imperative does not even enable us to do that, because we can always frame a universalizable maxim that permits us to do what we want while blocking others who want to do the same. For example, our lying debtor *would* will the universalization of a maxim permitting the making of false promises if it were sufficiently detailed to cover her situation and no others. A related criticism is that the first formulation of the imperative vindicates countless trivial or pernicious maxims so long as they can be consistently universalized; MacIntyre's examples include "always eat mussels on Mondays in March" and "persecute all those who hold false religous beliefs."[26] To be sure, the second formulation of the imperative—the command to treat people as ends, not means—does have some substantive content. But if the previous objections are valid, how can it do so and still be equivalent to the first formulation?

Manipulative Advertising and the Categorical Imperative

Despite the criticisms Kant's *Groundwork* has attracted, H. J. Paton probably was correct when he claimed that it "has exercised on human thought an influence almost ludicrously disproportionate to its size."[27] One reason for that influence, perhaps, is Kantian ethics' apparent ability to decisively condemn some social practices. At first glance, this certainly seems true of manipulative advertising.

As R. M. Hare has observed, manipulative advertising "is something that we prefer not to happen to us and therefore shall not will it as a universal maxim."[28] Suppose that, after having stumbled upon an enormously effective form of subliminal advertising, an ethical advertising agency subjects it to the first version of the imperative. The agency's maxim goes as follows: "In order to sell their clients' products and thereby make money, advertisers may employ subliminal advertising and other manipulative techniques whenever those methods have good prospects of success." Presumably, our agency's members would not will this maxim's universalization because the maxim would allow other advertisers to manipulate *them*. Specifically, the maxim's universalization would enable other advertisers to dictate one's consumption choices, and perhaps to affect one's basic values by stimulating a propensity to consume. The same seems true of any other person or group contemplating the use of manipulative advertising. Therefore, the practice would be wrong no matter who tries it, and the government presumably would be justified in suppressing it.

This Kantian argument may resemble an approach to regulating advertising that was briefly mentioned in chapter 1: Ivan Preston's proposed rule requiring advertisers to promise by implication that *they* believe in their own claims and are willing to rely on them.[29] The similarity is that Preston's rule requires advertisers, in effect, to universalize their claims. In any event, our simple Kantian argument runs afoul of a problem suggested earlier. An advertising agency might evade the first formulation of the imperative by framing its maxim narrowly enough to permit it to use manipulative techniques, while blocking such efforts by competitors. To defeat this ploy, maybe we could adopt a supplemental principle commanding that maxims be stated at a reasonably high level of generality. So far as I can determine, though, Kant did not state such a principle in the *Groundwork*. Another problem with the previous argument concerns a possibility discussed in chapter 2. What if manipulative advertising's elimination would destroy the economy? With this possibility introduced, the applicable maxim might read: "In order to sell their clients' products, make money, *and thereby keep the economy humming*, advertisers may employ subliminal advertising and other manipulative techniques whenever those methods have good prospects of success." Because the alternatives seem so dire, perhaps our hypothetical ethical advertisers—and society as a whole—would will this maxim's universalization even though in doing so they would will their own manipulation.

The preceding argument comes uncomfortably close to making consequences dictate an action's rightness or wrongness and thereby undermining the strict deontology of Kant's ethics. In any event, however, the argument is of no avail against the second major formulation of the imperative. A common interpretation of Kant's command to treat people as ends rather than means is that we must respect their rationality by offering them reasons for any action we propose, rather than trying to use or manipulate them.[30] As MacIntyre expresses this idea,

> What Kant means by treating someone as an end rather than as a means seems to be as follows. . . . I may propose a course of action to someone either by offering him reasons for so acting or by trying to influence him in non-rational ways. If I do the former I treat him as a rational will . . . for in offering him reasons I offer him an impersonal consideration for him to evaluate. . . . By contrast an attempt at non-rational suasion embodies an attempt to make the agent a mere instrument of *my* will, without any regard for *his* rationality.[31]

Purely informative advertising arguably meets this standard. As its name suggests, manipulative advertising plainly does not.[32] Advertisers who employ manipulative techniques obviously try to use consumers as means to their own ends—and just as obviously do so through nonrational appeals. Subliminal advertising is characterized precisely by its attempt to bypass conscious, rational reflection. Associative advertising tries to defeat the reasoned evaluation of products by linking them to the satisfaction of powerful human inclinations. Under the second formulation of the categorical imperative, therefore, manipulative ads apparently are wrong irrespective of their consequences—including the collapse of the economy. Among chapter 1's smorgasbord of political responses to manipulative advertising, Kantian arguments should favor those that promise to eliminate it entirely. If manipulative advertising is unconditionally wrong, there is a duty not to practice it, and the political authorities presumably have a duty to suppress it—all of it.

Maybe, however, associative advertisements can be characterized as rational appeals that consumers can evaluate for themselves. As we saw in chapter 2, such advertisements may provide added value or extra utility by making purchasers of a product experience the pleasurable ideas the ad has associated with the product. For example, an ad for Chance Encounter perfume might suggest that love is just around the corner for its female buyers. Perhaps this ad could be construed as making the following rational pitch: "For $75, we're offering you this physical product (the perfume), plus a pleasing psychic state (the expectation of love). We think it's a good deal, but you can decide." While this appeal might satisfy the second formulation of the imperative, few advertisers are likely to employ it. By making explicit the association between the product and a desirable mental state, the appeal highlights that association's implausibility. Once approached in this way, even the loneliest woman is unlikely to believe that Chance Encounter will improve her emotional condition. Of course, a less explicit association might do the trick. But this nonrational appeal would fail to satisfy the second formulation of the imperative.[33]

MANIPULATIVE ADVERTISING AND HUMAN AUTONOMY

After a considerable wait, we finally appear to have found a solid ethical basis for condemning manipulative advertising. Although manipulative advertisers might be able to evade the first formulation of Kant's categorical imperative, they hardly seem able to duck the second. Indeed, the imperative's second formulation almost seems to have been designed with manipulative advertising in mind. That formulation clearly bans manipulative advertising when it is consciously used to make consumers buy particular products. But it may encounter difficulties when we consider manipulative advertising's other assumed effect—stimulating the propensity to consume—because the second formulation's emphasis is on the manipulator, his actions, and his motives. This should not be a problem where the desire to consume results from manipulative ads that are intended to make consumers buy particular products. Here, the advertiser clearly acted wrongly under Kant's criterion. But, as I suggested in chapter 1, *informative* advertising also may help make people consumers. In this case, arguably, even an advertiser who sincerely endeavors to treat people as ends may nonetheless inadvertently manipulate them.

Perhaps we can seal off this loophole with a shift in emphasis. Rather than focusing on the manipulator, why not emphasize manipulative advertising's impact on its *targets*? When a manipulative advertiser uses people or treats them as ends, he or she undermines their capacity for rational, self-directed choice. This seems equivalent to saying that she he or undermines their *autonomy*. Manipulated consumers arguably lose autonomy both when they are stimulated to consume and when they are made to buy a particular product, and this is true no matter what the advertiser's motives were or what tactics were employed. By focusing on autonomy, therefore, perhaps we can both retain the moral thrust of the categorical imperative's second formulation, and have a basis for condemning informative advertising that stimulates the propensity to consume.

Because it involves consequences, however, this shift in emphasis seems to contradict Kant's deontology. It also seems inconsistent with his conception of autonomy, which he defined as the free will's embrace of the moral law set by the categorical imperative.[34] Kant to the contrary notwithstanding, though, business ethicists' evaluations of manipulative advertising often stress its implications for human autonomy. Unfortunately, these people—and philosophers in general—have not always agreed on the definition of autonomy. In addition, not all ethicists agree that manipulative advertising violates autonomy. After briefly considering two conceptions of autonomy and their implications for manipulative advertising, this section examines an important claim that manipulative advertising is consistent with autonomy.

Two Conceptions of Autonomy

Kant's conception of autonomy may bother some readers. A will that finds its freedom only in the moral law, they might say, is not free at all. And those who propound such notions of freedom are wittingly or unwittingly providing ideological ammunition to authoritarians of all stripes.[35] Thus, this view would continue, we need a conception of autonomy that does not constrain the ends the will might pursue. Thomas E. Hill provides such a conception when he contrasts Kant's notion of autonomy to what he calls "Sartrean autonomy." This is both "a denial that human choices are subject to causal determination" and "a denial that there are objective moral and rational constraints on our choices."[36] From this formulation, however, one might wonder whether Hill's Sartrean autonomy defeats authoritarianism at the cost of moral nihilism. One also might wonder whether this conception of autonomy is even possible. For example, if one accepts a scientific picture of reality and the determinism this probably implies, one will not accept the notion that human choices are free from causal determination.[37] And even if one does not make these assumptions, one may wonder whether an uncaused and indeterminate, yet causally efficacious, will does not reduce human behavior to chance.[38] But we need not pursue these questions here. Because this chapter assumes that manipulative advertising both makes people consumers and dictates their product choices, it necessarily overcomes Hill's Sartrean autonomy.

The same fate befalls another of the conceptions Hill considers. Here, autonomy probably is consistent with causal determination from outside the will. On this conception, the autonomous person possesses observable character traits that presumably result from a certain upbringing and a certain social environment. These include independence of judgment, rationality, deliberation, self-control, emotional independence, self-reliance, and self-esteem.[39] Of course, someone who truly has these attributes should be fairly resistant to manipulative advertising. Thus, my assumption that such advertising is effective seems to require an explanation of why people now lack the character traits that would enable them to withstand it. As we saw in chapter 1, Richard Lippke has provided a possible answer,[40] which is, basically, that people now lack this "determinate" kind of autonomy because both American society and advertising itself contribute to prevent its emergence.

According to Lippke, advertising suppresses autonomy by helping create a consumer culture rather than by dictating particular product choices. One reason for its effectiveness is the presence of background social conditions that inhibit the development of autonomy. These include the power of corporations; their hierarchical, authoritarian bureaucratic structures; unequal exposure to quality education; and the mass media's mindless programming. In the vacuum these conditions tend to create, advertising triumphs because it is pervasive, it is not challenged, and it begins its work early in life. This might be unobjectionable if advertising were a force for autonomy, but in fact advertising suppresses autonomy's development because of what Lippke calls advertising's implicit content. This involves a number of distinct messages whose central theme is that we should embrace consumerism and the infantile mental habits that support it. To Lippke, in sum, people lack autonomy because American society stunts its growth, and because this opens the door to advertising messages that kill it completely.

Manipulation and Autonomy Reconciled?

The preceding discussion suggests a conclusion that may have seemed obvious early in our inquiry: that however autonomy is conceived, it cannot coexist with effective manipulative advertising. Thus, if autonomy is a good thing, manipulative advertising is bad because it suppresses autonomy. In a 1982 article, however, Robert Arrington set out to demonstrate the opposite.[41] In his most important argument to that effect,[42] Arrington asserted that "there is something wrong in setting up the issue over advertising and behavior control as a question whether our desires are truly ours *or* are created in us by advertisements. Induced and autonomous desires do not separate into two mutually exclusive classes."[43] Even if manipulative advertising makes us buy things, therefore, we still may be acting autonomously when we do so. Indeed, even subliminal seduction may be consistent with autonomy.[44]

How can this be? As one might expect, the key to Arrington's argument is the conception of autonomy he advanced—a conception different from those set forth previously. In Arrington's view, a desire or an action is autonomous when one identifies with it during after-the-fact reflection. It is nonautonomous when, upon such reflection, it strikes one as alien, as something that does not express one's nature. As Arrington observes, a person may *feel* a desire even though he or she does not *acknowledge* it. For example, a kleptomaniac may be repelled by his or her own desire to steal.

> These are examples of desires which one might have but with which one would not identify. They are experienced as foreign to one's character or personality. Often a person will have . . . a second-order desire, that is to say, a desire *not* to have another desire. In such cases, the first-order desire is thought of as being nonautonomous, imposed on one. When on the contrary a person has a second-order desire to maintain and fulfill a first-order desire, then the first-order desire is truly his own, autonomous, original to him. So there is in fact a distinction between desires which are the agent's own and those which are not, but this is not the same as the distinction between desires which are innate to the agent and those which are externally induced.[45]

Under these criteria, does effective manipulative advertising violate human autonomy? Arrington's answer is: "Not necessarily and indeed not often."[46] His reason for this conclusion is that consumers ratify most of the desires advertising implants in them. This is demonstrated by, for example, the frequency with which they make repeat purchases of manipulatively advertised products.

Arrington's argument, then, is that most purchases caused by manipulative advertising are autonomous because we identify with those purchases when we engage in after-the-fact, second-order reflection about them. Of course, one might object that this identification occurs far less often than Arrington thinks it does. One also might object that because Arrington focuses solely on individual purchase decisions, he does not refute the claim that advertising reduces autonomy when it stimulates the propensity to consume.[47] But Arrington's argument is broad enough to meet this second objection. Just as I might ask myself whether I identify with my purchases, I might consider whether I really desire my consumer lifestyle. For many Americans, the answer to the second question almost certainly would be "yes."

The real problems with Arrington's argument lie elsewhere. Implicit in that argument, I think, is the notion that our second-order reflection is, if not freer, at least more central to our identities than the first-order desires it surveys. But is this notion consistent with manipulative advertising's efficacy? If a particular manipulative ad is potent enough to make me buy a product, might it not also influence my second-order evaluation of the purchase?[48] More important, if advertising has made me a consumer, how could my second-order reflection on that fact ever be genuine? Even if I could step back and ask, "Is this consumer-person really me?," would not the answer invariably be, "Of course"? Thus, it seems that we need to scrutinize our second-order desires to see whether we truly desire *them*. But if advertising really manipulates, how can we be sure about the purity of this third-order reflection? The only way to be certain, it seems, is to engage in fourth-order reflection. However, because advertising may also influence us at this level, and because the same may be true at subsequent levels, it seems that ensuring the autonomy of our character and our choices requires that we undertake an endless series of evaluations.

This infinite-regress problem arises in some recent philosophical literature on autonomy, which apparently has been dominated by conceptions like Arrington's.[49] To Gerald Dworkin, for example,

> [A]utonomy . . . is linked with the identification of a person with his projects, values, aims, goals, desires, and so forth. It is only when a person identifies with the influences that motivate him, assimilates them to himself, views himself as the kind of person who wishes to be moved in particular ways, that these influences are to be identified as "his." If, on the contrary, a person resents being motivated in certain ways, is alienated from these influences, would prefer to be the kind of person who is motivated in different ways, then these influences, which may be causally effective are not viewed by him as "his."[50]

But, Dworkin continues, this condition cannot be the entire story about autonomy. The second-order identifications one makes, or the choice of the type of person one wants to be, may have itself been so strongly influenced by others that we cannot regard it as being one's own.[51] Thus, the second-order reflection must be "procedurally independent" as well as authentic: "A person is autonomous if he identifies with his desires, goals, and values, and such identification is not itself influenced in ways which make the process of identification in some way alien to the individual."[52]

However, as Dworkin recognized and critics of his conception have affirmed, determining the procedural independence of a second-order reflection may require an infinite series of reflections.[53] His main response was that people either cannot or do not carry such reflections very far up the ladder.[54] But while this no doubt is true, it seems consistent with manipulative advertising's suppression of procedural independence and autonomy. Another response to the infinite-regress problem is that one can "terminate such a series of acts without cutting it off arbitrarily. When a person identifies himself *decisively* with one of his first-order desires, this commitment 'resounds' throughout the potentially endless array of higher orders."[55] "The decisiveness of the commitment he has made means that he has decided that no further question about his second-order volition, at any higher order, remains to be asked."[56] But while such commitments no doubt occur, without higher order reflection how can we be sure that they are genuinely our own? In other words, such commitments seem consistent with advertising's suppression of procedural autonomy. Indeed, if manipulative advertising really works, those "commitments" may come straight from Madison Avenue.

Arrington, readers will recall, was trying to reconcile advertising's manipulativeness with human autonomy. For the reasons just developed, that reconciliation appears to fail.[57] The reason is that Arrington's criterion for an autonomous purchase decision—second-order reflection—might itself be influenced by advertising. Ensuring the purity of that reflection seems to require an infinite series of subsequent reflections. To be sure, we have good reasons to think that this process is impossible and also have plausible ways to abort it. But by doing so, we merely revisit the dilemma that made the infinite series necessary in the first place: the questionable procedural independence of our second-order reflections about advertising and its influence on us.

However, Arrington no doubt was familiar with the literature on his conception of autonomy. Nonetheless, he chose not to address it in his article. Perhaps this was because he rejected the idea that procedural independence is necessary for autonomy. On that assumption, the only evident reason to regard a manipulated consumer's choice as "his own" or "her own" is his or her identification with it. But if this is the criterion, any manipulation of human beings that generates the appropriate subjective attitudes is consistent with autonomy. The more effective and extensive the manipulation, in fact, the more "autonomous" would be the identifications resulting from it. However we might define autonomy, I think, most of us would exclude such situations from that definition.

Implications for Political Action

When it manipulates, therefore, advertising violates autonomy under several common conceptions of the term. For that reason, it is wrong, and presumably it ought to be suppressed. Manipulative advertising's effect on consumer choice presumably would best be corrected by regulating the most effective—that is the most autonomy-inhibiting—ads of this kind. Due to the possibility, discussed in chapter 1, that all advertising helps stimulate the propensity to consume, regulation addressed to *that* problem might best protect autonomy if it simply seeks to eliminate as much advertising as possible—through bans, taxation, or other limits. Another possibility, one suggested by Lippke in chapter 1, is to attack the social conditions that (assertedly) make people susceptible to advertising's proconsumption message. However, autonomy considerations might *not* justify proposals like those made by John Kenneth Galbraith. The reason is that his agenda is too easily characterized as paternalistic.

MANIPULATIVE ADVERTISING, THE VIRTUES, AND THE GOOD LIFE

Manipulative advertising, then, suppresses autonomy in several senses of the term. But is autonomy really such a great thing? In particular, does it tell us how to conduct our lives? For example, consider Hill's Sartrean conception of autonomy. Under that variant of autonomy, not only is the autonomous person free from causal determination, he or she is free from all objective rational and moral restraints as well. Such a person, it seems, can do virtually anything.

To a greater or lesser extent, the other ethical theories or values we have examined are also vulnerable to the charge of indeterminacy. Almost any conception of autonomy raises the question:

autonomy for what? As for Kantian ethics, we have seen that the first major formulation of the categorical imperative is notoriously manipulable. Worse yet, no definite moral rules flow directly from it; instead, it evaluates maxims whose origins lie elsewhere. Its only substantive content (so to speak) is the notion of universalizability. Although the second major formulation of the imperative does have substantive content, it merely commands that we treat other people as rational beings when we propose a course of action to them. But it does not tell them (or us) what to do by dictating the rational mode of life. Finally, while utilitarianism has a definite criterion to guide our actions, that criterion seems consistent with any number of concrete behaviors. To all appearances, different people maximize utility in different ways, including some that ordinary morality would condemn.

The General Nature of Virtue Ethics

Missing in the ethical theories surveyed thus far and in the debate over advertising, some would complain, is the idea that certain kinds of behavior, states of character, sorts of desires, and modes of life are good or bad *in themselves*. For example, John Waide criticizes one defender of advertising for assuming "that in a satisfying life one has many satisfied desires—*which* desires is not important."[58] To Waide, moreover, "Arrington's defense of advertising . . . seems to assume that we have no standard to which we can appeal to judge whether a desire enhances a life."[59]

Such a standard, Stanley Benn has remarked, is "some objective assessment of what constitutes excellence in human beings."[60] The attributes that define human excellence often are called the virtues. James Rachels has defined them as traits of character, manifested in habitual action, that it is good for a person to have.[61] Of course, this definition is sufficiently capacious to include any trait that someone, somewhere might for some reason regard as good. It might even include the capacity for maximizing pleasure. The states of character typically praised by virtue ethicists, however, are the familiar traditional virtues. Rachels's list, for instance, includes compassion, conscientiousness, courage, generosity, honesty, loyalty, self-control, and self-reliance.[62] Besides focusing on particular virtues and vices, virtue ethics also may seek to identify the best or highest kinds of life. According to MacIntyre, for example,

Aristotle thought that the exercise of our rational faculties is the highest human excellence.[63]

In recent years, this virtue ethics has attracted increased attention from philosophers. For at least the past three centuries, however, other ethical views probably have been more popular. The most likely reason is what might loosely be called the modern worldview. Virtue ethics probably is most convincing if it is based on a teleological conception of human nature in which human beings are seen as striving to realize some determinate form or end that is a standard for evaluating their lives.[64] Today, however, most people view humanity as part of a nature that, if it has any place for ends or moral standards, relegates them to human consciousness and thereby renders them merely subjective.[65] A significant contributor to this conception of nature, of course, is modern science.

Virtue Ethics by Any Other Name

Even if virtue ethics has not been especially popular among post–seventeenth century philosophers, it still is very much the stuff of everyday life. We continually evaluate people with reference to particular virtues and vices. No doubt Kantians, utilitarians, and advocates of autonomy do the same in their day-to-day existences. Indeed, the form of autonomy characterized by independent judgment, deliberation, self-control, and self-reliance *is* a set of virtues.[66] The virtues also seem to have influenced Kant's ethics. According to MacIntyre,

> Kant is not of course himself in any doubt as to *which* maxims are in fact the expression of the moral law; virtuous plain men and women did not have to wait for philosophy to tell them in what a good will consisted and Kant never doubted for a moment that the maxims which he had learnt from his own virtuous parents were those which had to be vindicated by a rational test.[67]

Indeed, the four stated applications of the categorical imperative in Kant's *Groundwork* are that it is wrong to commit suicide, to make false promises, to refuse to develop one's abilities, and to ignore the distress of others.[68]

Utilitarianism also shares some common ground with virtue ethics. Many of the traditional virtues—honesty in particular—are so essential to society's functioning that significant utility would be lost in their absence.[69] In addition, the good life envisioned by most proponents of virtue ethics, while probably not a life of maximum pleasure, is not a life of self-denial either.[70] Sometimes, however, philosophers appear to believe that what is virtuous must also be utility maximizing, or at least that vice inevitably means lost utility. After agreeing with Friedrich Hayek about Galbraith's dependence effect, for example, Alan Goldman tried to resuscitate Galbraith's position. As I observed in chapter 2, Hayek's triumph over Galbraith was a limited one; he undercut Galbraith's argument that consumerism generates little utility, but he did not show that consumer goods are more desirable than Galbraith's public goods. Goldman tried to bolster Galbraith's position on consumerism by supplying an "independent criterion for wants worth fulfilling."[71]

> One weak criterion that can be adopted from a want-regarding or utilitarian moral theory relates to whether satisfaction of the desires in question increases overall satisfaction in the long run, whether it contributes to fulfilled or worthwhile lives. Desires are irrational when their satisfaction is incompatible with more fundamental or long-range preferences, either because of harmful side effects or because of the creation of more unsatisfied desires. Alcoholism is an example of such irrational desire, the satisfaction of which is harmful overall. Desires for junk food, tobacco, and certain kinds of conspicuous consumption are other examples, at least for certain consumers. Processes that create and feed such desires are not utility maximizing, since even the satisfaction of these desires lowers the subject's general level of utility in the long run.[72]

To Goldman, of course, advertising is one of those processes. Although consumers may develop resistance to individual ads, he believed, they have more difficulty resisting the consumer lifestyle advertising propounds. But this means that they are unlikely to maximize utility in the long run.

Here, of course, I assume for purposes of argument that manipulative advertising both dictates product choices and stimulates the propensity to consume. Even on those assumptions, however, is it so obvious that such advertising causes consumers to lose utility (or at least Benthamite utility) in the specific ways Goldman suggests? In my experience, at least, alcohol consumption, junk food ingestion, and smoking are pleasurable activities. Some consumers of these items never experience the physical and mental ills at which Goldman hints. For those who do suffer such ills, it is by no means clear that the utility lost thereby exceeds the utility gained during years of drinking, smoking, and eating unwisely. On simple Benthamite grounds, for example, how can one be sure that a painful death from lung, liver, or colon cancer outweighs the years of fun that may have caused it? (In some cases, moreover, such overindulgence may mean a quick exit by heart attack or stroke.) Finally, while it seems true that people who eschew alcohol, junk food, and tobacco live longer than their more self-indulgent brethren, it is unclear whether this has major implications for utility. The abstainers still must die—perhaps as painfully as the self-indulgent. And while they probably will live longer, since when is old age a high-utility experience?

The Denigration of Consumerism

Of course, Goldman's argument may ultimately be correct. My point, however, is that his confidence about advertising's consequences for utility is unjustified. One explanation for that confidence is his apparent belief that many of the activities advertising encourages are relatively lacking in virtue, and that for that reason they simply cannot be utility maximizing. Consider for example his use of the terms "wants worth fulfilling" and "fulfilled and worthwhile lives." If I am correct in this surmise, maybe an implicit virtue ethics influenced Goldman's overtly utilitarian argument against manipulative advertising.

In any event, a tacit virtue ethics seems to have influenced many other attacks on advertising, most of which involve the express or implied assumption that consumerism is a low, base, insipid mode of life. As Michael Schudson observes, such criticism generally "sees the emergence of a consumer culture as a devolution of manners, morals, and even manhood, from a work-oriented production ethic of the past to the consumption, 'lifestyle'-obsessed, ethic-less pursuits of the present."[73] According to Benn, for example, "advertising that presents consumption as a self-justifying activity, that attributes value to things, rather than to what they do to and for a person, is essentially corrupting in that it promotes a misconception of the nature of man."[74] A similar view may underlie Christopher Lasch's assertion that, by promoting consumption as a way of life, advertising "manufactures a product of its own: the consumer, perpetually unsatisfied, restless, anxious, and bored."[75]

Galbraith seemed to hold similar views. As one observer has remarked,

> Moralists and ascetics have long challenged the supremacy of material values and the inordinate estimation of wealth; and in the case of Galbraith it is difficult not to suspect that this challenge, together with the implicit puritanism one detects in so much of his work, may be traced back to the "uncompromising Calvinism" of his childhood in Iona Station, Ontario, where as elsewhere hard work and minimal luxury were characteristic of the Protestant Ethic. . . . Possibly because of a childhood spent (like Veblen) in a world both agrarian and puritanical, Galbraith has a definite propensity to regard rapid and continual change in the direction of commodity-affluence as the stormy petrol of national decadence.[76]

Despite its usual resort to utilitarian arguments, *The Affluent Society* provides some evidence for the preceding assertions. The book's frontmatter includes the following quotation from Alfred Marshall: "The economist, like everyone else, must concern himself with the ultimate aims of man." To Galbraith, the acquisition of consumer goods plainly did not rank high among those aims. This is most evident in his constant demand for a better balance between public and private goods.[77] Among its other bad consequences, Galbraith thought, our overemphasis on private goods corrupts the young by giving them too much mobility (via the automobile); by exposing them to the questionable messages contained in television, comic books, and the like; by stimulating them with drugs and pornography; and by generally weakening their ability to withstand all these stimuli.[78] Were we to put more emphasis on public goods, he apparently believed, these influences might be overcome by more and better education. This might make more people value "esoteric desires" such as music, the fine arts, travel, and literary and scientific interests.[79] It also could stimulate something even more important: the desire to know, understand, and reason.

The foregoing discussion suggests that Galbraith's political ideas might best be justified by some kind of virtue ethics. As we saw in chapter 2, those ideas are not easy to justify on utilitarian grounds. But Galbraith usually made utilitarian arguments. How, then, can his preoccupation with the good life be rendered consistent with his professed utilitarianism? Like Goldman, Galbraith may have assumed that intrinsically good behaviors also make for the greatest human satisfaction in the long run. If Galbraith had been able to flesh out and justify this apparent assumption, perhaps his utilitarian argument against manipulative advertising could have withstood Hayek's assault on it. In that event, he would have had an independent basis for his belief that public goods generate more utility than private goods. But my previous remarks about Goldman suggest how difficult that demonstration can be.

However, Galbraith could also have overcome Hayek by convincingly making the *nonutilitarian* argument that some wants are intrinsically superior to others—specifically, that a life devoted to public goods is intrinsically superior to a life devoted to consumption. On that assumption, questions of comparative utility would not matter. But while it would have been interesting to watch the dean of post–World War II American liberalism employ premodern philosophical ideas, so far as I know Galbraith never made the attempt. Another attack during the 1950s on advertising and consumerism, however, clearly did involve such ideas. Despite their similarities, Joseph Wood Krutch's *Human Nature and the Human Condition* has not survived the years as well as Galbraith's *The Affluent Society*. One reason, perhaps, is Krutch's considerably more radical attack on modern society. Although advertising plays a minor role within Krutch's book, a critique of the practice nonetheless emerges from his larger concerns.

Krutch exemplifies a tendency discussed in chapter 1: the propensity to view American society as a kind of machine devoted to the production of physical things, and to see advertising as the motor that moves its parts. In order for this machine to keep humming, more and more production is necessary. "What we call prosperity depends upon continual expansion, especially of manufactured goods, and we believe that we cannot stop producing too much without finding ourselves soon incapable of producing enough."[80] This ever-increasing production, in turn, depends on

ever-increasing consumption. For that reason, it is hardly surprising that we are inundated with advertising.

> If we could convincingly accuse the advertisers of greed, or
> even of mere self-interest, we might reasonably ask why they
> should be allowed to invade our homes, destroy the beauty of
> the countryside, and deface the sky. But if "prosperity" as
> currently defined is the only reasonable meaning or measure
> of the good life, then a strong case can be made for the
> commonly accepted contention that when I am urged to trade
> in my car, buy a new washing machine, or try some new gadget,
> the profit motive of the seller is of less than secondary impor-
> tance. Primarily, as he will eagerly explain, he is performing a
> public service by explaining to me my duty to support prosper-
> ity by behaving in the only manner by which prosperity can
> be maintained.[81]

On these assumptions, in fact, advertisers have a moral duty to
manipulate and consumers a moral duty to buy.[82]

In Krutch's view, two widespread ideas go some way toward
explaining the condition just described. The first is the familiar
scientific-technological mindset that seeks to dominate nature for
the satisfaction of human wants and that ignores most other values
in the process. The second is a pervasive relativism whose practical
message is that one should conform to the society of which one is
part. Because in America the first attitude tends to dominate, the
second enjoins us to go with the national flow by embracing
consumerism. As a determined foe of both relativism and the
scientific-technological mentality,[83] Krutch naturally rejected this
injunction. Indeed, he called advertising "permissive exploita-
tion."[84] He did so in part for the economic reasons discussed in
chapter 2. More important, Krutch thought that advertising exploits
people by diverting them from their true nature.

According to Krutch, one manifestation of the prevailing relativism is a tendency to define "normal" as "average," rather than as a
standard or norm for human behavior.[85] Without such a criterion,
he thought, it is difficult to reject the modern consensus.[86] Thus,
Krutch tried to argue that human beings have a more or less
determinate nature—a nature that is largely inconsistent with
modern consumerism and the relativism that counsels our acceptance of it.[87] The specifics of those arguments need not concern us

here. For present purposes, the point is Krutch's use of virtue ethics broadly conceived to attack consumerism and advertising.

Manipulative Advertising and Some Specific Virtues

. Krutch's argument, then, was that advertising is wrong because it stimulates a consumeristic lifestyle that violates human nature. Thus, his critique emphasizes advertising's stimulation of the propensity to consume rather than its ability to distort consumer choices among products and services. Another alleged inconsistency between advertising and the good life probably involves both of these assumed effects. According to this argument, advertising is wrong not so much because consumerism is contrary to human nature, as because it deprives its victims of certain specific virtues.[88]

Associative advertising performs its mission by producing an irrational inclination to believe that the purchase of a particular product will satisfy some desire extraneous to that product. By doing so, such advertising necessarily overcomes the rationality, reflectiveness, and self-awareness that would otherwise enable consumers to resist it. Aristotle believed that we acquire virtues and vices by the habitual performance of good and bad activities.[89] On that assumption, continued submission to associative advertising should tend to weaken consumers' possession of such virtues as self-control, self-discipline, moderation, and self-reliance.[90] Advertising also should undercut these virtues when it stimulates the propensity to consume. People who live to buy consumer products are not especially likely to be models of self-awareness and self-restraint. This would be true, I think, even if consumer products rank high among life's good things. In other words, advertising might be condemned for undermining these virtues even if critics such as Galbraith and Krutch were wrong in their evaluation of consumerism as such. And even if virtue is intrinsically worthless, it still might have instrumental value. Even if money and possessions are all that matter, that is, you are unlikely to acquire much of either without cultivating at least some of the traditional virtues.

Implications for the Critics' Agenda

This section of the chapter is primarily concerned with corruptions that arise directly from *manipulation itself*, rather than from the particular things manipulative advertising might make people buy. Even though an ad for whiskey might make little Billy an alcoholic and thereby warp his life, for example, that corruption is not my main concern here. As we have seen, advertising might corrupt simply by manipulating. It might do so by making people consumers and thereby preventing realization of the good life, or by inhibiting the development of certain specific virtues in the ways just described.

The most important "regulatory implication" of virtue ethics probably is the support it gives to Galbraith's position. If advertising makes people consumers, and if consumerism is a low and insipid way to live, then drastic measures may be necessary. In lieu of Galbraith's social surgery, these measures at least should include significant curbs on the volume of advertising. As we will see in chapter 6, moreover, the critics' general worldview probably becomes most coherent on assumptions akin to those made by virtue ethics.

INITIAL CONCLUSIONS

Critics of advertising who make any of the various political proposals described in chapter 1 need to show that advertising's manipulativeness is a bad thing. Otherwise, why bother with political efforts to counteract its influence? In short, such critics need a moral argument for their position. Although advertising's traditional foes rarely attempted such arguments, business ethicists have tried to remedy the deficiency. If chapters 2 and 3 are correct, that effort has met with considerable, albeit incomplete, success. Advertising's implications for utility may justify piecemeal regulation of certain forms of manipulative advertising, but they provide little support for more ambitious transformations of American society. Also, manipulative advertising may evade censure under the first major formulation of Kant's categorical imperative. On the other hand, it almost certainly stands condemned under the imperative's second major formulation. However autonomy is conceived, moreover, manipulative advertising violates that value as well. Finally, advertising probably inhibits the realization of certain traditional virtues if it manipulates, and it also seems to prevent some conceptions of the good life from being realized. Manipulative advertising's wrongfulness, therefore, seems somewhat ethical-theory relative; although Kant's ethics, autonomy, and virtue ethics provide grounds for condemning it, this is much less true of utilitarianism. Because autonomy and virtue ethics are difficult to reconcile, moreover, those who value one or the other probably cannot invoke both to attack manipulative advertising.

NOTES

1. William K. Frankena, *Ethics*, 2d ed. (Englewood Cliffs, N.J.: Prentice-Hall, 1973), 15.

2. W. D. Ross, *The Right and the Good* (1930; Indianapolis: Hackett Publishing, 1988), 34–35.

3. Ibid., 35.

4. Ibid., 19–24. Frankena, *Ethics*, 43–56 sets out an approach that resembles the one advanced by Ross.

5. Ross, *The Right and the Good*, 19; 20–21, note 1.

6. The duty of beneficence "rest[s] on the mere fact that there are other beings in the world whose condition we can make better in respect of virtue, or of intelligence, *or of pleasure*." Ibid., 21 (emphasis added).

7. Immanuel Kant, *Groundwork of the Metaphysic of Morals*, trans. and ed. H. J. Paton (New York: Harper Torchbooks, 1964).

8. Ibid., 61 (emphasis in original).

9. Ibid., 62.

10. Ibid., 68 (emphasis in original).

11. Ibid., 80.

12. Ibid., 81.

13. Ibid., 82.

14. Ibid., 84.

15. "Since I have robbed the will of every inducement that might arise for it as a consequence of obeying any particular law, nothing is left but the conformity of actions to universal law as such, and this alone must serve the will as its principle." Ibid., 70. See also 88.

16. Ibid., 88 (emphasis in original). A maxim is "a subjective principle of action." Ibid., note *.

17. Ibid., 90.

18. James Rachels, *The Elements of Moral Philosophy*, 2d ed. (New York: McGraw-Hill, 1993), 128.

19. Kant, *Groundwork*, 96.

20. Ibid., 97.

21. See, for example, Rachels, *The Elements of Moral Philosophy*, chap. 9.

22. Ibid., 128.

23. Steven B. Smith, *Hegel's Critique of Liberalism: Rights in Context* (Chicago: University of Chicago Press, 1989), 74–75.

24. Kant, *Groundwork*, 22. This material comes from H. J. Paton's translator's analysis of *Groundwork*.

25. Alasdair MacIntyre, *A Short History of Ethics* (New York: Collier, 1966), 197.

26. Alasdair MacIntyre, *After Virtue: A Study in Moral Theory*, 2d ed. (Notre Dame, Ind.: University of Notre Dame Press, 1984), 45–46.

27. Kant, *Groundwork*, 8 (translator's preface).

28. R. M. Hare, "Commentary," *Business and Professional Ethics Journal* 3 (1984): 28.

29. Ivan L. Preston, *The Tangled Web They Weave: Truth, Falsity, and Advertisers* (Madison: University of Wisconsin Press, 1994), 186–95.

30. "The beings we are talking about are *rational* beings, and 'treating them as ends-in-themselves' means *respecting their rationality*. Thus, we may never *manipulate* people, or *use* people, to achieve our purposes, no matter how good those purposes may be." Rachels, *The Elements of Philosophy*, 129 (emphasis in original).

31. MacIntyre, *After Virtue*, 46.

32. For arguments to this effect, see Tom L. Beauchamp, "Manipulative Advertising," *Business and Professional Ethics Journal* 3 (1984): 17; Hare, "Commentary," 28.

33. One remaining possibility, which I will not pursue owing to its speculative nature, is that Theodore Levitt was correct when he asserted that deep down consumers know that they are being manipulated when they buy associatively advertised products. Theodore Levitt, "The Morality (?) of Advertising," *Harvard Business Review* (July-August 1970): 90. If on some level they are aware of the "manipulation," are consumers genuinely being used and treated as means?

34. See, for example, Kant, *Groundwork*, 108, 114. This suggests that Kant's notion of autonomy focuses on the *advertiser* rather than on the consumer. Because this is so contrary to our usual notions about advertising and autonomy, I ignore Kant's conception of autonomy in this book.

35. See Isaiah Berlin, "Two Concepts of Liberty," in *Four Essays on Liberty* (London: Oxford University Press, 1977), 118–72 and, especially, 131–34.

36. Thomas E. Hill, Jr., "The Kantian Conception of Autonomy," in *The Inner Citadel: Essays on Individual Autonomy*, ed. John Christman

(New York: Oxford University Press, 1989), 94. In this and all subsequent remarks concerning Hill's "Sartrean autonomy," my concern is with the concept as Hill formulated it, and not with what Sartre wrote. Also, I am not imputing any particular conception of autonomy to Hill himself.

37. Ibid., 102 (raising the issue). As Hill notes, while modern physics may be indeterministic at the subatomic level, "most seem to agree that this makes little practical difference when we turn to the explanation and prediction of large-scale objects, such as human bodies."

38. To F. H. Bradley, for example, this must be true if human behavior is free from all causal determination. Bradley's argument, essentially, was that any force, principle, factor, or innate attribute that would affect the will's behavior and make it nonrandom also would constrain its freedom. The perfectly free will, in other words, would have to be the perfectly indeterminate and arbitrary will. F. H. Bradley, *Ethical Studies*, 2d ed. (1927; London: Oxford University Press, 1962), 11.

39. Hill, "The Kantian Conception," 92–93. Stanley Benn once sounded a similar note when he suggested that within the liberal tradition, "a man's capacity for making responsible choices among alternative ways of life" is high among the human excellences. Stanley I. Benn, "Freedom and Persuasion," *Australasian Journal of Philosophy* 45 (1967): 274.

40. Richard L. Lippke, "Advertising and the Social Conditions of Autonomy," *Business and Professional Ethics Journal* 8, no. 4 (1990): 37–48. A similar argument appears in Richard L. Lippke, *Radical Business Ethics* (Lanham, Md.: Rowman & Littlefield, 1995), chap. 5.

41. Robert L. Arrington, "Advertising and Behavior Control," *Journal of Business Ethics* 1 (1982): 3–12.

42. Arrington also maintained that even when manipulative advertising works, advertisers do not control, but instead only influence, consumers. His argument, however, depended on an extremely strong definition of "control": one in which the controlling party (e.g., an advertiser) must intend to ensure that *all* of the necessary conditions of an action (here, a purchase) are satisfied. Ibid., 10–11.

43. Ibid., 7 (emphasis in original).

44. Ibid.

45. Ibid.

46. Ibid.

47. Lippke, "Advertising and the Social Conditions of Autonomy," 39.

48. If manipulative advertising is genuinely effective, for example, it might cause people to make repeat purchases and thus undermine Arrington's argument that those purchases show our genuine acceptance

of the advertised product. Roger Crisp, "Persuasive Advertising, Autonomy, and the Creation of Desire," *Journal of Business Ethics* 6 (1987): 415.

49. John Christman, "Autonomy and Personal History," *Canadian Journal of Philosophy* 21, no. 1 (1991): 4 (calling a conception like Arrington's the received model).

50. Gerald Dworkin, "The Concept of Autonomy," in *The Inner Citadel: Essays on Individual Autonomy*, ed. John Christman (New York: Oxford University Press, 1989), 60. See also Harry G. Frankfurt, "Freedom of Will and the Concept of a Person," in *The Inner Citadel: Essays on Individual Autonomy*, ed. John Christman (New York: Oxford University Press, 1989), 63–76.

51. Dworkin, "The Concept of Autonomy," 61.

52. Ibid.

53. Ibid. Those critics include Christman, "Autonomy and Personal History," 7–8; and Irving Thalberg, "Hierarchical Analyses of Unfree Action," in *The Inner Citadel: Essays on Individual Autonomy*, ed. John Christman (New York: Oxford University Press, 1989), 130.

54. Dworkin, "The Concept of Autonomy," 62.

55. Frankfurt, "Freedom of Will," 71 (emphasis in original).

56. Ibid.

57. Again, Theodore Levitt's article provides a possible rejoinder to this conclusion. See Levitt, "The Morality (?) of Advertising," 84–92. His article can be read as contending that at some level people know they are being manipulated, and that they submit to avoid an inescapably dreary human existence. This might mean that the submission is more or less voluntary and almost certainly rational under the circumstances. In that event, it might be deemed autonomous as well. Because this argument is so speculative, however, I do not explore it.

Also, one might maintain that my acceptance of Hayek's argument in chapter 2 is inconsistent with my rejection of Arrington's argument here. These two arguments have at least one common feature: they try to make the preservation of some human good—utility in Hayek's case, autonomy in Arrington's—consistent with manipulative advertising's effectiveness. Because utility and autonomy are different things, however, the alleged inconsistency does not exist. In other words, manipulative advertising might suppress autonomy while still maximizing utility. This would be true, for example, if it produces a nation of robotically happy consumers.

58. John Waide, "The Making of Self and World in Advertising," *Journal of Business Ethics* 6 (1987): 77 (emphasis in original; criticizing Theodore Levitt).

59. Ibid.

60. Benn, "Freedom and Persuasion," 273.

61. Rachels, *The Elements of Moral Philosophy*, 163.

62. Ibid. Rachels's full list includes benevolence, civility, compassion, conscientiousness, cooperativeness, courage, courteousness, dependability, fairness, friendliness, generosity, honesty, industriousness, justice, loyalty, moderation, reasonableness, self-confidence, self-control, self-discipline, self-reliance, tactfulness, thoughtfulness, and tolerance.

63. MacIntyre, *A Short History of Ethics*, 62–63.

64. For an account of this kind, see Henry B. Veatch, *Aristotle: A Contemporary Appreciation* (Bloomington: Indiana University Press, 1974), 94–118. On its centrality to Aristotle's ethics, see MacIntyre, *A Short History of Ethics*, 62–63.

65. For a brief statement of this very familiar point, see Veatch, *Aristotle*, 97–98.

66. Benn, "Freedom and Persuasion," 273–74.

67. MacIntyre, *After Virtue*, 44.

68. Kant, *Groundwork*, 89–91, 96–98.

69. For a utilitarian justification of several traditional virtues, see Henry Sidgwick, *The Methods of Ethics*, 7th ed. (1907; Indianapolis: Hackett Publishing, 1981), 424–25, 430–39, 448–53.

70. See, for example, MacIntyre, *A Short History of Ethics*, 63, 80–82 (describing the role of pleasure in Aristotle's ethics).

71. Alan H. Goldman, *The Moral Foundations of Professional Ethics* (Totowa, N.J.: Rowman & Littlefield, 1982), 254 (italics omitted).

72. Ibid., 254–55. I should add that Goldman seems to be neither a utilitarian nor an exponent of virtue ethics.

73. Michael Schudson, *Advertising, the Uneasy Persuasion: Its Dubious Impact on American Society* (n.p.: Basic Books, 1986), 6–7.

74. Benn, "Freedom and Persuasion," 273–74.

75. Christopher Lasch, *The Culture of Narcissism: American Life in an Age of Diminishing Expectations* (New York: W. W. Norton, 1978), 72. To Lasch, however, advertising apparently is as much a response to this restlessness, anxiousness, and boredom as it is their creator. Those conditions, that is, have other causes as well. In Lasch's view, for example, advertising "plays seductively on the malaise of industrial civilization" and "addresses itself to the spiritual desolation of modern life and proposes consumption as the cure" (pp. 72, 73).

76. David A. Reisman, *Galbraith and Market Capitalism* (New York: New York University Press, 1980), 90.

77. John Kenneth Galbraith, *The Affluent Society* (Boston: Houghton-Mifflin, 1958), 132–37, 251–69.

78. Ibid., 256–58.

79. Ibid., 279–80.

80. Joseph Wood Krutch, *Human Nature and the Human Condition* (New York: Random House, 1959), 22.

81. Ibid., 28–29.

82. Ibid., 35, 37.

83. See Joseph Wood Krutch, *The Modern Temper: A Study and a Confession* (1929; New York: Harvest Books, 1956); Joseph Wood Krutch, *The Measure of Man: On Human Values, Survival, and the Modern Temper* (Indianapolis: Charter Books, 1962).

84. Krutch, *Human Nature and the Human Condition*, 44–52.

85. Ibid., 89–95.

86. Ibid., 164–67.

87. Ibid., chap. 10.

88. This belief apparently is common among the general populace. See Richard W. Pollay and Banwari Mittal, "Here's the Beef: Factors, Determinants, and Segments in Consumer Criticism of Advertising," *Journal of Marketing* 57 (July 1993): 102, 109.

We might also inquire whether the use of manipulative advertising corrupts its *practitioners* as well as the consumers at whom it is aimed, but this question seems relatively insignificant in context. For a brief discussion of this issue, see Waide, "The Making of Self and World," 74–75.

89. Aristotle, *The Ethics of Aristotle*, trans. J.A.K. Thomson (Harmondsworth, England: Penguin Books, 1953), 55–56. This is book 2, chap. 1 of the *Nichomachean Ethics*.

90. Cf. Waide, "The Making of Self and World," 75–76.

Chapter 4

MANIPULATIVE ADVERTISING
AND CONSUMER CHOICE

Although chapters 2 and 3 do not condemn manipulative advertising unequivocally, they provide ample grounds for declaring it wrong. Those chapters, however, assume that advertising manipulates. Specifically, they assume that advertising makes people consumers by stimulating the propensity to consume, and then dictates the particular product and service choices consumers make. At a first approximation, what would happen if both these assumptions are untrue? In that event, most of advertising's alleged positive and negative consequences for utility simply would not occur. Similarly, it appears unlikely that advertising would render its targets less virtuous. If advertising fails to manipulate, why should we assume that it affects human character? In addition, it is difficult to see how ineffective advertising can be criticized for robbing consumers of their autonomy. Because Kant's ethical theory so strongly downplays consequences, however, advertising's inability to manipulate might not disturb a Kantian critique of that activity.

To many readers, these possibilities may seem irrelevant. As chapter 1 revealed, a significant body of critical opinion has long proclaimed advertising's powers. Often joining hands with advertising's critics on this particular issue is the advertising industry itself. Business routinely displays its belief in advertising's effectiveness by spending huge sums on it. Still, because the efficacy question is so important to the critics' political agenda and the ethical evaluation of manipulative advertising on which that agenda depends, the subject deserves examination. Chapters 4 and 5 attempt to make that examination by considering a sampling of the relevant research on advertising's effectiveness, one that I believe is representative. This chapter presents evidence on manipulative advertising's ability to affect the competitive process by causing people to buy particular goods and services. It begins by sketching some general reasons for skepticism about manipulative advertising's ability to dictate consumer choice. Then it considers research on the effectiveness of two particular manipulative techniques: subliminal advertising and advertising associating the product with sex. The chapter concludes by reconsidering chapter 2's discussion of the economic debate on advertising's competitive impact. Chapter 5 examines some research and informed speculation on advertising and the propensity to consume.

Although chapters 4 and 5 cannot and do not consider every relevant source, most of the materials they do examine support the same conclusion: advertising's foes overestimate its power. This obviously is not to say that manipulative advertising never works or that the firms employing it invariably are wasting their money; nor (God forbid) is it to suggest what amount businesses should spend on advertising or what strategies advertisers should pursue. Rather, it is to assert a negative proposition: that "strong" views about advertising's power are dubious. In that event, most ethical criticisms of advertising except those based on Kantian ethics become correspondingly dubious. Kantian objections aside, therefore, the critics' political agenda has relatively little to support it.

SOME GENERAL REASONS FOR SKEPTICISM

Two obvious sources of information on manipulative advertising's effectiveness are scholarly writing by business school marketing faculty members and popular books on advertising. Within the former, some say, advertising's efficacy is widely assumed.[1] The same probably is true of general-readership works, where the John Kenneth Galbraiths, the Vance Packards, and the Wilson Bryan Keys have long seemed dominant. As chapters 2 and 3 suggest, many business ethicists join the marketing scholars and the popular writers in assuming that advertising works.[2] Normally allied with these groups on this particular question, of course, is the advertising industry itself.[3] One source notes the "remarkable fact that there is little doubt about the effectiveness of advertising amongst its most rabid opponents, as well as amongst its most fervent supporters."[4] To another, "[a]n instinctive (and in most cases unsubstantiated) belief in the power of advertising is a truism of the advertising business, and is an article of faith devoutly accepted by observers of all persuasions, whether defenders or opponents of the art."[5]

Anyone with an ounce of skepticism, however, might wonder just what this consensus actually proves. Should we expect advertisers to downgrade the techniques that provide their livelihood? Is there any reason to think that business ethicists, many of whom are philosophers, really know much about advertising?[6] Little in the articles they write suggests much familiarity with the pertinent marketing literature or with any economic arguments other than Galbraith's. As for that literature, recent years have witnessed increasing dissent from the prevailing orthodoxy. Journal titles such as "Advertising: Strong Force or Weak Force?" and "Advertising's Effect on Sales: Proven or Just Assumed?" suggest as much.[7] The same is true of writing aimed at the educated public. For example, the first sentence of the preface to the paperback edition of Michael Schudson's *Advertising, the Uneasy Persuasion* states that "[a]dvertising is much less powerful than advertisers and critics of advertising claim, and advertising agencies are stabbing in the dark much more than they are practicing precision microsurgery on the public consciousness."[8] Just in case an unwary reader had missed his point, Schudson nailed it home one page later.

> In the common view, advertising associates a given brand or product with a prestigious person or a romanticized lifestyle, and suggests that the use of the product will transform the consumer into a more beautiful, more desirable, or more energetic human being. The consumer, believing or half-believing this, and consciously or subconsciously coaxed by the ad's suggestion, buys the product. With most Americans most of the time . . . this notion that advertising directly affects consumer choice explains scarcely anything about why consumers buy what they do.[9]

Other popular writers echo Schudson's remarks. According to Philip Gold, for example, "Consumers have always been notoriously fickle and unreliable, and advertising has yet to reach a level of manipulative or therapeutic competence that can guarantee consistent, predictable success."[10]

The Uncertain Impact of Individual Ads

One reason for skepticism about advertising's manipulativeness is the difficulty of measuring the effect of an individual ad or campaign on sales of the advertised product. (This is true despite the sizable expenditures and sophisticated techniques advertisers deploy toward that end.[11]) The problem is a simple and familiar one: too many variables. Because so many factors affect the sales of a product, marketers find it virtually impossible to isolate advertising's contribution.[12] In the words of two academic writers, "[t]he relationship between the frequency or intensity of advertising and the size of its effect is often non-observable. In general, the specific contribution of advertising cannot be extracted from the mixture of simultaneous phenomena and effects taking place."[13] Sometimes even advertising professionals admit this problem. According to David Ogilvy, "For all their research, most advertisers never know for sure whether their advertisements sell. Too many other factors cloud the equation."[14] Because they are so contrary to advertisers' economic interests, such statements deserve attention.

These "simultaneous phenomena" and "other factors" fall into two groups. The first group comprises the seller's promotional efforts. Advertising is only one part—and sometimes a small part—of a marketing mix that includes direct contact by sales representatives; discounts, coupons, and sweepstakes; packaging, shelf displays, and other in-store displays; and the development and nurturing of effective avenues of distribution.[15] The second group of phenomena concern the external environment in which the seller's promotional efforts operate—for example, the state of the economy and the efforts of competitors. An example from Eric Clark combines both sets of factors:

> [H]ow can you tell whether an advertising campaign sells what
> it is promoting? How can you isolate the effect of the advertis-

ing from all the other factors involved? Take, say, a new soft drink. How much of its sales do you attribute to the advertising and how much to other things such as the hot weather, the number of shops that have been persuaded to stock it, its position on supermarket shelves, the shape of the bottle, the price and so on?[16]

Shortly thereafter, Clark quotes a source who claims that, in a normal marketing situation, as many as fifty factors might affect a product's sales.

The Hierarchy-of-Effects Approach

Because it is so difficult to measure an ad's impact, academic and professional advertising researchers tend not to use sales as a measure of advertising effectiveness. Instead, they often try to measure factors such as whether consumers remember an ad or whether it changes their attitudes. Such factors, researchers assume, give some indication of an ad's ability to sell the product.[17] This tactic has been formalized in what is known as the hierarchy-of-effects approach.[18] The general idea behind this approach is that once consumers are exposed to an effective ad, they move through a series of stages culminating in the decision to purchase the advertised product. These stages may be characterized abstractly; the most common such characterizations are the *cognitive* (thinking) stage, the *affective* (feeling) stage, and the *conative* (doing) stage. They may also be characterized with more particularity—for example, by a movement from awareness, to knowledge, to liking, to preference, to conviction, and finally to purchase. A much-cited hierarchy-of-effects approach[19] combines these two sets of stages much as follows:

Cognitive ———→ Affective ———→ Conative

Awareness → Knowledge → Liking → Preference → Conviction → Purchase.

A favorable response at one step is a necessary, but not a sufficient, condition for a favorable response at the next step.[20] The farther a consumer progresses through the stages, however, the greater is the likelihood of a purchase.[21]

If such a scheme accurately describes the steps through which consumers proceed before buying products, and if those steps are measurable, the hierarchy-of-effects approach might be useful in determining the effectiveness of particular advertisements. For example, if consumers recall manipulative advertisement M better than they recall informative advertisement I, or if they like the product M advertises better than I's product after being exposed to M and I, this might suggest that M is more effective than I. If such results are replicated over many tests, moreover, we might have some reason to believe that manipulative ads generally produce more sales than their informative counterparts.

However, the hierarchy-of-effects approach, while probably useful to advertising researchers, hardly solves all the measurement problems suggested earlier.[22] For one thing, researchers have suggested many such hierarchies, some of which introduce different stages, and some of which present the same stages in different sequences.[23] In addition, critics claim that empirical validation for both the hierarchy-of-effects approach in general, and individual approaches in particular, is either absent or insufficient.[24] Occasionally, advertising practitioners provide concrete examples. For example, Ogilvy strenuously maintains that neither sales nor brand preference is predicted by product recall (which presumably correlates with awareness and knowledge).[25] Finally, some researchers even claim that there is little or no evidence that attitudinal changes cause purchases.[26]

Additional Reasons for Skepticism

However the questions about the hierarchy-of-effects approach finally are resolved, contemporary skeptics about advertising's power make other arguments to bolster their case. For example, they note the number of new products that fail despite heavy promotion. Examples of the former include the Edsel, Lady Gillette shaving cream, paper apparel, and Billy Beer.[27] More telling in this connection, perhaps, is the high rate—perhaps as high as 90 percent—at which new products fail.[28] In addition, some products succeed despite little or no advertising effort. Examples include marijuana, cocaine, some scholarly books, race horses, and generic products of all kinds.[29]

   The skeptics also make various points that bear more directly on the hierarchy-of-effects approach. One is that people often pay little attention to advertising.[30] For instance, studies have shown that during commercial breaks television viewers often turn their attention elsewhere or even absent themselves from the room.[31] Clark presents advertising research indicating that of the seven and one-half hours of television commercials watched by the average American family during a week, only one hour and twenty-seven minutes' worth actually are seen.[32] Even when an ad is seen, Clark immediately adds, it may not be attended to: "[t]he majority of the ads that are seen never 'break through.' "[33] "Of those which are attended to," he continues, "only about half are correctly comprehended and fewer than 5 percent are actively recalled for as long as twenty-four hours."[34] (As we have seen, moreover, recall may be a poor predictor of advertising effectiveness.) Even when an advertisement is seen, attended to, and recalled, furthermore, advertisers confront another obstacle to success: popular skepticism about advertising.[35] For example, a 1966 compendium of several different poll questions on the subject suggested that roughly half of the American people apparently find fault with the truthfulness of advertising.[36] Skepticism about television advertising seems especially pronounced.[37] This skepticism may help explain why people pay relatively little attention to advertising. In Schudson's blunt formulation, people tune out advertisements because "advertising is propaganda and everyone knows it."[38]

   A last set of reasons for questioning manipulative advertising's effectiveness assumes that ads actually generate some sales. The most important of these is captured by the slogan, "Good advertising kills a bad product." As Schudson describes this process, effective advertising "can lead a consumer to try a product once. If it is a bad product, the consumer will shun it thereafter and let others know, too, that it is a bad product."[39] In addition, even ads that are perceived, believed, and highly effective might cancel each other out.[40] Finally, consumer tastes are influenced by the attitudes and purchases of other consumers as well as by advertising.[41] Galbraith's discussion of emulation in chapter 1 suggests his agreement on this point.[42] Another possible influence on consumer tastes is a process called prescription: the tendency for particular social roles or positions to require that their holders possess certain material things.[43] Thus a banker, for example, might be strongly

Chapter 1's discussion of subliminal advertising concluded by questioning whether anyone has articulated convincing reasons to believe that it affects consumer behavior. Nonetheless, a rationale for subliminal advertising's efficacy can be cobbled together from the literature, mainly from Wilson Bryan Key's *Subliminal Seduction*. The rationale's first component is the truism that subliminal messages are not perceived by consumers. This means that "[u]nlike supraliminal communications, the recipient cannot consciously evaluate and discount the received message."[46] The rationale's second component is the notion that human behavior is largely determined by a subconscious with great abilities to assimilate and retain information. In *Subliminal Seduction*, Key asserts that the unconscious dominates human behavior.[47] Unlike the conscious mind, moreover, the unconscious takes in and retains virtually all the information presented to it by external messages such as advertisements.[48] Then Key combines these contentions into one bold statement:

> [T]he human nervous system is capable of assimilating symbolic content at incredible speeds. Lineal conscious rationalization of content occurs much more slowly. The conscious mind discriminates, decides, evaluates, resists, or accepts. The unconscious, apparently, merely stores units of information, much of which influences attitudes or behavior at the conscious level in ways about which science knows virtually nothing. The mass communication industry long ago realized the resistance to advertising which develops at the conscious level. However, there is little if any resistance encountered at the unconscious level, to which marketing appeals are now directed.[49]

Because the stimuli setting this process in motion are subliminal, finally, there is no hope that we can overcome them through conscious mental effort.

This suggested argument for subliminal advertising's effectiveness encounters any number of problems. Although the question is best left to psychologists, it is doubtful whether Key's assumptions about the powers of the unconscious would command anything like universal support. Another problem is that Key's account seems to presuppose two systems for processing sensory inputs—one conscious and one unconscious. According to Timothy Moore, however, there is no psychological evidence to support this assumption.[50] A further difficulty with Key's account is its failure to explain why, amidst the data the unconscious supposedly takes in and retains, subliminal information affects it so profoundly. This is particularly true if we assume that the unconscious already possesses ingrained desires, aversions, drives, and the like. As Moore observes, finally, Key cites no studies or other documentation for the effects he attributes to embedded messages.[51] Instead, he "appears to invent whatever features of perception and memory would be necessary to achieve the results imputed to embedded stimuli."[52]

So far as I can determine, therefore, there is no compelling theoretical argument to support the proposition that subliminal advertising works. This obviously does not preclude the possibility that someone already has developed such a rationale, or that one will emerge in the future. Any argument of this kind, however, must confront certain theoretical arguments *against* subliminal advertising's effectiveness. The literature suggests at least two such arguments. The first rests on the principle that more intense stimuli generally have a greater influence on human behavior than weak stimuli.[53] Because subliminal messages plainly are weak stimuli, it is questionable whether they affect people to any significant degree. The weakness of subliminal stimuli also may explain why subliminal communication is said to be "inefficient," or incapable of generating experimental responses that are much higher than random.[54] Another apparent implication of the weakness of subliminal stimuli is that, unless elaborate precautions are taken, supraliminal material such as the film or commercial in which the subliminal stimuli reside almost certainly would "wash out" those stimuli.[55]

A second theoretical reason for doubting subliminal advertising's effectiveness is that people actively process and transform the perceptions they receive. In other words, a simple stimulus-response model does not describe the way in which we actually respond to messages and other stimuli.[56] According to Moore,

> Perhaps the single most important lesson to be learned from cognitive psychology in the last decade is that the meaning of a stimulus does not reside in the stimulus itself. Meaning is constructed by the receiver in active, complex and often spe-

cialized ways. With respect to advertising the selectivity of
attention and the active control over subsequent processing of
the input means that stimulation is not a sufficient condition
for any response at all, let alone some particular response.[57]

Thus, subliminal advertising may be ineffective when its message
conflicts with the consumer's emotions, preferences, or values.[58]
To illustrate the point, consider advertising stimuli that reside
somewhere between the subliminal and the supraliminal—those
that may be perceived but are not attended to.

> [W]hy do people who dislike beer or liquor still refrain from
> purchasing it when they have for years been receiving sublimi-
> nal impressions from bill boards while driving along, from
> newspapers and magazines while flipping the pages, from
> radios while switching from station to station? Why don't men
> purchase corsets and dresses, after years of subliminally "see-
> ing" them? Why do young adults still not wear hats? Or women
> smoke cigars?[59]

This argument gains strength when we consider advertisers' im-
perfect success with commercial messages that clearly are perceived and understood. As Moore remarks, why attribute special
powers to a subliminal message if that same message lacks those
powers when delivered supraliminally?[60]

Employing theoretical arguments to assess subliminal advertising's effectiveness, however, can carry one only so far. What does
the empirical research on subliminal advertising tell us about its
effectiveness? So far as I am aware, only one study has tried to
determine whether subliminal advertising can trigger a decision to
purchase or some other behavioral effect, and in that study the
subliminal appeal was ineffective.[61] Most research on the impact
of subliminal advertising has involved its ability to generate responses that fit somewhere in the hierarchy of effects. The evidence
on subliminal advertising's ability to generate such responses is
mixed.[62] To make the weak case for subliminal advertising's effectiveness as strong as possible, the following discussion emphasizes
the studies in which subliminal advertising did produce a cognitive,
affective, or conative response.

In one study, visual subliminal communication apparently generated a product preference.[63] In that study, different groups of

university students watched a film telling them how to wash woolens. For one of the groups, the film contained a subliminal presentation of a woolen cleaning product called Zero. In a questionnaire administered after the film, the students exposed to the Zero message showed a marked preference for that product, as compared with a control group and a group exposed to a subliminal message for a different product. From this, the authors concluded that "academic marketers may have been too quick to discount the ability of subliminal presentations to impact upon consumer decision making."[64] However, there is at least one published academic marketing study in which a visual subliminal message did not produce an affective response.[65]

Embedded subliminal messages also have produced significant responses on occasion. In one study, certain groups of students viewed actual magazine advertisements for Chivas Regal whiskey and Marlboro Lights cigarettes which the authors judged to contain sexual embeds.[66] (The Chivas ad was said to contain the image of a nude female seen from the back; and the Marlboro ad, a representation of male genitals.) Other groups viewed the same ads with the embeds removed. The students then rated the ads through questions measuring four general attributes: "cognitive" (trustworthy, informative, and believable), "affective" (appealing, attractive, and impressive), "conative" (try, buy, and seek out product), and "sexual" (sensual, erotic, and exciting). The version of the Chivas ad with the embed rated higher on all four measures than its nude-free counterpart, but a comparison of the original Marlboro ad and its gelded companion generated no significant differences. However, the authors obtained significant results for both ads when they tested students' skin resistance (apparently a measure of arousal) during exposure to the ads. Despite these positive results, however, there are other published academic marketing studies in which embedded subliminal stimuli produced no significant effects.[67]

Even if subliminal advertising reliably generates cognitive, affective, or conative responses, however, there is reason to doubt whether this finding would have positive implications for advertising practice. As chapter 1 noted, the signal intensity threshold at which stimuli begin to be consciously perceived varies both for one individual and between individuals. Also, there should be a signal intensity below which subliminal stimuli are ineffective. Thus, advertisers who use subliminal messages must walk a fine line when setting the message's strength.[68] If the intensity is too high, some people may consciously detect the message, which could undermine both the ad campaign and the advertiser's credibility by making the subliminal appeal public knowledge. (This apparently has happened at least once.[69]) On the other hand, setting the intensity too low might mean that some consumers are not affected at all. This problem may not plague embedded messages, but another difficulty affects both them and visual stimuli. In lab experiments, the subjects concentrate on the visual material containing the subliminal message, but this is much less likely to occur in real-life advertisements or broadcasts.[70] Like advertising generally, therefore, the effectiveness of subliminal appeals should suffer from consumers' inattention to commercial messages.

All in all, subliminal advertising seems to promise only meager benefits to firms that employ it. There apparently is no convincing theoretical argument for its effectiveness. In addition, researchers have adduced theoretical reasons why its impact should be slight. To my knowledge, moreover, no research concludes that subliminal stimuli boost sales. Furthermore, while some studies find that subliminal messages push consumers part way up the hierarchy of effects, others find that they produce no affective response. Finally, even if subliminal advertising reliably generates affective reactions under experimental conditions, advertisers may have difficulty replicating those results in practice.

Sex in Advertising

As Gold observes, advertising has "long employed sex appeal as one of its heaviest-duty weapons."[71] It has done so since at least the beginning of this century, and perhaps earlier.[72] Sex-related advertisements employ a variety of approaches. Those most often examined in the marketing literature are nude or partially nude models, sexual suggestiveness (usually by physical interaction between the male and female models), physically attractive models, and the so-called decorative model (a model, usually female, whose only function is to adorn the product as a stimulus). Although there is a widespread perception that such appeals have increased in frequency and explicitness during recent decades, the first perception may be inaccurate.[73] A comparison of ad content in six general-interest, women's, and men's magazines for the years 1964 and 1984 concluded that (1) the percentage of advertisements with sexual content remained constant, although their absolute number rose as total ads increased; (2) the numerical increase occurred mainly in the general-interest magazines; (3) sexual illustrations have become more overt; (4) the sexual element in ads is more likely to be visual than verbal, a tendency that has increased over time; and (5) female models are more likely to be portrayed as suggestively clad, partially clad, or nude than are male models.[74]

The effectiveness of sex as an advertising tool is unclear. Schudson regards it as neither regularly effective nor regularly ineffective.[75] As Clark observes, however, there are great rewards for using it effectively. "Does Calvin Klein look like he's short of a bob or two?"[76] But as Clark also notes, the sensitivities of certain groups (e.g., some women and older people) make it a dangerous weapon as well.[77] Two recent surveys of academic work on sex-related advertising are similarly ambivalent. One begins by stating that "past research casts some doubt on the efficacy of this form of advertising."[78] The other opens with a sentence that echoes Schudson: "Studies of erotic communication appeals indicate that the effects of such appeals vary; reactions are sometimes positive, sometimes negative."[79] As will become apparent, one reason for these ambivalent conclusions is the range of variables that affect the efficacy question. These include (1) the type of sexual appeal made (e.g., nude, decorative model, etc.), (2) the gender of the model(s) in the ad (male, female, or both), (3) the gender of the person witnessing the ad (which may interact with the previous factor), (4) the informational content of the ad (low or high), (5) whether a sexual appeal is natural for the advertised product (e.g., perfume versus fertilizer), and (6) the variables the relevant study is testing (e.g., cognitive, affective, or conative).

To consider the effect of such factors, I will use as my point of departure a fairly recent and comprehensive academic study.[80] The four-color advertisement that was the basis for the study could hardly have been more manipulative in intent. It touted Travel Fox sports shoes, a product intended for males and females, age eighteen to thirty-four, by showing side profiles of an adult male and female from the chest down. Each was completely nude except for the Travel Fox shoes and matching socks. The positioning of the two models clearly suggested that they were engaged in sexual intercourse. Only one line of copy appeared below this illustration; it emphasized the soft leather construction of the shoes and the colors available. Four versions of the ad (plus some controls) were displayed to different groups of college students on a large screen. One version was the original ad and another was the original with more copy information; a third and fourth were sex-free versions with low and high copy information, respectively. (The sex-free versions only depicted the shoes themselves, with copy immediately beneath.) All versions included the Travel Fox brand name. After the presentation, the students filled out a questionnaire concerning the ads they had seen. Among other things, the questions measured brand recall, recall of copy information, various affective reactions, and intent to purchase the product.

The students' brand recall, between the high-sex and no-sex presentations, did not differ significantly, but did increase on the higher information ads. The former finding is somewhat consistent with other studies involving nudity and decorative models—studies which contain little to suggest that sex increases brand recall.[81] However, decorative models do seem to increase recognition and recall of the advertisement itself.[82] The same probably is true for nudity. Thus, as one article on that technique suggested, "[w]hile an illustration of a nude female may gain the interest and attention of a viewer, an advertisement depicting a nonsexual scene appears to be more effective in obtaining brand recall."[83]

The students' recall of the advertising copy (as opposed to the ad itself) in the Travel Fox ads resembled their recall of the product's brand name. As before, recall was greater for the high-information ads. Here, though, the no-sex ads resulted in significantly greater recall than their high-sex counterparts. In fact, the no-sex/low-information presentation elicited greater recall than the high-sex/high-information presentation. Other studies have concluded that decorative models have little effect on the reading and retention of information presented in advertisements.[84] As one such study concludes, these results and those of the preceding paragraph concerning recall of the ad

> confirm what advertising practitioners have assumed all along: putting an attractive or sexy female in an ad to adorn the product is an effective attention-getting device. . . . [T]he results convincingly demonstrate that portraying decorative female

models in an ad's illustration will improve ad recognition. This
does not mean, however, that the presence of decorative
models will lead to a reading of the ad's body copy.[85]

The same probably holds for other kinds of sexual advertising
content.

The results thus far suggest that sex in advertising is good for
increasing ad recognition, but for little else. However, the latter
conclusion changes considerably when attention turns to affective
factors. In the Travel Fox study, the high-sex ads were regarded
more favorably than the low-sex versions, and they also were
judged more interesting and original. In addition, positive attitude
toward the brand was higher for students exposed to the high-sex
ads. (The increases were most pronounced for the interest and
originality ratings.) But the high-sex ads also were viewed as more
offensive. Some other studies seem to display consistent results.[86]
However, gender differences assume importance in this connection. As one might expect, there is evidence that male viewers tend
to rate female models and female nudity more highly than male
models and male nudity, while female viewers favor male models
and male nudity.[87] There also is evidence that women are more apt
to dislike sexual suggestiveness.[88] Clark maintains that women
seem to find innuendo most offensive. "Nudity does not worry
them as long as the image is attractive and bereft of pornographic
overtones."[89] Finally, the student subjects exposed to the high-sex
Travel Fox ads indicated that they would be more likely to purchase
the shoes than those who were exposed to the no-sex ads. (The
difference, while significant, was not huge.) However, one field
study suggests that physical attractiveness does not affect purchase
intentions.[90] Another study involved male and female decorative
models of varying degrees of attractiveness who appeared in ads
for coffee and for perfume, cologne, or aftershave lotion.[91] When
the male model appeared in the advertisement, female subjects
expressed a stronger intention to purchase than did male subjects,
but the attractiveness of the male model did not influence the
results. The attractiveness of the female model did not affect female
subjects. For the male subjects who viewed a female model, the
nature of the product was an important factor. When the product
was perfume, cologne, or aftershave, the more attractive female
model produced higher intention-to-purchase scores. For the coffee

ad, however, the unattractive female model generated a greater intention to purchase.

The nature of the product may also have been a factor in the shoe study, whose ads "tended to position the Travel Fox brand as a fashion-type product, where the use of a sexual appeal might have been perceived as being appropriate."[92] In addition, the authors conceded that their study might have been biased by its use of student subjects, who may have been relatively tolerant of, or attracted to, sexually explicit advertising. Finally, like the subliminal advertising studies, this study did not reflect real-world conditions because its subjects presumably paid close attention to the presentations.

All things considered, the research discussed here seems consistent with the remarks that opened this section. Sex in advertising is a mixed bag for the firms that employ it. Although some sexual ploys promise great rewards, such tactics must be used with care. Because they evidently enhance recall of the ad itself, sexual themes probably enable it to attract consumers' attention. However, they apparently do nothing to increase recall of either the brand or of advertising copy, and indeed may detract from it. Nonetheless, attractive, decorative, or nude models and sexually explicit depictions of them also seem to induce more favorable attitudes toward the ad. Here, though, gender differences come into play. In particular, people of one gender tend not to react to nudes of the same gender, and some people (especially some women) are turned off by certain sexually explicit materials. Although there is evidence that sexual material can increase the intention to purchase, there also is evidence to the contrary. Finally, as with subliminal advertising, I am not aware of any work that examines the effect of sex on the actual sales of the products in whose ads it appears.

REVISITING THE ECONOMIC DEBATE OVER ADVERTISING

Thus far, this chapter has suggested various reasons for skepticism about manipulative advertising's power to determine consumer choice, and has examined two particular manipulative techniques whose benefits to advertisers collectively seem modest. Chapter 2's discussion of the protracted economic debate over advertising's impact on competition also looks consistent with the conclusion that manipulative advertising's impact on competition, while real, is limited. The discussion concluded that it is uncertain how much utility consumers lose from advertising's supposed ability to foster and sustain anticompetitive pricing. Because the argument that advertising has such effects depended to a considerable degree on its ability to manipulate consumers, this inconclusion also raises questions about the effectiveness of manipulative advertising.

A Review of the Arguments

The Traditional Critique of Advertising. As we saw in chapter 2,[93] the traditional economic critique of advertising assumes that it often is manipulative. The result is increased product differentiation in consumers' minds; an important example is the creation of irrational brand loyalties. This means that demand becomes less elastic, which in turn means that firms can raise prices without losing too many sales. Thus, because consumers pay more per unit, they lose economic welfare and utility.

Consumers also lose welfare and utility, the critique continues, because advertising helps promote economic concentration, which makes it easier for firms to collude in oligopolistic pricing. One way that advertising promotes concentration is by helping create economies of scale in production. The first firms to make large advertising outlays steal sales from competitors. The resulting increases in revenues and profits enable those firms to invest in more efficient plant and equipment, which should further increase scale economies and profits. This, in turn, permits the purchase of still more advertising, which can further increase sales and weaken competitors. As a result, some competitors may fall by the wayside. This should make it easier for the remaining competitors to manage prices within the industry and to further increase their profits. All these effects might occur to some degree even if advertising is nonmanipulative, but obviously the whole process works better on the assumption that advertising manipulates.

According to the traditional critique, advertising also helps promote concentration by increasing barriers to entry. For one thing, new entrants may have to make large advertising expenditures to overcome the brand loyalties established by manipulative advertising. In addition, the traditional critique asserts, there are economies of scale in *advertising* as well as in production. Within a certain range of advertising expenditures, therefore, each extra dollar of advertising generates more than a dollar in sales. If existing firms within the industry are large enough to operate within this range and potential entrants are not, the latter may be deterred from entering the industry because they will be less competitive. This leaves the field open to the existing firms within the industry.

The New Defense of Advertising. Due to the processes just described, the traditional critique concludes, consumers lose welfare and utility—principally through the higher prices oligopolistic competitors can charge. (Another reason consumers may lose utility is that in the relatively uncompetitive environment manipulative advertising helps produce, product innovation may decline.[94]) Since at least the 1970s, however, the traditional economic critique of advertising has come under increasing attack.

Unlike the traditional view, this new defense of advertising regards it as primarily *informative* rather than manipulative. This means that advertising does not create tastes, artificially differentiate products, produce irrational brand loyalties, and reduce elasticity of demand. On the contrary, it provides information that rational consumers assess for themselves. This includes information about alternative products and services and their prices. Because consumers rationally evaluate such information and act accordingly, they seek out the cheapest products and services of equivalent quality. This naturally forces prices down and maximizes consumers' utility per dollar spent.

The new defense of advertising also rejects the traditional critique's claim that advertising sustains oligopoly. One argument for this claim was that advertising-induced brand loyalties create barriers to entry by forcing new entrants to make disproportionately high advertising expenditures. According to the new view, however, advertising does not create such loyalties in the first place. In addition, some defenders doubt whether there are economies of scale in advertising. If so, large existing firms lose another potential advantage over would-be competitors. Finally, the new defense of advertising emphasizes how advertising *helps* new entrants who offer superior or lower priced products. If advertising is informative and consumers are rational, such firms can make these facts known with some assurance that consumers will respond appropriately.

In sum, the new defense of advertising sees it as a force for competition. In the view of its proponents, it tends to lower prices and thus give consumers more utility per dollar spent. Advertising also provides information about higher utility products and services and thus facilitates their purchase. Furthermore, it increases consumer utility by reducing the cost of searching for superior products and services. Finally, advertising is a powerful stimulus to efficiency and innovation because it rewards firms that market cheaper and/or better products and services and penalizes those that do not.

The Results of the Research

Chapter 2 tried to summarize the voluminous, detailed, and contentious body of empirical research created by proponents of the two views just discussed.[95] The best way to attack the problem, one might think, would be to establish the relationship (if any) between advertising expenditures and the elasticity of demand within particular industries. Establishing the needed relationship, however, requires that researchers establish the relationship between level of advertising and price. Due to the many factors that affect a product's price, it evidently has not been possible to isolate advertising's effect on it. As a result, researchers have used industry concentration and industry profits as indirect measures of the market power whose existence might better be captured by elasticity of demand.

Industry Concentration. The traditional critique of advertising identified several ways in which advertising can increase industry concentration, which assertedly makes it easier for the industry's members to collude in oligopolistic pricing. In the critique, advertising's ability to increase concentration depended partially, but not entirely, on its ability to manipulate consumers. Thus, a solid relationship between advertising expenditure and concentration might support the assertion that advertising indeed does manipulate. Advertising's defenders, on the other hand, maintain for various reasons that advertising tends to defeat the emergence of oligopoly. If the relationship between advertising and concentration is weak or nonexistent, we might have some reason to accept these claims. In particular, we might have some reason to accept the central claim made by advertising's defenders—that it informs rather than manipulates. As we saw in chapter 2, the research on this question apparently tends to favor the first view, but not very convincingly. Despite some evidence that advertising causes concentration, in other words, the significance of this evidence is unclear.

Industry Profits. According to the traditional critique, one reason why firms that advertise heavily reap additional profits is the inelastic demand that permits them to raise prices without suffering severe losses in sales. This inelastic demand, of course, supposedly derives from brand loyalties created by advertising's manipulative powers. Thus, if there is reason to think that more advertising means more profits, there may also be reason to think that it is manipulative. Chapter 2's summary of the research on the relationship between advertising and profits revealed some evidence that the two indeed are associated. But it also revealed accounting disputes that might undermine the association. Perhaps more importantly, that discussion suggested that the association may exist because firms tend to spend less on advertising when business turns bad. Thus, the research on the advertising–profits relationship seems inconclusive.

Brand Loyalty. According to the traditional critique, advertising's manipulativeness manifests itself primarily in the creation of irrational brand loyalties. Thus, a solid relationship between advertising expenditure and the existence of brand loyalty might help cement the claim that advertising manipulates. As chapter 2 made clear, however, the limited research on this question apparently suggests the opposite.

In Conclusion. Like its counterpart in chapter 2, this section does not attempt to resolve the economic debate over advertising's impact. Instead, it seeks to determine what light the debate sheds on advertising's ability to manipulate consumer purchase decisions. Overall, the evidence suggests that while advertising has some manipulative power, that power is not great. This conclusion, of course, is consistent with the conclusions reached by this chapter's other inquiries.

WHY THEN DO FIRMS ADVERTISE?

If manipulative advertising is a relatively weak force, some readers may ask, why does business spend so much money on it?

As we saw in chapter 1, something like half of all advertising may qualify as manipulative under the definitions employed there. Are we really to believe that America's largest and most sophisticated corporations would throw good money after bad, year after year, on a service that is of only modest benefit to them? One answer to these questions is to ask another: Are you sure that businesspeople always behave rationally?[96] The main reason firms spend so much money on manipulative advertising, however, derives from a much-quoted piece of business folk wisdom: "I know that at least half of my advertising money is being wasted. My problem is—I do not know which half."[97] The remainder of this section elaborates on this remark; what it says about advertising in general should apply to manipulative advertising in particular.

The business perception that a sizable portion of one's advertising budget is wasted fits in with the general thrust of this chapter. Its implication is that firms invest heavily in advertising because the alternative looks even less appealing. For one thing, a particular campaign might work, or at least might make some difference. Except in cases where good advertising kills a bad product or a particular pitch turns off a particular audience, it is unlikely that advertising will appreciably *harm* sales. For all these reasons, it is reasonable to expect that one's competitors will advertise. Thus, our decision maker's firm may be at a disadvantage if it does not do the same. If the firm's sales decline, the responsible manager may have difficulty explaining why he failed to advertise while the competitors did. For rational firms, in sum, it may well seem less risky to advertise than not to advertise. Indeed, it may be rational to overspend on advertising. If you believe that half of your advertising will work but do not know which half, you probably will buy more advertising than you ideally would need.

As we will see in chapter 5, the most important determinant of advertising expenditures may be the money firms have available to spend for that purpose at any particular time. Chapter 5 also presents some empirical evidence supporting the previous paragraph's surmises. In a 1992 article describing a survey of British advertisers, the authors concluded that (1) firms find it difficult to estimate the effectiveness of advertising, (2) one reason they advertise is that they do not know any more efficient and economical way to generate sales, and (3) another reason they advertise is their fear that sales would drop if they did not.[98] With regard to the first and third points, the authors observe that "[w]hen it comes to evaluating effectiveness it is not seen as being particularly easy. Indeed, advertising aims more at reinforcing the name of the brand than at pushing sales which have reached a stable level."[99]

The previous sentence underlines another reason why it may be rational to advertise even though advertising's effect on sales is uncertain. As another source remarks, advertising's main role is to reassure repeat buyers and to reinforce their brand choices.[100] When performing this role, advertising is "essentially defensive"; thus, "[t]o focus on new buyers . . . is to waste money on illusions."[101] To be sure, assessing advertising's ability to stabilize demand by retaining existing purchasers may be just as difficult as determining its power to generate new sales. Perhaps, however, it is easier to keep existing buyers loyal than to generate new ones. If so, advertising may succeed at that task even if it is not especially efficacious overall. On that assumption, we have a rational explanation for some advertising expenditures that is consistent with advertising's relative ineffectiveness.

ETHICAL IMPLICATIONS

Manipulative advertising almost certainly is less effective in getting people to buy particular products than many of its foes maintain. As we have seen, there are many general reasons for questioning its efficacy. Turning to specific forms of the practice, the effect of subliminal techniques seems slight, while associating products with sexual themes is a mixed bag for advertisers. At best, finally, the lengthy economic debate on advertising's competitive impact provides only moderate—and indirect—support for the claim that advertising successfully manipulates. With all these reasons to downplay manipulative advertising's effectiveness, why do so many firms spend so much money on it? The answer, essentially, is that doing so seems the best of a bad bargain. In an environment of uncertainty, the perceived risks of refusing to employ manipulative techniques exceed their cost.

But if manipulative advertising is not especially effective in getting consumers to buy things, what happens to the ethical criticisms it received in chapters 2 and 3? We now reconsider those criticisms in the order in which they appeared earlier. For the most part, this chapter's findings weaken their force. As a result, they also weaken the critics' argument that advertising's manipulativeness justifies one or more of the political responses sketched in chapter 1.

The Utilitarian Arguments

Chapter 2's crude cost-benefit analysis of manipulative advertising suggested that it might reduce aggregate utility through (1) the money firms spend for it (a cost probably passed on to consumers), (2) its ability to steer consumers toward suboptimum products, (3) the pain consumers suffer when associative advertising's false expectations are dashed, (4) the higher prices it produces by generating brand loyalties and by helping create and sustain oligopoly (the traditional economic critique), and (5) its ability to steer consumers away from more satisfying public goods by stimulating the propensity to consume (Galbraith's argument). On the positive side of the ledger, chapter 2 concluded that manipulative advertising might generate utility by (1) stimulating the economy as it increases the propensity to consume, (2) creating economies of scale in the process, (3) giving consumers pleasing product-related associations, and (4) helping provide free or cheap mass media. The chapter also entertained the possibility that, even if manipulative advertising reduces aggregate utility on balance, the costs of getting to a more felicitous organization of society could deter the transition.

How did these positive and negative effects balance out? Chapter 2 disposed of two of them (the costs of advertising and the benefits of cheap media) by assuming that they largely cancel each other out. The chapter also maintained that Galbraith was wrong in arguing that manipulated consumption necessarily generates low utility, and that there is no particular reason to believe that his public goods would make people happier. But chapter 2 also argued that the net utility effects attributable to manipulative advertising's impact on consumer purchase decisions—the "suboptimum products," "dashed expectations," and "pleasing associations" arguments, plus the traditional economic critique—probably are negative, albeit moderately so. This might support some kinds of regulation for some particular types of ads. But chapter 2 concluded that utilitarian arguments could not justify more radical steps of the kind Galbraith proposed, or even less stringent steps such as restrictions on the amount of advertising. The main reason was manipulative advertising's assumed ability to stimulate consumption and scale economies, and thus to increase utility. These utility gains, I assumed, are not outweighed by the losses resulting from manipulative advertising's impact on competition. Also relevant here were the possible transition costs of moving to some (professedly) higher utility new order.

In chapter 4, we have considered only manipulative advertising's ability to affect consumer choice. Therefore, this chapter's arguments do not affect my previous conclusions regarding advertising's stimulation of the economy and its generation of scale economies, Galbraith's argument, the money spent on advertising, and its subsidization of the mass media. But they do affect the various utilitarian arguments that depend on manipulative advertising's presumed ability to affect consumer purchase decisions. Our conclusions concerning one of those arguments, the traditional economic critique of advertising, of course remain unchanged from chapter 2. But this chapter does impact the others. If manipulative advertising is not especially effective in getting people to buy things, it also causes relatively few utility losses from the purchase of suboptimum products. The same is true for the thesis that purchasers of associatively advertised products will lose utility as the hopes generated by the associations prove illusory. On the other side of the ledger, manipulative advertising's relative ineffectiveness also limits the utility gains consumers derive from pleasing product associations. Chapter 2 concluded that, when taken together, these various effects meant less utility. Now, with three of the four effects suppressed to some degree, it seems that those losses may not be as significant as previously believed. This probably weakens, but does not destroy, the case for piecemeal regulation of manipulative advertising. And it further weakens the already feeble arguments for limitations on the volume of advertising and for social surgery of one kind or another. However, most of the asserted utility gains and losses pertinent to this last argument involve advertising's asserted ability to stimulate consumption—a topic addressed in chapter 5.

The Categorical Imperative

As chapter 3 made clear, Kantian ethics is avowedly anticonsequentialist. For that reason, this chapter's revised estimate of manipulative advertising's powers should not affect the largely negative evaluation it received under at least one major formulation of the categorical imperative. Because manipulative advertising's relative ineffectiveness might change the application of each formulation, however, we need to examine this assumption with more care.

Under the first version of the imperative, a maxim permitting manipulative advertising now might read: "In order to sell their clients' products and thereby make money, advertisers may employ subliminal advertising and other manipulative techniques whenever those methods have good prospects of success, even though those prospects are uncertain." Presumably advertisers would not will even this diluted maxim's universalization, since doing so still might entail that they would suffer manipulation in their personal capacities. As before, however, advertisers might evade condemnation by framing their maxim so narrowly that they escape its application.

Under the second formulation of the categorical imperative, advertisers still would be endeavoring to undermine consumers' rationality and therefore to treat them as means—albeit with less prospect of success. It seems unlikely that quantitative considerations—the number of consumers whose rational evaluation of products actually is affected by manipulative advertising—would have mattered to Kant. A bad will is a bad will, no matter what the efficacy of its tactics. Therefore, manipulative advertising presumably should be suppressed even though its effect on competition is not severe.

Autonomy

This chapter's conclusions about manipulative advertising's efficacy blunt, but do not completely eliminate, the objection that it reduces human autonomy. This is true under all the conceptions of autonomy discussed in chapter 3. If it is relatively ineffective, manipulative advertising is less of a threat to the inner freedom of a will possessing Thomas Hill's "Sartrean autonomy," and to the integrity of a self possessing "autonomous" character traits such as independent judgment. In addition, consumers would often remain autonomous in Robert Arrington's sense of the term because their second-order identification with their purchases is more likely to be procedurally independent. Of course, even if manipulative advertising does not greatly affect competition, it still may reduce autonomy by stimulating the propensity to consume. Chapter 5 considers this possibility.

Virtue Ethics

Chapter 3 discussed two overlapping ways in which manipulative advertising might offend an ethics that stresses the virtues. The first is that manipulative advertising is objectionable because it stimulates the propensity to consume, and a life devoted to consumption is far from the best life. Because it involves manipulative advertising's assumed ability to make people consumers rather than its effect on consumption choices, this argument's discussion must await chapter 5. The second criticism is that manipulative advertising tends to rob its targets of certain specific virtues. These include rationality, reflectiveness, self-awareness, self-control, self-discipline, self-reliance, and moderation. This second effect of manipulative advertising probably arises both from its asserted ability to affect competition and its ability to stimulate consumption. Here, we consider only the former; discussion of the latter is deferred until chapter 5.

This chapter's conclusions about manipulative advertising's efficacy raise questions about its ability to corrupt consumers. Its somewhat limited ability to generate sales suggests that its effect on consumers' character is correspondingly limited. Against this conclusion, one might maintain that manipulative advertising corrupts even if it does not sell products. But the effectiveness of associative advertising, at least, seems to depend upon the corruptions listed earlier. When it works, such advertising links the product to the satisfaction of some desire that it is unlikely to satisfy in fact. The desire's ability to sway consumers—to make them suspend their rational faculties—is critical to its success. When it is effective, therefore, associative advertising should make consumers less rational, reflective, self-disciplined, and moderate. If such virtues must be practiced to be maintained, and if their abandonment on one occasion weakens their future hold, the effects of a successful associative ad may linger. The present point, though, is that because associative advertising does not work especially well, this criticism packs less weight than it did in chapter 3. As a result, chapter 3's suggestion that regulators might focus on associative advertising now seems less persuasive as well.

NOTES

1. For example, a recent marketing journal article asserts that "[t]he literature on communication and advertising effects seems to be biased toward advertising effectiveness." Theo B. C. Poiesz and Henry S. J. Robben, "Individual Reactions to Advertising: Theoretical and Methodological Developments," *International Journal of Advertising* 13 (1994): 35. Other observers concur. As one declares, "An assumption underlying the majority of studies of advertising's effectiveness is that advertising *is* effective, and that we need only to develop more sophisticated measurement tools and we shall then be able to quantify the payoff." John P. Jones, "Advertising: Strong Force or Weak Force? Two Views an Ocean Apart," *International Journal of Advertising* 9 (1990): 235 (emphasis in original). See also 235–37; and Hugh Murray, "Advertising's Effect on Sales—Proven or Just Assumed?," *International Journal of Advertising* 5 (1986): 15–18.

2. For example, this view is at least implicit, and sometimes explicit, in Robert L. Arrington, "Advertising and Behavior Control," *Journal of Business Ethics* 1 (1982): 3–12; Tom L. Beauchamp, "Manipulative Advertising," *Business & Professional Ethics Journal* 3 (1984): 1–22; David Braybrooke, "Skepticism of Wants, and Certain Subversive Effects of Corporations on American Values," in *Ethical Theory and Business*, ed. Tom L. Beauchamp and Norman E. Bowie (Englewood Cliffs, N.J.: Prentice-Hall, 1979), 502–8; Roger Crisp, "Persuasive Advertising, Autonomy, and the Creation of Desire," *Journal of Business Ethics* 6 (1987): 413–18; and John Waide, "The Making of Self and World in Advertising," *Journal of Business Ethics* 6 (1987): 73–79. On occasion, business ethicists deny that advertising has much impact on consumer purchase decisions but affirm that it does generate a propensity to consume. See, for example, Richard L. Lippke, "Advertising and the Social Conditions of Autonomy," *Business and Professional Ethics Journal* 8, no. 4 (1990): 38–39.

3. Occasionally, however, suggestions to the contrary appear within the industry. See, for example, Rance Crain, "Power of Advertising More Like a Myth," *Advertising Age*, 10 January 1994, 24. Another example, one discussed at various points in the chapter, is the work of David Ogilvy.

4. Murray, "Advertising's Effect on Sales," 16.

5. Jones, "Advertising: Strong Force or Weak Force?," 235–36.

6. On the "deficient sense of fact" manifested by many philosophers, see Richard A. Posner, *Overcoming Law* (Cambridge, Mass.: Harvard University Press, 1995), chap. 22.

7. Jones, "Advertising: Strong Force or Weak Force?," 233–46; Murray, "Advertising's Effect on Sales," 15–36.

8. Michael Schudson, *Advertising, the Uneasy Persuasion: Its Dubious Impact on American Society* (n.p.: Basic Books, 1986), xiii.

9. Ibid., xiv.

10. Philip Gold, *Advertising, Politics, and American Culture: From Salesmanship to Therapy* (New York: Paragon House, 1987), 22.

11. For an extended discussion of those techniques, see Eric Clark, *The Want Makers. The World of Advertising: How They Make You Buy* (New York: Viking Penguin, 1988), chaps. 2, 3.

12. However, this point may not apply to "direct response" (direct mail and direct personal contact) promotion or to department store advertising. David Ogilvy, *Confessions of an Advertising Man* (1963; New York: Atheneum, 1987), xiii, 91–92; David Ogilvy, *Ogilvy on Advertising* (New York: Vintage Books, 1985), 23. The reason is that here the ad and any response to it succeed each other fairly quickly.

13. Poiesz and Robben, "Individual Reactions to Advertising," 26.

14. Ogilvy, *Ogilvy on Advertising*, 23. To the same effect is Ogilvy, *Confessions*, xiii.

15. Mark S. Albion and Paul W. Faris, *The Advertising Controversy: Evidence on the Economic Effects of Advertising* (Boston: Auburn House, 1981), 8–9; Schudson, *Advertising, the Uneasy Persuasion*, 20–23.

16. Clark, *The Want Makers*, 106.

17. Ibid.

18. For a detailed description and critique of the many such approaches, see Thomas E. Barry and Daniel J. Howard, "A Review and Critique of the Hierarchy of Effects in Advertising," *International Journal of Advertising* 9 (1990): 121–35. See also Albion and Farris, *The Advertising Controversy*, 3–8; Murray, "Advertising's Effect on Sales," 18–23.

19. Barry and Howard, "A Review and Critique," 122 (sketching an approach developed by R. C. Lavidge and G. A. Steiner).

20. Ibid., 123.

21. Murray, "Advertising's Effect on Sales," 19.

22. For various criticisms of the approach, see Barry and Howard, "Review and Critique," 127–33; Murray, "Advertising's Effect on Sales," 19–23.

23. Barry and Howard, "Review and Critique," 124–27.

24. Ibid., 128–29; see also Murray, "Advertising's Effect on Sales," 19.

25. Ogilvy, *Ogilvy on Advertising*, 161.

26. "[T]hese models assume, without evidence, that there is a unidirectional flow of causality from change in awareness to change in buying habits." Murray, "Advertising's Effect on Sales," 20. Murray then discusses some sources who suggest that changes in attitude may *follow* the purchase rather than precede it.

27. Schudson, *Advertising, the Uneasy Persuasion*, 36, 38; Geoffrey P. Lantos, "Advertising: Looking Glass or Molder of the Masses?," *Journal of Public Policy and Marketing* 6 (1987): 113.

28. See, for example, Clark, *The Want Makers*, 35 (fewer than 10 percent of all new products launched in America are still around three years later); Jones, "Advertising: Strong Force or Weak Force?," 239 (failure rate may be as high as 95 percent); Lantos, "Advertising: Looking Glass or Molder?," 113 (failure rate may be as high as 80 percent). Of course, these estimates depend on, among other things, how a "new product" and its "failure" are defined. For a good general discussion presenting a wide range of estimated failure rates, some of them much lower than those just quoted, see Schudson, *Advertising, the Uneasy Persuasion*, 36–37.

29. Schudson, *Advertising, the Uneasy Persuasion*, 32–34. For some other examples, see ibid., 35–36; Lantos, "Advertising: Looking Glass or Molder?," 121; Vincent P. Norris, "The Economic Effects of Advertising: A Review of the Literature," *Current Issues and Research in Advertising* 2 (1984): 46.

30. Schudson, *Advertising, the Uneasy Persuasion*, 3–4.

31. Francis Buttle, "What Do People Do with Advertising?," *International Journal of Advertising* 10 (1991): 98–99 (citing many studies). Ogilvy, who concurs on this general point, attributes it to the barrage of advertisements to which Americans are subjected. Ogilvy, *Confessions*, 97.

32. Clark, *The Want Makers*, 62.

33. Ibid., 63.

34. Ibid.

35. See, for example, Schudson, *Advertising, the Uneasy Persuasion*, 110–11.

36. Stephen A. Greyser and Raymond A. Bauer, "Americans and Advertising: Thirty Years of Public Opinion," *Public Opinion Quarterly* 30 (Spring 1966): 73; see ibid., 73–75. For some later negative poll data on advertising and advertisers, see John O'Toole, *The Trouble with Advertising* (New York: Times Books, 1985), 3–4, 5–6. However, some of the polls discussed by Greyser and Bauer contained responses suggesting a belief that advertising's veracity is improving. In addition, their article also suggested that Americans generally (1) are favorable toward advertising, (2) believe that it contributes to a higher standard of living, and (3) believe that it results in higher prices.

37. Schudson, *Advertising, the Uneasy Persuasion*, 108–9.

38. Ibid., 4.

39. Ibid., 19; see also Ogilvy, *Confessions*, 156; Ogilvy, *Ogilvy on Advertising*, 215. As Schudson notes, however, this particular objection to advertising's effectiveness depends on consumers' ability to evaluate the product and thus does not apply where they are unable or relatively unable to judge product quality (e.g., sales of life insurance).

40. Robert M. Solow, "The Truth Further Refined: A Comment on Marris," *Public Interest* 11 (Spring 1968): 49. See also F. A. Hayek, "The *Non Sequitur* of the 'Dependence Effect,'" *Southern Economic Journal* 27 (1961): 347.

41. Robin Marris, "Galbraith, Solow, and the Truth about Corporations," *Public Interest* 11 (Spring 1968): 39.

42. John Kenneth Galbraith, *The Affluent Society* (Boston: Houghton Mifflin, 1958), 154–55.

43. David A. Reisman, *Galbraith and Market Capitalism* (New York: New York University Press, 1980), 88.

44. Thorolf Helgesen, "The Rationality of Advertising Decisions: Conceptual Issues and Some Empirical Findings from a Norwegian Study," *Journal of Advertising Research* 32, no. 6 (November-December 1992): 22; Jones, "Advertising: Strong Force or Weak Force?," 235; Poiesz and Robben, "Individual Reactions to Advertising," 25.

45. Timothy E. Moore, "Subliminal Advertising: What You See Is What You Get," *Journal of Marketing* 46 (Spring 1982): 39.

46. Scot Silverglate, "Subliminal Perception and the First Amendment: Yelling Fire in a Crowded Mind?," *University of Miami Law Review* 44 (1990): 1252.

47. Wilson Bryan Key, *Subliminal Seduction: Ad Media's Manipulation of a Not So Innocent America* (New York: Penguin, 1981), 47.

48. Ibid., 50–55.

49. Ibid., 61.

50. Moore, "Subliminal Advertising," 45.

51. Ibid.

52. Ibid.

53. Ibid., 46. It also seems to be true that the effectiveness of subliminal stimuli increases with their intensity. Sid C. Dudley, "Subliminal Advertising: What Is the Controversy About?," *Akron Business and Economic Review* 18, no. 2 (Summer 1987): 16. As Dudley points out, this suggests that completely supraliminal messages are more effective than subliminal ones.

54. Melvin L. De Fleur and Robert M. Petranoff, "A Televised Test of Subliminal Persuasion," *Public Opinion Quarterly* 23 (Summer 1959): 179.

55. Moore, "Subliminal Advertising," 41. This argument applies to embedded stimuli as well. J. Steven Kelly, "Subliminal Embeds in Print Advertising: A Challenge to Advertising Ethics," *Journal of Advertising* 8 (1979): 23.

56. De Fleur and Petranoff, "A Televised Test," 180.

57. Moore, "Subliminal Advertising," 43.

58. Alvin W. Rose, "Motivation Research and Subliminal Advertising," *Social Research* 25 (Fall 1958): 279–80.

59. Ibid., 280–81. The words "subliminal" and "subliminally," however, do not seem accurate in this context. Making much the same point are De Fleur and Petranoff, "A Televised Test," 180.

60. Moore, "Subliminal Advertising," 43.

61. De Fleur and Petranoff, "A Televised Test," 170–79.

62. Also, one writer has asserted that several researchers on subliminal advertising have abandoned their projects and have not sought publication because they were unable to show that the advertising had any affective or behavioral impact. Joel Saegert, "Another Look at Subliminal Perception," *Journal of Advertising Research* 19, no. 1 (1979): 55.

63. Ronnie Cuperfain and T. K. Clarke, "A New Perspective of [sic] Subliminal Perception," *Journal of Advertising* 14, no. 1 (1985): 36–41.

64. Ibid., 40. However, a similar subliminal presentation involving Woolite failed to generate significant results. The authors suggested that this failure may have been due to the students' low familiarity with Woolite as opposed to Zero, which may have rendered them unable "to build a satisfactory impression from the subliminal stimulus." They also surmised that the Woolite message may have fallen below the students' subliminal threshold owing to its color.

65. Sharon E. Beatty and Del I. Hawkins, "Subliminal Stimulation: Some New Data and Interpretation," *Journal of Advertising* 18, no. 3 (1989): 4–8. This study replicated a study conducted by Hawkins nineteen years earlier. See Del Hawkins, "The Effects of Subliminal Stimulation on Drive Level and Brand Performance," *Journal of Marketing Research* 7 (August 1970): 322–26. However, it failed to repeat the affective responses found in the first study.

66. William E. Kilbourne, Scott Painton, and Danny Ridley, "The Effect of Sexual Embedding on Responses to Magazine Advertisements," *Journal of Advertising* 14, no. 2 (1985): 48–56.

67. Myron Gable, Henry T. Wilkens, Lynn Harris, and Richard Feinberg, "An Evaluation of Subliminally Embedded Sexual Stimuli in Graphics," *Journal of Advertising* 16, no. 1 (1987): 26–28 (embeds did not generate consistent preferences for products in which they appeared); Kelly, "Subliminal Embeds," 21–23 (no significant difference in recall).

68. Moore, "Subliminal Advertising," 41. Researchers face a similar problem. If the stimulus is too strong, some viewers may perceive it supraliminally, thus biasing the study. Ibid., 39; see also Dudley, "Subliminal Advertising," 15.

69. As noted in chapter 1, during the 1973 Christmas shopping season, some viewers of a televised children's toy commercial spotted an attempted subliminal message to "Get it," and then complained to the FCC and the FTC. Diane Kiesel, "Subliminal Seduction: Old Ideas, New Worries," *American Bar Association Journal* 70 (July 1984): 27.

70. Beatty and Hawkins, "Subliminal Stimulation," 7.

71. Gold, *Advertising, Politics, and American Culture*, 82.

72. Clark, *The Want Makers*, 113 (since at least the beginning of this century); Schudson, *Advertising, the Uneasy Persuasion*, 58–59 (providing some nineteenth-century examples).

73. Another reason to question this perception is the number of fairly recent suggestions in the advertising media that sex is falling out of favor as a promotional ploy. See, for example, Warren Berger, "No Sex Please, We're Skittish," *Advertising Age*, 5 October 1992, 12C; Anthony Vagnoni, editorial, *Advertising Age*, 5 October 1992, 3C; John P. Cortez and Ira Teinowitz, "More Trouble Brews for Stroh Bikini Team," *Advertising Age*, 9 December 1991, 45; Ira Teinowitz, "This Bud's for Her: Women to Get 'Equal Roles' in New A-B Campaign," *Advertising Age*, 28 October 1991, 1.

74. Lawrence Soley and Gary Kurzbard, "Sex in Advertising: A Comparison of 1964 and 1984 Magazine Advertisements," *Journal of Advertising* 15, no. 3 (1986): 53.

75. Schudson, *Advertising, the Uneasy Persuasion*, 84.

76. Clark, *The Want Makers*, 113 (quoting an advertising executive).

77. Ibid., 113, 114.

78. Jessica Severn, George E. Belch, and Michael A. Belch, "The Effects of Sexual and Non-Sexual Advertising Appeals and Information Level on Cognitive Processing and Communication Effectiveness," *Journal of Advertising* 19, no. 1 (1990): 14.

79. Michael S. LaTour, Robert E. Pitts, and David C. Snook-Luther, "Female Nudity, Arousal, and Ad Response: An Experimental Investigation," *Journal of Advertising* 19, no. 4 (1990): 52.

80. Severn, Belch, and Belch, "The Effects of Sexual and Non-Sexual Advertising," 14–22.

81. Robert W. Chestnut, Charles C. LaChance, and Amy Lubitz, "The 'Decorative' Female Model: Sexual Stimuli and the Recognition of Advertisements," *Journal of Advertising* 6 (1977): 13, 14 (decorative model had little influence on recognition of brand name). However, one study involving a nude male model showed significantly increased brand recall

among male viewers, but only a statistically insignificant increase among female viewers. Robert H. Davis and John A. Welsch, "A New Viewpoint on Nudes in Advertising and Brand Recall," *International Journal of Advertising* 2 (1983): 145. Another study reported that significantly more brand names were recalled for nonsexual ads than for those depicting a nude female. M. Wayne Alexander and Ben Judd, Jr., "Do Nudes in Ads Enhance Brand Recall?," *Journal of Advertising Research* 18, no. 1 (1979): 49–50. Also, this study found that although nudity generally increased brand recall, brand recall did not rise significantly as the nudity of the model increased.

82. Chestnut, LaChance, and Lubitz, "The 'Decorative' Female Model," 13 (decorative model increases recognition of ad); Leonard N. Reid and Lawrence C. Soley, "Another Look at the 'Decorative' Female Model: The Recognition of Visual and Verbal Ad Components," *Current Issues and Research in Advertising 1981*, 128 (recognition of ad illustration is significantly better when decorative female models are present than when they are absent). Another study found that male observers' attention to an ad increased in the presence of a decorative female model, decreased in the presence of a decorative male model, and was unaffected by the presence of decorative male and female models together. Leonard N. Reid and Lawrence C. Soley, "Decorative Models and the Readership of Magazine Ads," *Journal of Advertising Research* 23 (April-May 1983): 30.

83. Alexander and Judd, "Do Nudes in Ads Enhance Brand Recall?," 50.

84. Reid and Soley, "Another Look," 129 (presence or absence of decorative female model does not significantly affect recognition of ad's body copy); Reid and Soley, "Decorative Models," 30 (decorative male model, decorative female model, or both does not affect male subjects' reading of ad copy). Also, another study concluded that male and female decorative models had no effect on the subjects' cognitive evaluations of advertisements (as measured by attributes like "believable," "informative," and "clear"). Michael J. Baker and Gilbert A. Churchill, Jr., "The Impact of Physically Attractive Models on Advertising Evaluations," *Journal of Marketing Research* 14 (November 1977): 547.

85. Reid and Soley, "Another Look," 130.

86. Baker and Churchill, "The Impact of Physically Attractive Models," 547 (both males and females rate ads with more attractive models more highly than ads with less attractive models). In Michael A. Belch, Barbro E. Holgerson, George E. Belch, and Jerry Koppman, "Psychophysical and Cognitive Responses to Sex in Advertising," *Advances in Consumer Research* 9 (1981): 425–26, the authors concluded that (1) nudity and sexual suggestiveness cause physiological responses in sub-

jects, (2) nudity generally increases an ad's interest and appeal, and (3) suggestiveness produces mixed results. So far as I can tell, the data presentation in Donald Sciglimpaglia, Michael A. Belch, and Richard F. Cain, "Demographic and Cognitive Factors Influencing Viewers' Evaluations of 'Sexy' Advertisements," *Advances in Consumer Research* 6 (1979): 62, 63–64 lend some support to the view that nudity makes ads more interesting and appealing, but also more offensive. The text of the last two studies, their data, and its presentation make definite statements about their results somewhat difficult.

87. Baker & Churchill, "The Impact of Physically Attractive Models," 547 (ad with female model evaluated more favorably by male subjects, and ad with male model evaluated more highly by female subjects); Belch et al., 426 (study data suggest that ads targeted at a specific sex should not employ nudes of the same sex); Sciglimpaglia et al., 63 (males tend to evaluate male nudity poorly and females positively; reverse true for female nudity).

88. Belch et al., "Psychophysical and Cognitive Responses," 425–26 (female subjects rate sexually suggestive ads as more offensive, less appealing, and less interesting as degree of suggestiveness increases; therefore, ads employing sexual suggestiveness probably are not useful for attracting favorable reactions from women); Sciglimpaglia, Belch, and Cain, "Demographic and Cognitive Factors," 63 (female subjects evaluated male-female suggestive ad negatively, while male subjects evaluated it positively).

89. Clark, *The Want Makers*, 117.

90. This study involved videotaped pitches for grocery products (a soft drink and three cheeses) with male and female "spokespersons" of different degrees of attractiveness. Different tapes were shown to different shoppers in a grocery store, each of whom then completed a questionnaire. The subjects also sampled the products. In addition, they essentially were volunteers, so the representativeness of the sample was a problem. For neither the drink nor the cheeses was the attractiveness of the spokesperson a significant factor behind the respondents' purchase intentions. Marjorie J. Caballero, James R. Lumpkin, and Charles S. Madden, "Using Physical Attractiveness as an Advertising Tool: An Empirical Test of the Attraction Phenomenon," *Journal of Advertising Research* 29, no. 4 (August-September 1989): 18–21.

91. Baker and Churchill, "The Impact of Physically Attractive Models," 552.

92. Severn, Belch, and Belch, "The Effects of Sexual and Non-Sexual Advertising," 21.

93. The sources for the assertions made below can be found in chapter 2.

94. Julian L. Simon, *Issues in the Economics of Advertising* (Urbana: University of Illinois Press, 1970), 218 (sketching a common view).

95. For the relevant sources, see the appropriate notes in chapter 2.

96. Michael B. Metzger and Charles C. Schwenk, "Decision Making Models, Devil's Advocacy, and the Control of Corporate Crime," *American Business Law Journal* 28, no. 3 (Fall 1990): 342–50 (discussing the many reasons for irrational organizational behavior).

97. Schudson, *Advertising, the Uneasy Persuasion*, 85.

98. M. P. Flandin, E. Martin, and L. P. Simkin, "Advertising Effectiveness Research: A Survey of Agencies, Clients and Conflicts," *International Journal of Advertising* 11 (1992): 204–5, 207. For more discussion of this article, see chapter 5.

99. Ibid., 205.

100. Murray, "Advertising's Effect on Sales," 32. Prior to this, however, Murray also observed that another important function of advertising is to get consumers to try the product (p. 31).

101. Ibid., 32.

Chapter 5

ADVERTISING AND THE PROPENSITY TO CONSUME

Although chapter 4 did not eliminate all the ethical objections to manipulative advertising, it weakened most of them. For that reason, it also weakened the case for the critics' political agenda. However, chapter 4 did not consider advertising's asserted ability to stimulate consumption: to make people consumers in the first place. For some of advertising's foes, it is *this* effect of advertising that is critical. As we saw in chapter 1, for example, John Kenneth Galbraith put more stress on advertising's stimulation of consumption than on its competitive impact, and Richard Lippke emphasized the former while dismissing the latter. As a result, some critics of advertising have a fallback position that is unaffected by its less-than-stunning impact on consumer choice among products and services. The reason, of course, is that advertising might decrease aggregate utility, violate Immanuel Kant's categorical imperative, reduce personal autonomy, and render people less virtuous by increasing the propensity to consume even if it does not seriously affect competition. In addition, advertising might do so in ways that justify the more ambitious components of the critics' practical agenda. Although advertising's distortion of consumer choice might be addressed by familiar kinds of regulation, stronger medicine would seem necessary to counteract its encouragement of the consumerist lifestyle.

This chapter tries to assess the claim that advertising socializes people to a life of consumption. It begins with some general reasons for skepticism about this assertion. Then it considers whether these initial reasons can be overcome by the argument that advertising has done its work slowly and almost imperceptibly over time. Then the chapter examines what is probably the most important argument for advertising's ability to stimulate consumerism: that the demonstrated link between advertising expenditure and total consumption is best explained on this assumption. After that, the chapter considers some scattered contemporary evidence on the existence of a direct link between advertising and the propensity to consume. Because it finds all these arguments for advertising's influence less than persuasive, the chapter concludes that advertising most likely plays only a minor role in producing the desire to consume. Indeed, its influence on the propensity to consume may be even weaker than its influence on consumer choice.

In the preceding paragraphs, I used the term "advertising" rather than "manipulative advertising." The "empirical" portions of this chapter usually do the same. For the most part, that is, the chapter discusses advertising in general rather than manipulative advertising in particular. It does so primarily because the studies it cites and discusses do the same. Those studies employ advertising expenditure statistics that do not, and almost certainly could not, distinguish between informative and manipulative advertising. Thus, advertising in general must stand in for manipulative advertising here. It is questionable whether this use of aggregate advertising data especially matters. As we saw in chapter 1, it seems that well over half of all advertising qualifies as manipulative. Furthermore, manipulative advertising and informative advertising hardly form airtight compartments.

THREE REASONS FOR SKEPTICISM

Does advertising stimulate the propensity to consume? Admittedly, advertising's omnipresence and relentlessness suggest that it must have *some* effect on popular attitudes. But how much? So much that it, in effect, changes people from nonconsumers to consumers? Casual reflection suggests at least three difficulties with this contention.

We begin with a plainly observable fact: by and large, Americans avidly pursue material things. What might explain this phenomenon? One possibility is that people simply are that way—that they have an inbred and apparently inexhaustible desire to consume. Because this desire extends beyond the basic requirements of survival, however, we might wonder to what extent it is innate. But even if the propensity to consume is partly due to environmental influences, why assume that advertising looms large among those influences? Just as advertising is only one of many variables affecting consumer purchase decisions, it is not the only social force shaping popular values. Family socialization, peer group influence, and emulation are some of the more obvious alternative possibilities. Because these other factors cannot be held constant, this at least means that advertising's contribution to consumerism cannot be measured accurately.[1] As chapter 4 argued, finally, advertising's impact on consumer purchase decisions seems to be modest. This casts further doubt on its ability to create a consumer consciousness.

ADVERTISING'S HISTORICAL INFLUENCE

At a minimum, I think, the three considerations just adduced create some doubt about advertising's power to stimulate consumption. But at most, they show only that its influence is not dramatic. Thus, we might salvage the critics' argument by maintaining that advertising has worked its will slowly and by degrees over time. This hypothesis is consistent with my suggestion that because advertising's current impact on consumer choice is modest, its current influence on the propensity to consume is correspondingly modest. The hypothesis also is consistent with the possibility that social forces other than advertising help make people consumers. To be sure, the argument might run, family and peer-group pressures help make people consumers *today*, but this is only because advertising has created those pressures over time. It did so by slowly altering the personal attitudes that create those pressures in the first place. Once those attitudes become entrenched, they naturally exert an independent influence. But advertising created them, and it helps sustain them to this day. For this reason, consumerism is not innate, and our feeling that it is innate only shows how profound advertising's long-term influence has been.

Of course, my suggested hypothesis is difficult, if not impossible, to prove or disprove. But maybe we can form some judgment about the likelihood of its being true. To that end, this section examines two historical discussions of advertising's influence on consumption. For the most part, these two discussions do not parallel each other especially well. Thus, I make no effort to evaluate them on a point-by-point basis. Taken together, however, they do little to aid the critics' cause.

Borden on Advertising and Abundance

In chapter 24 of his 1942 classic on the economic effects of advertising,[2] Neil Borden sought to identify the processes through which the United States and England achieved their huge rise in national income during the post-medieval period. Borden admitted that due to the many factors underlying this achievement, any attempt to isolate advertising's precise role is hopeless. Nonetheless, he advanced some hypotheses on that subject.

Borden first observed that modern economic abundance could not have been achieved without the emergence of a large-scale productive machine, effective methods of delivering its output to purchasers, and the management skills needed for running each. Then he considered the possibility that advertising played a role in making the economic machinery more productive. Some economists and some defenders of advertising, he observed, have reasoned that "advertising and aggressive selling have led people to want things; and to get desired products they have been induced to work harder than they would have otherwise, with consequent increase in goods produced."[3] But while to Borden this account contained some truth, it ignored the fact that some people depend on others for employment and thus cannot increase their earnings at will through harder work. More important, "the study of demand [has] led to the conclusion that environment and social conditions have been stronger forces than advertising and selling in increasing people's wants for products."[4] The most important of these social factors were the increased social mobility accompanying the breakdown of the traditional medieval class structure, and a process of emulation through which wants spread to all segments of society. In the United States, which was comparatively free from medieval class distinctions at its inception, new wants spread to other income groups only after first being adopted by the rich.

Within this general framework, what role did advertising play in achieving greater production and consumption? A precondition for advertising's emergence, perhaps, was yet another social factor underlying economic expansion: the emergence of an entrepreneurial class which employed this and other aggressive selling methods. Once advertising emerged, Borden surmised, it stimulated consumption by producing the initial sales upon which the process of emulation depends. More important, advertising probably increased the general propensity to consume.

> The scale on which advertising and aggressive selling have been conducted in the United States supports the theory that they have probably been forces of considerable consequence in influencing people's views and attitudes. . . . Much of the advertising and selling have been carried on by men trained in the techniques of influencing people's attitudes and beliefs. Consequently they probably have been contributors to the propensity to consume, a propensity which is absent among people who have not had similar social backgrounds and have not been subjected to such conditioning, with the result that they have not developed similar consumption habits.[5]

The remainder of Borden's discussion largely assumed advertising's efficacy; based on that assumption, he considered additional ways in which it assisted the productive process. By stabilizing demand, for example, advertising increased profits, therefore stimulating investors to invest.

Simon's Reversal of Causation

The hypothesis we are examining asserts that advertising created the modern propensity to consume by slowly changing popular attitudes over time. By now, the hypothesis continues, those attitudes exert an independent causal influence—mainly, perhaps, in the socialization of children. Borden's arguments provide only moderate support for these assumptions. To be sure, Borden did think that advertising has been an important force behind the drive to consume. But he was tentative in asserting a link between advertising and consumerist attitudes, stating only that the former "probably" helped cause the latter. Also, Borden simply assumed this probabilistic link and did little or nothing to demonstrate it. More important, he thought that other factors, both social and economic, played a larger role. With the partial exception of emulation, furthermore, he did not regard these other factors as entirely, or even mainly, the product of advertising. For the most part, their origins evidently lay elsewhere.

Borden also emphasized the sheer scale of advertising and promotional expenditures. As we will see later in the chapter, both defenders and critics of advertising agree that there has been a strong relationship between advertising expenditures and consumption over time and across nations. Borden evidently assumed that such a relationship held for the nations and times he considered, and his self-appointed task was to identify advertising's causal role in producing the correlation. But what if, rather than causing consumption, advertising instead was its product? In a 1970 book, Julian Simon advanced exactly this argument.[6] Simon's aim was to examine why advertising appears in larger quantities when per capita income is high. He conceded that promotion sometimes stimulates industrial development and national income, but he declined to discuss that subject.[7] The processes he did discuss generally involved causation in the other direction: from economic development (measured by greater per capita income) to increased advertising.

Most of Simon's arguments were hypotheses based on the changes societies undergo when they move from communalism and agrarianism to individualism and an industrial, market-based economy. He identified twelve processes in all. Of the twelve, I discuss those that seem most clearly to involve causation from economic development or its concomitants to greater advertising.[8] The relevant processes tend to fall into more or less distinct groups. The first group involves the breakdown of premodern communal ties that normally is associated with economic development. Before the breakdown, Simon noted, people dealt mainly with friends and relatives, but over time those ties weakened and economic relations became more impersonal. Because this meant that buyers and sellers were less apt to know one another, the need for advertising grew. Increasing urbanization had similar consequences. In a small community, for example, you can easily ask people if they want to buy your dog or its pups; in a large city, you need to use a classified ad.[9] To Simon, the breakdown of communal ties also meant that people were less inclined to receive guidance from custom and traditional religious beliefs, and were more likely to rely on reason instrumentally conceived. Thus, they were less apt to buy particular goods because they had always been bought in the past, or because a religious creed dictated such purchases. This created an opening for advertising and a consequent incentive for sellers to employ it.

The second group of relevant processes involves the new attitudes and institutions that gradually replaced their more communal forebears (and that likewise seem associated with economic development). The breakup of traditional communal ties, Simon observed, went hand in hand with increasing individualism and more privately held property. Together, these two interrelated developments stimulated the growth of advertising by changing buyers' attitudes toward their purchases. A man who buys only for himself and his family probably will pay more attention to his purchases than someone who belongs to a tribe that holds everything in common. Such a person is a better target for advertising because he will be more interested in it.[10] Another concomitant of the new individualism was the emergence of increasingly differentiated wants. This made it more difficult for producers to find potential customers for their specific offerings, and thus forced them to advertise.

Thus far in my rendition of Simon, I have emphasized attitudinal factors underlying the rise of advertising. His third set of relevant processes included some material considerations that are central features of a developed economy. One of these considerations was the increasing division of labor. Along with differentiated wants, this made it necessary for producers to advertise.

> [I]f half the men in a community catch fish and half raise corn, any particular fisherman has a 50–50 chance that the first man he meets will be a trade partner. But if, instead, a man is the only fisher for shad in the village, and if there are only ten people in the village who like shad, the man needs to do more searching (that is, promotion) to find customers.[11]

Also impelling producers toward more advertising was another material change accompanying economic development: the increasing ability to manufacture goods on a large scale. For example, a shoemaker using crude tools may not produce much, but he can sell all his output to people living near his shop. But once he mechanizes the production of shoes, he must reach out to distant parties in order to sell his increased output. This most likely requires that he advertise.[12] Finally, improvements in transportation stimulated the use of advertising. By making it possible to ship goods over longer distances, better transportation increased the incentive to contact distant buyers with advertisements.

THE RELATIONSHIP BETWEEN AGGREGATE ADVERTISING AND CONSUMPTION EXPENDITURES

Simon's basic technique was to isolate certain features of the "modern" society that emerged from medievalism, each assertedly related to economic development, and to show how they necessitated more advertising. His account obviously presupposed a largely acquisitive, materialistic psychology; but it is unclear to me whether he saw this as innate, treated it as a presupposition of economic inquiry, or merely regarded it as an obvious feature of the modern (as opposed to the medieval) world. It also is unclear to me what would prove or disprove his hypotheses. But if they are at all accurate, they destroy my suggestion that behind the many forces that make most modern Americans consumers lies the historical influence of advertising. In Simon's view, it is the emergence of advertising that requires explaining, and he roots its emergence in certain features of early modern society. These, in turn, were related to the increase in economic abundance that marked this period. And while the causes of that phenomenon may not be clear, an increased propensity to produce and consume might be prominent among them. Thus, Simon's arguments are more consistent with the view that a greater propensity to consume generated more advertising, than with the reverse view advanced by Borden. As we saw earlier, moreover, Borden's arguments did not fully support my historical hypothesis in any event.

All things considered, therefore, it is unlikely that advertising's historical influence explains contemporary consumerism. But it is still possible that *today's* advertising has this effect. Although my three initial arguments may create some doubt on this score, they do not resolve the issue. As the preceding remarks about medieval society suggest, it is hardly obvious that consumerism is innate. Although it creates suspicions on this score, advertising's relative inability to direct consumer choice does not prove that advertising lacks the power to socialize. And even if we concede that many factors lie behind the propensity to consume, advertising might have pride of place among them. As we saw, and as will become more apparent later in this chapter, not even Simon would deny it some ability to promote consumption.

In recent years, the relationship between advertising and consumption has been the subject of empirical research. Such research usually follows one of two paths. The first, and most common, path involves the relationship between advertising expenditures and the general level of abundance.[13] The second path is to examine directly the relationship between advertising and the propensity to consume by employing quantitative measures of the latter. This section discusses the first path; and the following section, the second.

The Advertising–Consumption Link and Its Asserted Implications

In the economic debates over advertising's role, the opposed camps agree on relatively little. One area of consensus, however, is the correlation between advertising expenditures and the national product. Borden's book, for example, summarized data showing a strong temporal relationship between advertising activity and various indices of business activity (mainly production and sales).[14] In Borden's charts, which covered the American economy for the period from 1919 to 1940, advertising activity and business activity reliably fluctuated together. They did so even when the Great Depression caused each measure to fall by roughly 50 percent. As we will see shortly, Galbraith assumed a relationship between advertising expenditure and production in *The Affluent Society*. Later criticisms of Galbraith's dependence effect do not contest him on this particular point.[15] As one of these studies stated, "Only one Galbraithian assertion, the linkage between industrial development and advertising, can be considered noncontroversial."[16] This relationship apparently holds across countries. As the same study observed, "[N]ations with greater advertising expenditures tend to have higher rates of consumption."[17]

Presumably, measures such as national development and production are fairly reliable indices of national consumption—of the general level of abundance. Here, though, our concern is with the *propensity* to consume. So far, I have implicitly treated this as a psychological property. But it might also be defined quantitatively; to one author, it is "the real value of consumption expenditure weighted by real household disposable income."[18] Whatever definition we adopt, how is the correlation between advertising expenditure and national consumption supposed to demonstrate that advertising increases the propensity to consume? One possibility is to assert a causal model like the one previously stated and partly accepted by Borden:

Advertising ——→ Greater propensity to consume ——→
Harder and longer work ——→ Greater production.[19]

A reliable relationship between the first and last steps in this sequence (advertising expenditures and production) might make it plausible to assume that the intervening steps are true.

Galbraith apparently reasoned in this fashion when he wrote *The Affluent Society*'s chapter on the dependence effect.[20] The dependence effect, it will be recalled, is production's ability to create the wants that it also satisfies. To Galbraith, advertising was one of the forces through which the dependence effect operates (emulation is the other). From this, it seems to follow that advertising stimulates the propensity to consume. Galbraith also maintained that, by doing so, advertising causes the American consumer to resemble a squirrel who continually strives to keep abreast of a wheel propelled by its own efforts. Evidently, then, he also believed that increasing wants spur people toward harder work. Presumably, he also thought that harder work would result in more production, all other things being equal. Most important, Galbraith relied on the correlation between advertising expenditures and the general level of abundance to justify his claim that advertising stimulates the propensity to consume. After making that claim, he bolstered it with this statement: "A broad empirical relationship exists between what is spent on production of consumers' goods and what is spent synthesizing the desires for that production. . . . The path for an expansion of output must be paved by a suitable expansion in the advertising budget."[21]

Thus, Galbraith's argument proceeded from an accepted fact (the correlation between advertising expenditure and national consumption), to a particular causal relationship between those phenomena. But while he assumed the intervening links in Borden's suggested causal chain, he did not demonstrate them. In particular, Galbraith did not directly show that advertising increases the propensity to consume; apparently, he simply assumed this. One way to assess the correctness of his argument is to examine the relationship between advertising and the propensity to consume; the next section considers some miscellaneous evidence on this subject. Another is to attack the argument's assumption that, whatever the precise causal links between them, higher advertising expenditures produce higher consumption. The basis of the attack is the simple observation that, taken by itself, a correlation between two variables does not imply any particular causal relation between them. Specifically, a correlation between advertising expenditures and economic abundance does not prove that the former causes the latter. This section now examines two more or less distinct efforts to explain the causal relationship between these two variables. Echoing Simon's historical arguments, it concludes that economic growth probably stimulates advertising expenditures more than those expenditures stimulate economic activity.

The Macroeconomic Effects of Advertising

Some defenders of advertising agree with its critics that advertising increases the demand for consumer products and services. Of course, as I noted in chapter 1, each group evaluates the asserted relationship differently. This notwithstanding, the two groups also are united in their usual unwillingness or inability to substantiate their common claims about advertising's powers. In responding to this problem, some economists and marketing faculty members have initiated what Robert Jacobson and Franco Nicosia once called a "fourth research tradition" concerning advertising.[22] This tradition, they said, "is directly focused on the study of the macroeconomic effects of advertising—e.g., the search for some relationships between all advertising expenditures and various measures of aggregate demand in the economy."[23]

Most of the studies making up this fourth tradition in advertising research were published during the 1960s, 1970s, and 1980s. Some of them examine Galbraith's view of the advertising–consumption relation, while others assess advertising's usefulness as a tool for countering "down" cycles in the economy. They generally present a data base containing figures on advertising expenditures and consumer demand for certain places and historical periods. Then, they normally apply recondite mathematical and statistical techniques in an effort to determine causation between these variables. Naturally, these studies often encounter criticism for poor data selection, inappropriate methodology, erroneous causal assumptions, and so on.[24] An examination of their details and the technical controversies they have sparked is a topic for someone else's book. Fortunately for the nonexpert, however, several authors have summarized the research on advertising's causal relations with other macroeconomic variables. Although the results recounted in these summaries are mixed, overall they do not indicate that advertising strongly affects economic activity. Indeed, they sometimes suggest that, rather than being its product, increased economic activity generates greater advertising expenditure.

Some books on the economics of advertising scant the macroeconomic issues just discussed and, instead, emphasize the industry-level concerns treated in chapter 4. Nonetheless, they do make some comments on the subject. After discussing a few studies whose results were mixed, Mark Albion and Paul Faris concluded that, owing to the many factors affecting aggregate consumption, it is difficult to isolate advertising's impact.[25] But they seemed disinclined to believe that that impact is large.[26] In their brief treatment of the macroeconomic literature, Robert Ekelund and David Saurman focused on advertising's potential for smoothing out swings in the business cycle by stimulating demand during periods of inactivity. In their view, the studies on which they focused failed to show a clear causal relationship between advertising expenditure and the business cycle.[27]

Longer summaries of the literature sound the same themes. In 1984 Vincent Norris reviewed many of the studies discussed by Albion and Faris and Ekelund and Saurman, plus a few later efforts. During the course of that review, he stated:

> On its face, the notion that advertising "stimulates consumption" is persuasive. . . . This is, however, an example of what is variously called the "hypodermic needle," the "magic bullet,"

or the "push-button" theory of communication effects, which holds that persuasive communication "automatically" produces the intended effect. This "theory" (which it never really was) has been thoroughly discredited by a great amount of research during the last several decades.[28]

After this, Norris quoted an economist who analogized the claim that advertising causes consumption to the assertion that the rooster's crowing causes the sun to rise.[29]

Some of the research examined in Jacobsen and Nicosia's 1981 literature review, however, arguably did demonstrate a fairly strong relationship between advertising and consumption.[30] But Jacobson and Nicosia found methodological problems both with this work and with studies finding no causal relation between advertising and consumption. More important, they doubted whether any of the relevant research did much to establish or disprove its claims about causation or its absence. As they summarized the matter:

> Our review of past studies indicates the use of a variety of data, variables, and estimation procedures, as well as a variety of findings and interpretations of those findings. Underlying this variety, however, is the assumption of all the investigators that their approaches are capable of establishing *causality*, in the context of so-called "real-life" research designs. This assumption is highly questionable because, among several reasons, the statistical-inference procedures used in the studies (e.g., graphing, correlating, and regressing) are not in themselves suitable for discerning causality.[31]

Then, after describing an ideal research design, they presented the results of their own study. This study, which used yearly advertising and consumption data for the period from 1929 to 1977, found the following: (1) a significant within-the-year relationship between advertising and consumption, with the direction of causation unclear; (2) a possible causal relationship between consumption in the previous year and advertising in the current year; and (3) a negative relationship between advertising in the previous year and current-year consumption.[32] However, the authors admitted that their study also fell short of proving causation and achieving the ideal research design.

Two later studies went farther in rejecting the claim that advertising causes consumption. A 1983 effort by Rebecca Colwell
Quarles and Leo Jeffres used a technique called path analysis
evaluation, which purportedly can determine causal relationships
among quantitative variables collected at one point in time. After
applying that technique to 1974 data from fifty-odd nations, Quarles and Jeffres concluded that (1) there is two-way causation
between income and consumption, (2) economic development
(measured by energy use) causes advertising, and (3) consumption
also causes advertising.[33] In the process, they specifically rejected
Galbraith's claim that advertising causes consumption.[34] They also
found that, as between income and consumption, it is consumption
that really does the causal work in generating advertising.[35] These
findings, Quarles and Jeffres asserted, yield "a picture of spending,
severely constrained by disposable income—a world where advertising has little room to maneuver in any efforts to draw spending
from savings."[36] Rather than serving as high priest of the cult of
materialism, they concluded, advertising's role is "more like that
of an acolyte who follows and assists in the rituals of the greater
culture."[37] But they did allow that, in some contexts, some advertising messages might overcome the constraints of limited disposable income.[38]

Like Jacobson and Nicosia's article, Brian Sturgess's 1982 piece
criticized past work for tending to confuse correlation with causation, and for failing to use methods capable of detecting causation.[39]
His study applied allegedly superior methods to quarterly British
advertising and consumption expenditures covering the period
from 1969 to 1980. At its conclusion, Sturgess stated: "This paper,
employing Box-Jenkins modelling techniques to test the effect of
total advertising on aggregate consumption in the United Kingdom,
has not found any evidence that may lead one to reject the null
hypothesis of no relationship between the two variables in this
particular causal direction."[40] "Much past emphasis on this relationship," he concluded, "has been misplaced and the question may
hopefully be laid to rest."[41] Arguably, that is exactly what has
happened; so far as I can determine, little or no published work on
the advertising–consumption relationship has appeared since the
mid-1980s.

The Budgeting of Advertising

At this point, it may be useful to review the course of the argument thus far. The hypothesis we are examining assumes that advertising increases the propensity to consume, which stimulates increased efforts to earn money for this purpose, which in turn means more production for workers to consume. The temporal and cross-cultural correlation between the first and last steps in this hypothesis—advertising outlays and consumption—seems well established. And the hypothesis would gain plausibility if it could be shown that causation runs from the former to the latter: from advertising to consumption. But while the quantitative studies on the relationship between advertising and consumption are a mixed bag, on balance they do not support the view that the former causes the latter. Thus, they indirectly argue against the notion that advertising stimulates the propensity to consume.

However, this body of work is unlikely to persuade critics of advertising who hold that advertising actually does cause consumption. Indeed, if I were writing a brief for the critics on this issue, I would make several points. As with the studies discussed in chapter 4, I would suggest that the mixed results displayed here may well reflect their authors' ideological biases at least as much as the reality those people purport to examine. The arcane statistical methods the studies employ make it difficult for nonexpert readers to critique those studies and detect where they may have gone astray. In fact, who is to say that such methods have much purchase on reality at all? Many of the studies admit that it is difficult to prove causation in either direction between advertising and consumption. Worse yet, when the studies do speak to this question, they sometimes suggest that consumption causes advertising. A suggestion so contrary to everyday experience, I could conclude, can only mean that its authors are hopelessly lost in abstraction, and can only cast doubt on everything else they say.

In response to this last point, however, recall that Simon provided a number of reasons for thinking that economic development and its concomitants generate increased advertising. But while his arguments are interesting and suggestive, they hardly are conclusive here. For one thing, those arguments are little more than unsubstantiated theories about the causal processes accompanying economic modernization. As such, they are roughly as persuasive or unpersuasive as Borden's contrasting theories about those processes. As it turns out, however, there is a fairly simple explanation both for the established temporal correlation between contemporary advertising and consumption outlays, and for the latter's causing the former. The explanation is that firms traditionally have based their advertising expenditures on recent or anticipated sales, or on measures that should correlate with such sales. Aggregate advertising expenditure data should reflect all these individual firms' budgeting decisions. And aggregate consumption should approximate the sum of all the firms' sales. Thus, aggregate consumption and aggregate advertising expenditure correlate because as the former increases or decreases, the latter fairly quickly follows. For the same reason, consumption can be said to determine or cause advertising.

As noted earlier in the chapter, Borden presented data showing a strong temporal relationship between advertising activity and various measures of business activity such as production and sales. Immediately thereafter, he explained these results.

> The fluctuation of advertising expenditure in the manner
> indicated above is to be expected in view of the advertising
> budgeting practices of business organizations. Advertising
> tends to be closely related to sales outlook. Sales outlook for
> any product or service is influenced largely by business conditions. Advertising expenditures, like other expenditures, are
> ordinarily adjusted from time to time in accordance with
> current sales behavior and the probable trend.[42]

Lest Borden's position be thought a depression-era anomaly, some of the later quantitative studies use roughly similar assumptions to explain their findings. After noting the correlation between advertising expenditures and economic activity, Ekelund and Saurman asked why those expenditures are procyclical. The answer was simple: "Businesses typically determine current advertising outlays on the basis of past sales."[43] As noted earlier, one of Jacobsen and Nicosia's findings was that consumption in the previous year has an effect on advertising in the current year. This finding, they said, "indicates that a large percentage of advertisers determine their budget by applying this decision rule [the advertising-sales ratio], thereby using past sales as the base in the ratio."[44]

When first exposed to such arguments, critics of advertising may perhaps be excused for not taking them seriously. After all, the power of business and of Madison Avenue is central to their view of things. For such power to exist, its possessors must have powerful tools of social control and the rationality to put them to effective use. Yet if the previous arguments are correct, businesses continually *reduce* their advertising when sales slip, or somewhat thereafter. That is, they cut their advertising precisely when they need it most. This anomaly has not escaped the notice of advertising researchers. As two of them observed in 1994, "[i]n an economic downturn, [advertising] budgets usually suffer before other marketing budgets are restricted—as if communication is a necessity when money is available, and a luxury when budgets are tight."[45] Ten years earlier, Michael Schudson had quoted various experts who regarded firms' typical budgeting practices as "essentially illogical," "irrational," and "disturbing."[46]

Irrational or not, those practices seem to have prevailed until recently. Their existence is routinely noted in the literature.[47] More important, study after study has confirmed their prevalence.[48] The methods cited often are described as rule-of-thumb techniques. They base the advertising budget on, among other things, the previous year's sales or profits, estimated current-year sales or profits, the firm's liquid resources, and competitors' advertising outlays. Because all these measures should vary with the business cycle when aggregated, they should also correlate reasonably well with current aggregate consumption. Although more firms apparently have shifted to "rational" budgeting methods in recent years,[49] this is irrelevant for present purposes. Virtually all of the influential claims about advertising's powers occurred well before the change.

Confronted with all this, critics of advertising might maintain that the preceding research has to be bogus because businesspeople simply could not be so stupid as to proceed in the fashion described. Unfortunately for this argument, however, the traditional budgeting methods may not be especially irrational. More precisely, they may be a more or less sensible response to the situation many businesses face. The ideal budgeting method, some say, would push the level of advertising to the point where the next increment of spending just equals the profits resulting from the extra sales it produces.[50] But this ideal is difficult, perhaps impossible, to achieve in practice. As chapter 4 should have made clear, firms find it very hard to assess the impact of their advertising—in particular, to separate its contribution from all the other factors that affect sales. As a result, it also is very hard for them to measure the impact of advertising outlays at the margin.[51] Another problem is that, during bad times, firms may not always have the money to advertise at the optimum level. "In serious downturns," one source claims, "there is a simple lack of funds with which to finance advertising."[52] A third difficulty with the ideal method, one also noted in chapter 4, is that it may not jibe with some firms' reasons for advertising. For example, some businesses apparently use advertising less to generate short-term profits than to pursue long-term goals such as brand recognition among potential customers and brand loyalty among existing buyers.[53]

In light of considerations such as these, it hardly is surprising that many firms have opted simply to muddle through. As one source observed in 1968, "[t]he failure of analytical methods so far to provide a satisfactory guide to advertisers has led to a predictable confusion in the methods of decision-making they themselves employ."[54] Indeed, some businesspeople seem unsure whether advertising does them much good or are even a bit hostile toward it. According to a 1992 article describing a survey of leading British advertisers and clients, "[t]he overriding consensus is that there are no willing advertisers. Each time the decision is made to spend money on advertising it is only because the manufacturer or retailer does not know of a more efficient, more economical way of generating sales of his product."[55] As the authors later elaborate,

> Advertisers spend a lot of money on advertising and yet do not precisely know why. They all have different reasons and objectives for advertising and for those who are spending incredible amounts of money they often adhere to . . . [their] budgets only because nobody in the organization is ready to take the risk of cutting them down. Long-term effectiveness evaluation still remains a real enigma.[56]

In the words of a Nescafe executive, "We don't know if sales would drop if we stopped advertising but we are not ready to risk it."[57] The risk, however, might be worth taking. After complaining that field experiments involving lower advertising outlays are rare, Schudson recounts one case in which this tactic was used, and was followed by *higher* sales. He concluded that in all likelihood, many firms spend more on advertising than they need or ought to spend.[58]

OTHER MEASURES OF ADVERTISING'S INFLUENCE ON THE PROPENSITY TO CONSUME

The previous section mainly considered the validity of the following hypothesis:

Advertising ⎯⎯→ Propensity to consume ⎯⎯→ Harder work ⎯⎯→ More production and consumption.

The main argument for the hypothesis was the correlation between advertising expenditure and consumption or one of its surrogates. But as we have seen, it seems likely that advertising is at least as much consumption's product as its progenitor. To the extent that this is so, the previous hypothesis seems implausible.

But even if consumption tends to generate advertising, causation still may work in the other direction as well. In other words, advertising may stimulate consumption even as consumption also determines the level of advertising. Thus, it seems appropriate to consider other evidence on advertising and the propensity to consume. In his 1970 book, Simon summarized some scattered research of this kind, most of which tries to quantify the propensity to consume in one fashion or another and to relate it directly to advertising.[59] He began his account by observing that there is both empirical evidence and theory to question the assumption that advertising provokes consumption. The empirical evidence was the long-term stability of the average propensity to consume, despite an increase in the amount of advertising.[60] The theory, which he called "the 'spread-it-around' hypothesis," "implies that some constant proportion of income is 'taken off the top' for saving, and what is left is spent according to the prevailing tastes of the spending unit."[61] The alternative view is that advertising reduces saving by increasing consumption.

Despite this evidence and this theory, Simon evidently concluded that advertising has a slight positive effect on the propensity to consume.[62] Most of the other evidence and argumentation he presented pointed in that direction. By reducing the flow of advertising, for example, newspaper strikes have reduced sales at department stores and other establishments. Smaller communities, which tend to receive less advertising, also tend to have higher savings rates. In addition, advertising might stimulate consumption without generating any measurable increase in the propensity to consume. For instance, it might be true that advertising causes increased wants, moonlighting to satisfy those wants, and higher consumption. In such cases, however, the measured propensity to consume might remain the same because the individual is spending the same percentage of a higher wage base. But the *psychological* propensity to consume presumably would rise in such cases.

In a later chapter, Simon also made some remarks about *manipulative advertising*'s effect on aggregate demand. He suggested that automobile advertising (which often seems manipulative) may increase aggregate consumption by increasing the demand for cars.[63] For homogeneous package goods (HPGs) such as soft drinks, candy, cleaners, beer, gasoline, liquor, and cosmetics, however, the story was different. As we saw in chapter 1, advertising for these products tends to be noninformative because different brands supposedly differ relatively little in their objective characteristics. According to Simon, there is no reason to believe that advertising for these HPGs has any impact on total demand.[64] "In fact," he remarked, "it is a commonplace among package-goods advertisers that their job is to switch customers from other brands rather than to create new users."[65] As chapter 4 suggests, however, it is questionable how well they succeed.

CONCLUSIONS AND ETHICAL IMPLICATIONS

Advertising's omnipresence suggests that it plays *some* role in increasing and sustaining the propensity to consume; however, there is little reason to believe that it plays a significant role. Conceivably, human beings simply are natural consumers. Even if this is not true, it hardly is obvious that advertising ranks high among the social forces impelling people toward consumption. Certainly chapter 4's conclusions about advertising's influence on consumer choice suggest nothing of the kind. To be sure, one might avoid these objections by hypothesizing that underlying all the present influences conducing toward consumption lies advertising's slow, patient work over time. But the hypothesis is not very convincing.

All these objections notwithstanding, advertising still may be the most important single force behind modern consumerism. Most arguments to this effect rest on the well-established temporal and cross-cultural correlation between the level of advertising expenditure and the level of production and consumption. But no particular causal relationship between two variables follows inexorably from their mere correlation. Indeed, research on the advertising–consumption relationship suggests that the latter probably causes the former more than the former causes the latter. The most important evidence for this claim is business firms' traditional tendency to base advertising expenditures on past sales or the like. The remaining arguments for the claim that advertising strongly influences consumption consist largely of miscellaneous studies like those introduced by Simon. But while these studies may suggest that advertising plays some role in stimulating the propensity to consume, they do not demonstrate that it plays an important role.

But what about the specifically *manipulative* advertising that was defined in chapter 1 and that is the concern of this book? Is advertising in general really a suitable proxy for this manipulative advertising? Is it not conceivable that while advertising as a whole does little to stimulate the propensity to consume, its manipulative component does the lion's share of the work in producing whatever consumption advertising does generate? Of course, almost anything is possible, but this particular hypothesis seems unlikely. First, chapter 1 suggested that manipulative appeals probably characterize well over half of all ads. Second, the line between manipulative advertising and informative advertising often is indistinct. Third, chapter 4 suggests that manipulative advertising is not hugely effective in its primary mission: getting consumers to buy particular products. If so, why assume that its powers increase when the propensity to consume is at issue?

Our reason for inquiring about manipulative advertising's ability to stimulate consumption, of course, is that topic's ethical implications. These, in turn, are important because the political agenda advanced by advertising's critics goes nowhere without a demonstration that manipulative advertising is wrong. Chapters 2 and 3 developed a solid, but not overwhelming, case that if advertising successfully manipulates, it indeed is wrong. By showing that manipulative advertising influences consumer choice only modestly, chapter 4 partially undermined this ethical case. As a result, it also weakened, but did not completely overcome, the case for piecemeal consumer protection regulations directed toward particular kinds of manipulative ads. Here, we are considering ethical problems arising from advertising's asserted ability to stimulate consumption. Because there is little reason to believe that manipulative advertising plays a major role in making people consumers, these problems now seem to be relatively minor ones. This goes some way toward undermining the more ambitious portions of the critics' political agenda—those calling for limits on the amount of advertising or increased control by an anticonsumerist elite.

Utilitarian Considerations

Chapter 2 assumed that manipulative advertising distorts consumer choice and stimulates the propensity to consume. If the first assumption is valid, that chapter concluded, manipulative advertising probably results in utility losses, and some regulations aimed at reducing those losses may be justified. By weakening the claim that manipulative advertising directs consumer purchase decisions, chapter 4 undermined, but did not completely destroy, these two claims. Chapter 2 also concluded that manipulative advertising probably does not generate utility losses when it increases the propensity to consume. In fact, by stimulating the economy and making economies of scale possible, it most likely *increases* utility. Although Galbraith argued that those gains are meager because little utility is generated through the satisfaction of artificially stimulated wants, this argument was found wanting. In its absence, all that remained to salvage Galbraith's case was the possibility that his public goods are a better source of utility than the private goods advertising causes us to pursue. But this is only a surmise. And even if the surmise is true, the transition costs of moving to Galbraith's preferred order might outweigh the gains realized thereby. Because it dealt only with manipulative advertising's impact on competition, chapter 4 did not change these conclusions.

Now, it seems that manipulative advertising is not a major reason for the consumerist impulse. If so, it is not *the* stimulus behind economic growth and the scale economies associated with it. This means that manipulative advertising is not the most important reason for the utility that economic growth produces. But while this conclusion may disappoint advertisers and businesspeople who assert the contrary, it gives little comfort to advertising's critics. If manipulative advertising does not do a great deal to stimulate consumption, Galbraith's argument seems weaker than ever. And while public goods may generate more utility than private goods, we still have no reason to assume this. Even though the transition costs of moving to a society dominated by the pursuit of public goods may be lower than imagined, therefore, we continue to lack a compelling motive to make the move. Of course, utilitarian critics of consumer capitalism may be able to supply those motive by telling us why less consumption will yield more utility. But advertising's manipulativeness will be of little help in that endeavor.

Kantian Criticisms

As we saw in chapter 3, manipulative advertising might violate the first formulation of Immanuel Kant's categorical imperative both when it dictates consumer choice and when it stimulates the propensity to consume. Initially, it appears that advertisers should be unwilling to universalize a maxim permitting manipulative advertising not only because this would entail that someone else would determine their purchase decisions, but also because others would dictate their basic values as well. But, as we also saw in chapter 3, this conclusion might be evaded by reformulating the maxim used to justify manipulative advertising. For example, suppose the suggested maxim now reads: "Advertisers may employ manipulative advertising to sell products and make money when by doing so they stimulate the propensity to consume and thereby keep the economy humming." Maybe a rational advertiser would will this maxim, even though it would entail his or her own manipulation. No such evasion, however, seemed possible for the second major formulation of the categorical imperative. As chapter 3 made clear, advertisers who employ manipulative advertising obviously treat consumers as means rather than as ends. Because Kant's ethics is deontological, moreover, it does not matter that by so acting, advertisers may stimulate economic growth. To be sure, advertisers may escape censure when consumerist attitudes are the innocent by-product of purely *informative* advertising. But this book evaluates only manipulative advertising as defined in chapter 1.

Do this chapter's findings change any of these conclusions? Here, it is important to note that, although the chapter has argued that manipulative advertising is only one factor behind the propensity to consume, it has not denied manipulative advertising's influence entirely. At first glance, therefore, it seems that chapter 3's conclusions should not change dramatically. Even if manipulative advertising is only one of many forces influencing our values, why should advertisers want to universalize a maxim allowing it? By doing so, they still would permit some outside influence over their own identities. After this chapter's arguments, moreover, advertisers would submit without much compensating assurance that they would help stimulate the economy by doing so. Even if manipulative advertising only stimulates consumption to some degree, furthermore, advertisers still treat people as means when they use it. As I suggested in chapter 4, it is unlikely that Kant would let an action's morality or immorality hinge on a quantitative consideration like the probability or magnitude of its bad consequences.[66] As a result, Kantianism still seems to justify an absolute ban on manipulative advertising.

Autonomy

Chapter 4 concluded that, because manipulative advertising's impact on consumer choice is less than advertised, the practice reduces human autonomy only to some degree. As that chapter observed, however, manipulative advertising still might significantly restrict autonomy by increasing the propensity to consume. Because manipulative advertising's effect on consumption seems relatively modest, however, its consequences for autonomy are correspondingly modest. This should be true no matter which conception of autonomy we emphasize. Thus, manipulative advertising deserves only mild condemnation on autonomy grounds. As a result, autonomy does not provide especially strong justifications for the critics' political agenda. Because his proposals depended on the autonomy supposedly lost when advertising promotes the propensity to consume, this seems particularly true of Richard Lippke's agenda.[67] However, autonomy still might justify the regulation or suppression of particular ads that clearly manipulate.

Virtue Ethics

Chapters 3 and 4 maintained that manipulative advertising might reduce virtue in two somewhat distinguishable ways. By making people consumers, it might prevent their living superior kinds of lives. In addition, it might weaken the hold of certain specific virtues such as rationality, reflectiveness, self-awareness, self-control, self-discipline, self-reliance, and moderation. The former consequence, I asserted, is attributable only to manipulative advertising's impact on the propensity to consume, while the latter depends on both of its asserted consequences. Here, of course, our concern is manipulative advertising's asserted ability to stimulate consumption.

By showing that manipulative advertising's impact on consumer purchase decisions is not pronounced, chapter 4 has largely eliminated one reason for thinking that manipulative advertising causes people to lose the specific virtues just mentioned. But two possibilities remain. First, advertising might also undermine those virtues by making people consumers. Through that same process, second, it might cost people virtue by steering them away from the highest kind of life. But as this chapter has argued, manipulative advertising is only one factor underlying the propensity to consume. Even if consumerism is contemptible, therefore, manipulative advertising is relatively blameless for its existence. Moreover, even if consumerism invariably makes people irrational, unreflective, undisciplined, and so forth, manipulative advertising is not the major reason those vices prevail.

The bottom line, therefore, is that advertising does not do a great deal to corrupt consumers because it does not manipulate very well. For that reason, virtue ethics does relatively little to justify the critics' practical agenda. As we will see in the next chapter, this is true even though the critics' general view of things probably is most coherent when it is based on virtue ethics.

NOTES

1. Geoffrey P. Lantos, "Advertising: Looking Glass or Molder of the Masses?," *Journal of Public Policy and Marketing* 6 (1987): 108.

2. Neil H. Borden, *The Economic Effects of Advertising* (Chicago: Richard D. Irwin, 1942), chap. 24.

3. Ibid., 685.

4. Ibid.

5. Ibid., 692.

6. Julian Simon, *Issues in the Economics of Advertising* (Urbana: University of Illinois Press, 1970), chap. 7.

7. Ibid., 186. However, Simon certainly thought that advertising may sometimes help induce economic growth. Shortly after the quoted statement, for example, he maintained that promotion surely has a stimulating effect on the development of new consumer-durable industries. Ibid., 186–87.

8. The others are (1) the emergence of printing and greater literacy (which were a precondition for increased print advertising), (2) the existence of wealth above the subsistence level (which leads to new wants as the satisfaction of old ones creates diminishing marginal utilities, and thus creates new advertising opportunities), (3) monetization (whose relation to increased advertising strikes me as indirect), and (4) the emergence of promotional know-how, and of a desire to promote (whose relation to increased advertising is direct, but whose link to economic development seems much less so).

9. Simon, *Issues in The Economics of Advertising*, 179.

10. Ibid., 181.

11. Ibid., 182–83.

12. Ibid., 177.

13. This is not the same as the relationship between advertising expenditures and sales or profits within an industry, or made by particular firms within an industry. Chapter 4 considered work of this kind. See Robert Jacobson and Franco M. Nicosia, "Advertising and Public Policy: The Macroeconomic Effects of Advertising," *Journal of Marketing Research* 18 (February 1981): 29–30 (making this distinction).

14. Borden, *The Economic Effects of Advertising*, 716–20.

15. See, for example, Rebecca Colwell Quarles and Leo W. Jeffres, "Advertising and National Consumption: A Path Analytic Re-Examination of the Galbraithian Argument," *Journal of Advertising* 12, no. 2 (1983): 6; Brian T. Sturgess, "Dispelling the Myth: The Effects of Total Advertising Expenditure on Aggregate Consumption," *Journal of Advertising* 1 (1982): 203–5 (later renamed the *International Journal of Advertising*).

16. Quarles and Jeffres, "Advertising and National Consumption," 6.

17. Ibid., 4. See also Simon, *Issues in the Economics of Advertising*, 167–70 (providing data).

18. Sturgess, "Dispelling the Myth," 204.

19. Borden, *The Economic Effects of Advertising*, 685.

20. John Kenneth Galbraith, *The Affluent Society* (Boston: Houghton Mifflin, 1957), chap. 11.

21. Ibid., 155–56.

22. Jacobson and Nicosia, "Advertising and Public Policy," 30. The authors' other advertising research traditions concerned (1) studies on the effects of advertising for a specific brand, product, or company image; (2) efforts by trade associations and government bodies to determine whether advertising contributes to sales for a product or a product class; and (3) studies on the economic impact of advertising at the industry level (e.g., those discussed in chapter 4 of this book). See ibid., 29–30.

23. Ibid., 30.

24. For example, ibid., 31–33.

25. Mark S. Albion and Paul W. Faris, *The Advertising Controversy: Evidence on the Economic Effects of Advertising* (Boston: Auburn House, 1981), 82–84.

26. Ibid., 85.

27. Robert B. Ekelund, Jr., and David S. Saurman, *Advertising and the Market Process: A Modern Economic View* (San Francisco: Pacific Research Institute for Public Policy, 1988), 177; see ibid., 175–78.

28. Vincent P. Norris, "The Economic Effects of Advertising: A Review of the Literature," *Current Issues and Research in Advertising* 2 (1984): 68. See ibid., 67–71.

29. Ibid., 69, citing Mueller, "Monopoly with Real Money," *Washington Monthly* 3 (April 1971): 36–43.

30. Jacobson and Nicosia, "Advertising and Public Policy," 31–32.

31. Ibid., 32.

32. Ibid., 36–37.

33. Quarles and Jeffres, "Advertising and National Consumption," 13; see ibid., 8–12.

34. Ibid., 10, 13.

35. Ibid., 10.

36. Ibid., 13.

37. Ibid.

38. Ibid.

39. Sturgess, "Dispelling the Myth," 205.

40. Ibid., 212.

41. Ibid.

42. Borden, *The Economic Effects of Advertising*, 719–21; see ibid., 721–26 (presenting data to substantiate the claim).

43. Ekelund and Saurman, *Advertising and the Market Process*, 176 (italics omitted).

44. Jacobson and Nicosia, "Advertising and Public Policy," 36 (italics omitted).

45. Theo B. C. Poiesz and Henry S. J. Robben, "Individual Reactions to Advertising: Theoretical and Methodological Developments," *International Journal of Advertising* 13 (1994): 27.

46. Michael Schudson, *Advertising, the Uneasy Persuasion: Its Dubious Impact on American Society* (n.p.: Basic Books, 1986), 17.

47. See, for example, Poiesz and Robben, "Individual Reactions to Advertising," 27; Sturgess, "Dispelling the Myth," 202.

48. Borden, *The Economic Effects of Advertising*, 719–26; Peter Doyle, "Economic Aspects of Advertising: A Survey," *Economic Journal* 78 (1968): 577; C. L. Hung and Douglas C. West, "Advertising Budgeting Methods in Canada, the UK and the USA," *International Journal of Advertising* 10 (1991): 239; Hugh Murray, "Advertising's Effect on Sales— Proven or Just Assumed?," *International Journal of Advertising* 5 (1986): 25; Schudson, *Advertising, the Uneasy Persuasion*, 17 (all citing studies).

49. Hung and West, "Advertising Budgeting Methods," 239–40.

50. Doyle, "Economic Aspects of Advertising," 573; Schudson, *Advertising, the Uneasy Persuasion, 17.*

51. Doyle, "Economic Aspects of Advertising," 573–74.

52. Ekelund and Saurman, *Advertising and the Market Process,* 176; see also Borden, *The Economic Effects of Advertising,"* 726–28.

53. Doyle, "Economic Aspects of Advertising," 574–75; M. P. Flandin, E. Martin, and L. P. Simkin, "Advertising Effectiveness Research: A Survey of Agencies, Clients, and Conflicts," *International Journal of Advertising* 11 (1992): 205.

54. Doyle, "Economic Aspects of Advertising," 576–77.

55. Flandin, Martin, and Simkin, "Advertising Effectiveness Research," 204.

56. Ibid., 207.

57. Ibid.

58. Schudson, *Advertising, the Uneasy Persuasion,* 18.

59. Simon, *Issues in the Economics of Advertising,* chap. 8.

60. Ibid., 194–95. Although Simon never defined what he meant by the term "propensity to consume," presumably he had some consumption/income ratio in mind. For example, one economist defines the propensity to consume as "the real value of consumption expenditure weighted by real household disposable income." Sturgess, "Dispelling the Myth," 204.

61. Simon, *Issues in the Economics of Advertising,* 195.

62. Ibid., 72 (referring to chapter 8).

63. Ibid., 267, 274.

64. Ibid., 275.

65. Ibid.

66. Kant's emphasis on the bad motives underlying immoral actions, however, raises a possible problem with these conclusions. Advertisers who employ manipulative techniques probably are more concerned with generating sales than with making people consumers. Thus, one might

argue that because they do not consciously intend to stimulate consumption, they are not using people for *that* end and are not acting with a bad will when that end is the issue. In such cases, though, advertisers still are acting with a bad motive, and presumably that would suffice to render their action immoral under Kantian criteria. If an action results from a bad will, why should it matter that the action's bad results are not those intended?

67. Richard L. Lippke, "Advertising and the Social Conditions of Autonomy," *Business and Professional Ethics Journal* 8, no. 4 (1990): 53–54. However, Lippke's argument depended in part on certain features of American society that tend to inhibit autonomy. But he simply assumed their existence and their tendency to stunt the development of autonomy.

Chapter 6

THE FAILURE OF THE
CRITICS' VISION

Before making the remarks that opened chapter 1, Robert Heilbroner distinguished two visions of economic life: his own and one
he called the capitalist vision. Heilbroner did not try to compare
these visions point by point or to refute the capitalist view. "No
such attempt is possible," he maintained, "because the two conceptions are so fundamentally different as to be beyond comparison."[1]
By a vision, Heilbroner evidently meant a picture of social, economic, and political reality containing a more or less coherent set
of descriptive and normative propositions. His capitalist vision
roughly corresponds to the advertising-as-information view that
has appeared at various points earlier. This book does not evaluate
that particular picture of advertising. Instead, my concern is the
validity of the vision that seems to unite advertising's critics.[2] This
chapter begins with a sketch of the critics' vision. This sketch is a
composite ideal type that probably does not reflect the views of any
one person. Restating points developed in earlier chapters, the chapter's next section critiques the critics' vision in general and its
political agenda in particular. After this, the chapter concludes
by summarizing this book's alternative vision (or antivision) of
advertising.

THE CRITICS' VISION

To the full-blown critic of advertising, the institution's ill effects are many. Among other things, such a person would say, advertising pollutes our everyday life, cheapens public discourse, and corrupts the mass media. In addition, our critic would continue, much advertising is manipulative. Thus, it is the main reason for America's excessive preoccupation with material things. Indeed, it may be the most important socializing and ordering force in our mass-consumption capitalist order. Advertising's manipulativeness also means that it distorts consumers' choices among goods and services, thereby diminishing the value consumers receive for their dollars. By creating and sustaining anticompetitive pricing practices, moreover, manipulative advertising further reduces consumers' economic well-being. To the archetypal critic, therefore, advertising gives us the worst of both worlds. By promoting excessive consumption, it prevents the achievement of a saner and more fulfilling existence. And by distorting competition, it prevents us from fully realizing whatever meager benefits consumerism brings.

The Ethical Critique

If the preceding picture is at all accurate, manipulative advertising looks like a morally dubious practice. Indeed, as the business ethicists have maintained, it seems wrong from several different ethical perspectives. Because advertisers who practice manipulation would not will a universal rule under which *they* would be subject to manipulative advertising, they violate the first major formulation of Immanuel Kant's categorical imperative. When advertisers develop and employ their stratagems, moreover, they basically use consumers as means to their ends, thereby violating the imperative's second major formulation as well. In the process, they also restrict personal autonomy. Advertisers do so both by making people consumers and by dictating their consumption choices.

Some defenders of advertising might say that the preceding arguments do not matter because advertising promotes and sustains economic abundance and thus increases utility. To its critics, however, advertising fails to keep its promise of maximizing wel-

fare. By manipulating consumer choice and supporting anticompetitive pricing, it prevents consumers from getting a decent yield of
happiness per dollar. Even if this were not true, critics add,
advertising decreases utility by making people consumers in the
first place. Consumerism is a poor path to felicity, some critics aver,
because it is not congruent with our real nature. At this point,
utilitarian criticisms of advertising blend into criticisms based on
virtue ethics. Because it is inconsistent with human nature, certain
critics might continue, advertising is wrong even if it does maximize
utility in some crude Benthamite sense. The superficial pleasures
of consumerism, they say, are not the stuff of which a truly
human—and hence genuinely satisfying—life is made. Besides
directing us away from this better existence, these critics conclude,
advertising inhibits consumers from developing certain specific
virtues—for example, moderation, rationality, and self-control.

The Need for Political Direction

Defenders of advertising (or at least critics of its critics) often
accuse those critics of elitism and paternalism. In its most common
form, the complaint says that foes of advertising want to impose
their own values on everyone else. According to one recent writer,
"The mere assertion by critics that there are products consumers
do not (read: should not) need or want is a claim by the critics that
they are members of the 'noble class' of intellectuals—the elite
class—who know what is best for the lower classes of unwashed
mobs."[3] John Kenneth Galbraith naturally has been a special target
of such attacks. According to one writer, for example,

> Galbraith believes that almost all the preferences in an affluent
> society are induced by elites; and that want-creation by a
> socially conscious political and intellectual meritocracy (on
> behalf of schools, hospitals, roads and theatres) is at least more
> tolerable than want-creation by the narrow and selfish men of
> the technostructure (on behalf of electric toothbrushes and
> private motor-cars). Thus, while Galbraith on the one hand
> attacks the blandishments of private advertising and salesman-
> ship, he on the other hand clearly sees himself as a crusader
> carrying on an unrelenting campaign of political and social
> propaganda on behalf of the kind of future society he person-
> ally most favours.[4]

Another variant of the complaint sees advertising's foes as merely the latest example of socialism's unending drive for control of the state apparatus and therefore of society. After attacking Galbraith's dependence effect, for instance, Friedrich Hayek added, "For over a hundred years we have been exhorted to embrace socialism because it would give us more goods. Since it has so lamentably failed to achieve this where it has been tried, we are now urged to adopt it because more goods after all are not important."[5] "The aim," he concluded, "is still progressively to increase the share of the resources whose use is determined by political authority and the coercion of any dissenting minority."[6]

These criticisms may not describe every foe of advertising, but they are not products of an overheated imagination either. As we saw in chapter 1, advertising's critics sometimes propound a more or less statist political agenda. The form the agenda takes usually varies with the type of manipulation a particular critic emphasizes. For critics who stress manipulative advertising's impact on consumer choice, the typical remedy is increased regulation of certain manipulative practices. (Of course, such proposals may be mixed with, or difficult to distinguish from, proposals for increased regulation of *deceptive* advertising.) The more ambitious political agenda, however, normally comes from critics who emphasize advertising's stimulation of the propensity to consume. Here, the proposals typically range from recommendations for controls on the volume of advertising to calls for a politically directed transformation of American life.

Typically, however, advertising's more radical critics do recommend that the changes they urge come about through democratic means. More important, the charge that such critics are elitists and authoritarians may be irrelevant if their principal arguments are correct. Those arguments are, basically, that advertising makes people consumers and then distorts their product choices and that, for these reasons, it is wrong. In that event, advertising's critics perhaps are justified in their practical agenda. Indeed, maybe they have a moral duty to suppress manipulative advertising. Whether they also are justified in creating some new society, however, presumably depends on *its* moral worth and on the costs of getting there.

The Coherence of the Critics' Vision

From the preceding discussion, it appears that the critics' vision of advertising has a high (albeit incomplete) degree of internal coherence; that is, its various components hang together fairly well. The critics' belief that much advertising manipulates is consistent with their belief that it is wrong; under several ethical criteria, in fact, manipulative advertising's badness presupposes its efficacy. Both beliefs, moreover, at least partly justify the vanguard role some critics assume. On the other hand, the critics' assumptions about advertising's power make it unclear how *they* are able to resist it. This is one reason I say that the coherence of their position is incomplete.

For the critics' vision to achieve the highest possible degree of coherence, however, at least one further assumption seems necessary. One obvious rejoinder to the critics' vision is that people naturally desire material things, and that this desire does not appreciably abate as more things are acquired. If so, there is no need to explain consumerism by attributing great powers to advertising. On this assumption, furthermore, advertising would not significantly restrict autonomy and people might reap great utility from consumer products and services. This means that some of the ethicists' moral arguments against advertising collapse. This, in turn, weakens the case for the critics' political agenda.

To become maximally coherent, then, the critics' vision needs a positive conception of human nature, or at least a definite idea of what it is not. As chapter 3 suggested, many critics seem to have a notion of the latter kind, at least. As I observed in that chapter, implicit in the views of many foes of advertising, except perhaps the Kantians and the proponents of autonomy,[7] is the idea that, whatever human nature might be, consumeristic materialism is not its genuine expression. This assumption makes it easy for critics to assume that manipulative advertising works. If one is strongly convinced that consumerism is unnatural, and if people nonetheless consume, the obvious explanation for the anomaly is that they are being manipulated. And one need not look far to find the manipulator. What else could it be but the ubiquitous phenomenon of advertising? Consumer goods advertising obviously tries to make people buy particular products. It also explicitly and implicitly touts consumption as a desirable way of life. Year after year, business firms spend huge sums on such appeals. If it were true that manipulative advertising does not work, would they continue to throw good money after bad?

The assumption that consumerism is unnatural also reinforces some of the ethical criticisms advertising has attracted. This is most evident in the case of virtue ethics, for which assertions about human nature tend to be normative. If we ought to act in accordance with our real nature, and if consumerism does not express that nature, then consumerism is wrong. Because it makes us consumers, advertising is wrong as well. It is an alien force that diverts human beings from their true ends. For that reason, some would say, advertising leads people to live lives that are unsatisfying as well as lacking in virtue. In other words, it does not maximize utility properly conceived. And even if the connection between virtue and utility is not as tight as this argument would have us believe, chapter 2 has supplied other reasons to believe that advertising robs people of utility.

Finally, the contention that consumerism is not a genuine expression of human nature helps to justify the critics' political agenda and to absolve them from charges of unjustified elitism and paternalism. It does so by bolstering their basic assertions that advertising manipulates and that it is wrong. On the latter assumption, as I noted earlier, advertising's foes may well have a moral duty to move American society in healthier directions. And the former assumption helps remove any qualms about the steps this duty might require: if people are being manipulated anyway, a critic might say, better by us than by those business types. If people are not naturally consumeristic, moreover, the critics' political agenda arguably is not manipulation at all. Rather, it is a means through which people become reunited with their real selves. Maybe Ralph Nader had something like this in mind when he recently averred, "You have to teach people what they want."[8]

THE FAILURE OF THE CRITICS' VISION

The critics' vision, then, seems most coherent when underpinned by views of human nature that are roughly consistent with virtue ethics.[9] As I briefly suggested earlier, this conception of human nature may not find favor with Kantians and (especially) devotees of autonomy. But if we assume that the best life also is the most satisfying life, they probably are consistent with utilitarianism. As we have just seen, those assumptions about human nature provide critics with some cover against charges of elitism, paternalism, and the like. Of course, the assumptions may be wrong, but debates about human nature are as interminable as they are inconclusive.

The critics' vision, then, is—or can be made—fairly coherent. If so, how might we critically assess it? The way to begin, I think, is by reviewing this book's ethical conclusions about manipulative advertising.

How Unethical Is Effective Manipulative Advertising?

Even if manipulative advertising really makes people consumers and directs their consumption choices, the ethical case against it is not open and shut. The main reason is that advertising is a mixed bag from a utilitarian perspective. Chapter 2 maintained that, while manipulative advertising probably reduces utility when it distorts consumer choice, this effect most likely is counterbalanced by the utility such advertising generates when it stimulates the propensity to consume. Because advertisers could frame a maxim that permits their own manipulative advertising while blocking others' efforts to manipulate *them*, furthermore, such advertising might escape censure under the first major formulation of Kant's categorical imperative. But it cannot escape the second, which almost seems to have been formulated with manipulative advertising in mind. Advertisers who employ manipulative techniques, that is, treat their targets as means rather than as rationally self-determined ends. Under almost any conception of the term, moreover, efficacious manipulative advertising restricts personal autonomy. And by encouraging a hedonistic consumer lifestyle and undermining certain specific virtues, it also offends virtue ethics.

The Initial Conclusions Revised

Chapters 4 and 5 maintained that, contrary to the beliefs of advertising's foes, it is not hugely effective in directing consumer choice and is only one factor behind the propensity to consume. How do these findings change the initial ethical conclusions just stated? If manipulative advertising is a relatively weak force, it is unlikely to reduce autonomy and virtue significantly. It also is unlikely to cost consumers significant utility by distorting their purchase decisions. And while manipulative advertising's weak influence on the propensity to consume may dismay defenders of the practice who think it promotes economic growth, that fact hardly helps its critics either. But the Kantian argument against manipulative advertising remains largely unaffected by chapters 4 and 5. To be sure, any attack based on the first major formulation of the imperative remains mired in the technicalities just noted. Because Kant's ethics is strongly deontological and emphasizes the motives underlying actions, however, the attack based on the imperative's second major formulation is not seriously affected by the assertion that advertising fails to manipulate especially well.[10] Advertisers who try to manipulate consumers are acting with a bad will whether they succeed or not.

Taming the Kantian Objection

If manipulative advertising is not hugely effective, therefore, three of the four major ethical arguments against it lose much of their force. But the second Kantian argument escapes largely intact. Just as a good will "would still shine like a jewel for its own sake" even if it accomplishes nothing,[11] a bad will deserves censure and punishment even though it works no bad consequences. Thus, Kant's ethics seems to remain both a serious moral objection to manipulative advertising and a possible justification for the critics' political agenda.

Even if Kantianism provides definitive reasons to condemn manipulative advertising, however, one might wonder whether it provides a good basis for some of the critics' practical proposals. If I was correct in my earlier surmise that some kind of virtue ethics best supports the critics' vision, Kant might not be the horse many of them personally would prefer to ride. To the extent that these moral views issue in elitism and even authoritarianism, moreover, they coexist uneasily with the strongly antipaternalistic thrust of Kant's moral philosophy. Underlying Kant's command to treat people as ends rather than means, for example, is the idea that when trying to move others to some action, one should respect their rationality by giving them reasons for so acting.[12] Thus, it seems that if advertising's critics are to act as sincere Kantians, they cannot themselves manipulate—even for good ends. Therefore, critics should make every effort to promote their agenda through rational democratic persuasion. In his or her efforts to persuade the public, furthermore, a Kantian critic of advertising presumably would have to use Kantian moral arguments. But those arguments might not resonate with as result-oriented a group as the American people. ("If manipulative advertising doesn't work all that well, why should we restructure American society along the lines you propose?" "Because advertisers and the businesses who employ them act with a *bad will*.")

Worse yet, it is unclear whether Kant's ethics justify the most ambitious portions of the critics' agenda, those involving a shift toward something like Galbraith's public goods.[13] As chapter 3 observed, Kantianism probably lends most support to efforts at reducing the volume of advertising or eliminating it entirely. More important, what is the necessary link between Kantianism and anticonsumerism? Why could Kant's ethics not permit a life of consumption? For example, maybe a maxim commanding consumption could be consistently universalized, and perhaps people would rationally choose such a life after being fairly presented with all the relevant arguments. Kant's ethics, in sum, may be a better vehicle for opposing manipulation than for attacking consumption as a way of life. For this reason, it might remain as an important support for other portions of the critics' political agenda—those that merely urge that government crack down on certain manipulative ads in order to promote free consumer choice.

Even if advertising's more aggressive critics might not want to use Kantian arguments, therefore, those arguments still seem relevant to some portions of the critics' agenda. Useful or not, moreover, they still constitute an unequivocal *moral* objection to manipulative advertising. This is due to Kant's strict deontology: his view that an action's consequences are irrelevant to its rightness or wrongness—and his corresponding emphasis on the motives underlying actions. This aspect of Kant's ethics, however, seems questionable once its implications become clear. It evidently says that we should always follow the categorical imperative's dictates— no matter what. Because the imperative is commonly regarded as commanding behaviors such as telling the truth and keeping promises, for example, Kant's apparent message is that nothing can

justify our telling a lie or breaking a promise. Few moral philosophers have wanted to go so far. Indeed, one wonders whether Kant
did either. According to James Rachels, Kant once considered
whether one is obligated to tell the truth to a would-be murderer
who inquires into the whereabouts of his intended victim.[14] Kant,
of course, thought that we are so obligated. But then he recoiled
from the likely consequences of that decision. Perhaps, he said, the
victim is not at the place our truth teller identified, in which case
the murder may never happen. In addition, he continued, suppose
that our moral agent lies to the murderer, but that the victim then
moves to the (apparently) false location he has identified. In that
event, the murder may occur, and the author of the lie might justly
be held responsible for it.

One weakness in Kant's moral philosophy, then, is its inability
to deal with moral duties that are implicated by an action's
consequences and that compete with the absolute dictates of his
categorical imperative. A common-sense way out of the dilemma
is to preserve those dictates (which after all have some intuitive
appeal) while weakening their force. This presumably would mean
that the rules deriving from the imperative must be weighed against
other moral concerns. This apparently unprincipled eclecticism
might find justification in several considerations. As my various
critical remarks in chapters 2 and 3 suggest, each of our ethical
theories, Kant's included, is subject to telling objections. In part for
that reason, morally reflective people often refuse to let any one of
them preempt the ethical universe. Instead, they consider various
kinds of moral claims that might be relevant to the evaluation of
an action, without necessarily letting any of them dominate. Perhaps they do so because the theories are not self-sufficient, but
rather are strands in a moral tradition from which they have been
arbitrarily ripped. Although that tradition may lack an ultimate
sanction, it is practically obligatory for most of us.[15]

If we accept this view, the Kantian denunciation of manipulative
advertising becomes only one consideration in our evaluation of it.
Thus, we might begin that evaluation by noting that advertisers
who employ manipulative advertising try to use consumers for
their ends through methods that short-circuit consumers' rational
faculties. But the advertisers' efforts are not especially successful.
This means that the utility losses resulting from manipulative
advertising are not huge, it does not greatly affect consumers'

autonomy, and it does not make them markedly less virtuous. To be sure, even these consequences are sufficient to make manipulative advertising wrong. But there are moral evils and there are moral evils, and these particular evils appear only somewhat serious. On the view I am propounding, therefore, these additional considerations make manipulative advertising less objectionable than if Kantian criteria were the only relevant factors. (Alternatively, we might say that the Kantian considerations make manipulative advertising more wrong than if its consequences were our only concern.)

Ethics and the Critics' Agenda

As I argued toward the end of chapter 1, critics of advertising badly need moral arguments to support their practical agenda. Otherwise, they are powerless to resist defenders of advertising who claim that its manipulativeness is a good thing. In recent years, business ethicists have tried to provide the necessary arguments. As we have seen, though, not all of those arguments succeed even if manipulative advertising works as well as its critics believe. And even fewer retain their original force once we discover that manipulative advertising is not especially effective. Furthermore, it is difficult to absolutize the one moral objection—the Kantian attack on manipulative advertising—that survives that realization intact. Our conclusion, then, is that while manipulative advertising no doubt is wrong, it is only somewhat wrong. Can that conclusion support the critics' political agenda? In considering this question, I turn the tables on the critics by considering, among other things, how *their proposals* fare under the ethical criteria previously used to evaluate advertising.

The Aggressive Portions of the Agenda. Under our ethical criteria, there is little justification for the most radical elements of the critics' agenda. Indeed, some of those criteria supply reasons *not* to pursue these aspects of the agenda. The aspects in question generally involve a politically directed transformation of American society away from consumerism and toward the pursuit of nonmaterial goods. As I have suggested, it is doubtful whether Kantian ethics can supply an affirmative justification for this goal. The reason is the rather abstract, almost procedural, nature of its norms. Each formulation of the categorical imperative seems consistent with various substantive modes of life, consumerism among them. The same general point applies when we shift from Kantianism to autonomy.[16] If this is the goal, and if people autonomously choose to be consumers, who is to say them nay? Of course, critics of advertising always can argue that if all the social forces conducing toward consumption were eliminated, people would not devote their lives to it. That assertion, however, is just an assertion. Even if the claim is true, moreover, it does not follow that people would choose a society devoted to Galbraith's public goods. And we now know that one of the social forces said to account for consumerism's predominance—manipulative advertising—is not a strong force in that direction.

To justify the most far-reaching portions of the critics' agenda, therefore, we need a moral theory that clearly dictates the right substantive conditions of human life. Although it often is criticized for being consistent with almost any kind of behavior, utilitarianism would fill the bill if it could be shown that a society devoted to the critics' agenda maximizes utility. (For practical purposes, it might suffice if someone could demonstrate that such a society yields more utility than one devoted to consumption.) Apparently, however, that demonstration has not been made. So far as I am aware, the only serious effort in this direction is Galbraith's argument that because little utility results from the satisfaction of artificially induced wants and because advertising generates consumer wants, consumerism yields relatively little utility. But as we saw in chapter 2, that argument is very dubious. Worse yet, advertising evidently is not the main force behind consumerism in any event. Although this concededly lessens the utility costs of realizing the critics' aims, it does not eliminate those costs entirely.

Earlier, I argued that the critics' vision is most coherent when it draws inspiration from some form of virtue ethics. As that argument might suggest, virtue ethics apparently provides the most satisfactory moral basis for the social order some of advertising's foes urge upon us. What they need is an argument some proponents of virtue ethics would readily accept: that a life devoted to material things is not the best life, and that a life devoted to other aims is intrinsically superior. Of course, these aims presumably would include, or presuppose, a certain level of material abundance. That qualification aside, however, some form of virtue ethics might well get advertising's critics where some of them want to go. As chapter

4's discussion might suggest, however, these people still would have trouble making virtue ethics persuasive in an ethos disinclined to accept it. More important for present purposes, advertising's manipulativeness seems peripheral to this virtue-based argument for a new America. To be sure, critics of this persuasion always can use advertising's manipulativeness to explain the American public's failure to choose the good life. But in doing so, they are not attacking manipulation as such, only manipulation for bad ends. In contrast to Kantianism, that is, virtue ethics is a potent weapon against consumerism, but it provides little reason to oppose manipulation. People of this kind would (and should) condemn consumerism even when it is freely chosen.

Earlier, I suggested that none of our ethical theories is satisfactory standing alone, and that each should strike some chord with morally reflective people. If so, the other three theories raise possible objections to our virtue-based argument for a significant transformation of American life. Some proposed transformations might be faulted for insufficiently recognizing the utility consumer goods can provide. In addition, autonomy and Kantian ethics might put some restrictions on the means through which the transformation is pursued. That transformation, these ethical views might say, ought to be the autonomously chosen result of a nonmanipulative decision process. Of course, it is by no means clear that the new order would prevail if such a decision process were adopted. Even though advertising is not the principal reason Americans are consumers, they continue to consume. And among the educated classes, at least, alternative ways of life have been propounded. Galbraith's many celebrated books are among the most obvious examples. In my experience, though, even his "educational and scientific estate" continues to embrace consumerism.

The Intermediate Steps. Foes of advertising also have proposed some less sweeping, but still fairly stringent, responses to it. These mainly involve efforts to reduce the *volume* of advertising by direct regulation, taxation, spending limits, and the like. The main target of such proposals, I think, is manipulative advertising's assumed stimulation of the propensity to consume; by reducing the volume of advertising, we might also reduce this effect. But why should we bother? As chapter 2 argued, these proposals cannot be justified on utilitarian grounds because manipulative advertising probably increases utility when it (allegedly) stimulates consumption. With the discovery that manipulative advertising does relatively little to make people consumers, moreover, autonomy and virtue ethics largely cease to be reasons for suppressing advertising. Of course, that discovery does not affect the Kantian arguments, and, as I maintained in chapter 3, the most natural implication of those arguments is that manipulative advertising should simply be eliminated. But as I have just argued, we should not absolutize such arguments. What they say, after all, is that we should suppress manipulative advertising because it is inspired by bad motives. Maybe the regulatory costs of such an effort—which would have to distinguish between informative and manipulative ads—are sufficient to overcome these arguments, which probably would not strike most Americans as too compelling anyway.

The More Modest Components of the Agenda. Arguments for the more stringent portions of the critics' agenda usually invoke advertising's asserted ability to stimulate consumption. However, the more modest components of the agenda, which mainly involve increased regulation of certain allegedly manipulative ads, depend on their presumed ability to distort consumer choice. To be sure, that ability is not as great as many believe. So far as their effect on competition is concerned, therefore, manipulative ads deserve only modest condemnation when considered together as a group. But when they do work, individual manipulative ads seem quite wrong indeed. As chapter 2 maintained, they probably cost consumers some utility on balance, and as chapter 3 made clear, they obviously restrict autonomy, just as clearly violate at least one version of the categorical imperative, and possibly inhibit a few specific virtues as well.

Because these wrongs almost certainly occur even if they do not predominate, they may sometimes justify regulations that crack down on certain kinds of manipulative ads. Unlike the more sweeping parts of that agenda, here the various ethical theories directly support the recommended action, because regulation might promote utility, rational choice, autonomy, and virtue in certain cases. Although I doubt whether these considerations justify extensive regulation of manipulative (as opposed to deceptive) advertising, they may well support targeted efforts against especially effective and damaging ads. Specific recommendations along these lines are beyond the scope of this book, but it might be useful to sketch a few considerations—most of them utilitarian—

that should govern whatever regulatory efforts might seem desirable.

The first and most obvious of these considerations, one whose difficulties were suggested in chapter 4, is the degree to which the suspect advertisement actually succeeds or fails in manipulating consumers. This consideration, for example, might argue against serious efforts to eliminate subliminal advertising. (Also weighing against such an effort are questions about the frequency with which subliminal ads are used and the difficulty of detecting them.) Another obvious consideration involves the regulatory and compliance costs of prohibiting particular ads. Consider for example the likely costs of a serious Federal Trade Commission effort to regulate sex in advertising under its "unfairness" jurisdiction.[17] Also high on the list of obvious considerations are the likely benefits of successful regulation. As we saw in chapter 2, for instance, manipulative advertising often is used to tout so-called homogeneous package goods (or HPGs): products that are said to differ relatively little from brand to brand. Unless the manipulative ad in question stimulates additional consumption of the *product* (not the brand) it touts, the most that regulation of manipulative HPG ads might accomplish is to shift demand from one HPG to another of equivalent utility. Still another, perhaps less obvious, consideration concerns the use of finite regulatory resources: might we not get more social benefit from prohibiting other social ills besides manipulative advertising? Then again, there may be cases where the calculus of costs and benefits clearly justifies regulation of particular manipulative ads. One possibility, a topic of some concern in mid-1996, is the increased regulation of cigarette advertising aimed at young people.[18]

THE ANTIVISION

Late in 1988, Galbraith contributed to a special *Advertising Age* issue on the business-government relationship.[19] His piece made it clear that his views on advertising had changed remarkably little in the thirty years since publication of *The Affluent Society*. As always, Galbraith maintained that advertising creates wants, shapes consumer behavior, enables firms to control their sales, makes America a consumer society, and keeps its economic wheels humming. In the process, he reaffirmed the dependence effect.

Galbraith also mentioned his many foes. "Virtually every critic of my case for want creation and demand management came up with the same adverse example—the Edsel. Then with the passage of time there was progress. The defense of consumer sovereignty shifted to the consumer resistance to the new formula of Coca-Cola."[20] Finally, Galbraith concluded, most observers came to realize that such examples were exceptions rather than the rule.

Evidently Galbraith had not read too widely among his academic foes. Besides demonstrating the tenacity with which critics of advertising hold to their vision, his article is interesting for another reason. That article's main concern was advertising's integration within economic theory, where Galbraith thought that its impact had not been adequately recognized. Noting the huge sums devoted to advertising and the talented people it employs, Galbraith asserted that there must be some intellectual explanation for this activity. The tendency to exclude advertising from economic thought, he maintained, "leaves it [the advertising industry] in a vaguely functionless limbo."[21]

To Galbraith, therefore, any adequate explanation of advertising must stress its functions—what it does. In his view, of course, its main role is to create and sustain our mass-consumption society by manipulating consumers. But the same assumption—that advertising must have important consequences—can be found in authors who do not share Galbraith's estimate of its power. Michael Schudson, for example, emphatically rejected views of that kind.[22] But like Galbraith, he felt compelled to affirm that advertising does something significant. For Schudson, advertising functions as "capitalist realism."[23] This basically means that like the "socialist realism" of Soviet art and literature in the 1930s, advertising celebrates and reaffirms the society of which it is a part. "Advertising," Schudson concludes, "is capitalism's way of saying 'I love you' to itself."[24]

The two visions of advertising mentioned in this book agree with Galbraith and Schudson that advertising does significant things. In the critics' vision, advertising's impact is much as Galbraith described it. In the vision of the advertising-as-information school, whose views I have briefly sketched from time to time, advertising helps the economy function efficiently by giving rational consumers the information they need to make informed product choices and thereby maximize their satisfactions. Due to the functions advertising performs in each case, our two visions link up with two general visions of economic life—for the critics, the notion that America is a corporate state; for the advertising-as-information people, laissez-faire capitalism. For this reason, our two visions also take different sides on one of the most important issues in the philosophy of social science: the debate between holism and methodological individualism.[25] As we saw in chapter 1, to some believers in the first vision, American society is an organized, almost organic, totality to whose functioning advertising powerfully contributes. To the advertising-as-information vision, by contrast, individuals are primary, society is nothing more than the sum of its human components, and advertising helps those people fulfill *their* ends—not the ends of some illusory social whole.

Compared to these two visions, the vision of advertising that emerges from this book is a poor thing. According to this last vision (or antivision), advertising does not perform grand functions, it is not central to American life, and thus it is not a significant force for either good or ill. To be sure, advertising is not inconsequential. For example, informative advertising helps laissez-faire capitalism function, and manipulative advertising sometimes successfully manipulates. Some manipulative advertising, however, evidently has little impact one way or the other. Combining these different effects to produce an overall assessment of advertising's impact permits no bold generalizations about its purpose, function, or meaning. In some cases, it helps businesses and consumers, in others it manipulates, and in still others it is just *there*. In greater or lesser measure, I think, advertising really does inhabit Galbraith's vaguely functionless limbo.

The components of my antivision have appeared again and again in this and preceding chapters. Nonetheless, it may be useful to restate them briefly here. The six most important of these conclusions are presented below.

1. *Much advertising aspires to manipulate consumers.* In this book, of course, manipulative advertising is defined as advertising that *attempts* to control consumers either by changing their desires or by associating the product with desires they already have. The latter tactic, which characterizes the most common form of manipulative advertising, the book calls associative advertising. Everyday experience and content analyses of advertising suggest that a significant portion of it is primarily associative. The other kind

of manipulative advertising, subliminal advertising, seems to utilize both tactics just listed. Although it is difficult to be sure about the incidence of subliminal advertising, it almost certainly has been used on at least a few occasions.

2. *When manipulative advertising actually manipulates, it probably is unethical.* Critics of advertising generally assume that it works in one or both of two senses. First, they may say, manipulative advertising affects competition by strongly influencing consumers' choices among products and brands. Second, advertising manipulates people by stimulating the propensity to consume—by making them consumers in the first place.

On these assumptions, advertising's manipulativeness apparently makes it vulnerable to several ethical objections. First, it violates at least one major formulation of Kant's categorical imperative. Under several conceptions of the term, moreover, it deprives its victims of autonomy. Finally, advertising's manipulativeness probably renders its victims less virtuous. Its evaluation under utilitarian criteria, however, is unclear.

3. *Manipulative advertising does not significantly distort competition.* After nearly 300 pages of technical analysis, Julian Simon ended his book on the economic effects of advertising by stating,

> [T]hose branches of advertising which are most in dispute—advertising for such products as beer, autos, soap, and aspirin—do not seem to have much effect on the economy in any way, direct or indirect, and hence from an economic point of view it is immaterial whether they are present or absent.[26]

Simon was discussing the so-called homogeneous package goods, or HPGs, which tend to be advertised manipulatively. He may have overstated the case for manipulative advertising's ineffectiveness, but probably not by a great deal.

There are at least three broad reasons for believing that manipulative advertising's effect on competition is modest. First, many general considerations suggest skepticism about advertising's powers. To take just one example, the number of variables affecting purchase decisions makes it difficult, if not impossible, to measure the impact of most individual ads. Second, general commentary and empirical work on two common forms of manipulative advertising—subliminal advertising and advertising utilizing sexual appeals—suggest that the former technique is of little use to advertisers and that the latter promises only moderate benefits. Finally, the extended debate on advertising's economic impact provides some reason to question the traditional economic critique of advertising, which assumes that it manipulates by creating irrational brand identifications.

4. *Advertising is only one force behind the propensity to consume.* For at least three reasons, the claim that advertising makes people consumers seems initially implausible. This claim coexists uneasily with the evidence that manipulative advertising's impact on competition is limited; it ignores the many other forces that push people toward consumerism; and it refuses to consider the possibility that human beings have a natural propensity to consume. These objections probably cannot be overcome by the claim that advertising has worked its will slowly and by degree over time. They also survive what is probably the most common argument for advertising's influence on the propensity to consume, an argument that relies on the established temporal and cross-cultural relationship between advertising expenditures and consumption. This argument often assumes that advertising influences consumption through the following causal chain:

Advertising ⟶ Greater propensity to consume ⟶
People work harder ⟶ More production and more consumption.

However, economic and statistical analyses of the advertising–consumption relationship generally are skeptical about the claim that it proves causation from the former to the latter. More important, there is an embarrassingly simple alternative explanation for the advertising–consumption relationship: most firms base advertising expenditure on sales or on some other measure that correlates with consumption. At most, finally, the scattered studies attempting to quantify the propensity to consume and to show a direct relationship between it and advertising provide only modest evidence that the latter causes the former.

5. *Manipulative advertising's modest impact on competition and on the propensity to consume significantly weakens the ethical case against it.* To state the matter more crudely, advertising's relative nonmanipulativeness renders it only somewhat unethical. To the extent that it does not manipulate, advertising is unlikely to reduce

autonomy or inhibit virtue. Also, manipulative advertising's relative ineffectiveness does not significantly change its uncertain implications for utility. Although the Kantian objection to manipulative advertising survives its questionable ability to manipulate, finally, this objection should not be regarded as a knockdown argument against such advertising.

6. *The more sweeping portions of the political agenda propounded by advertising's critics have virtually nothing to support them; however, this does not preclude piecemeal attempts to regulate especially effective and harmful forms of manipulative advertising.* These conclusions were developed at length in the previous section.

CONCLUSION

To a greater or lesser extent, critics of advertising who decry its manipulativeness also are critics of consumer capitalism. The former belief, of course, is useful ammunition against those who defend mass-consumption capitalism. If advertising directs consumer purchase decisions, how can defenders of consumer capitalism say that the consumer is sovereign? Worse yet, advertising's stimulation of the propensity to consume means that consumption itself is suspect. In addition to delegitimizing consumer capitalism, advertising's manipulativeness also helps its critics defend themselves against the inevitable charges of elitism and paternalism their own proposals attract. When faced with such attacks, they can point out that people already are being manipulated. Advertising's manipulativeness may even help the most radical critics justify their proposals for a social transformation. If people are consumers only because advertising makes them that way, the critics might say, surely they would choose our preferred form of life in advertising's absence. Now that the business ethics movement has demonstrated how wrong manipulative advertising is, they could add, we can see that anticonsumerism is morally superior too.

Of course, these arguments involve a *non sequitur*; you cannot reason directly from advertising's manipulativeness, its wrongness, or consumerism's illegitimacy to the desirability of some alternative order. This reasoning, after all, could justify any alternative arrangement, no matter how bad. Viewed in this light, the claim that advertising manipulates begins to look like radical social philosophy on the cheap. Worse yet for the critics, it turns out that advertising does not manipulate all that well. This means that their indictment of consumer capitalism largely fails too. But for the same reason that one cannot logically argue from consumer capitalism's illegitimacy to the superiority of some alternative order, one cannot proceed from consumer capitalism's *acceptability* to the conclusion that no alternative order could possibly be superior. Thus, critics of consumer capitalism might be advised to simply tell us why it is bad and why their alternatives are better. In all likelihood, such an argument would have to be based on some kind of virtue ethics. For the reasons just stated, the claim that advertising manipulates is unlikely to be of much help in this endeavor. And capitalism's critics should stop trying to use it as a crutch. Manipulative advertising simply cannot bear that intellectual weight.

NOTES

1. Robert L. Heilbroner, "The Demand for the Supply Side," *New York Review of Books*, 11 June 1981, 37.

2. These two more or less elite visions of advertising have counterparts at the popular level. One survey of the attitudes of college students toward advertising classified 28 percent of the sample as "contented consumers" who enjoy advertising. These people believe that advertising is informative and good for the economy and that it does not mislead, corrupt, or make people materialistic. Another 20% of the sample was made up of "critical cynics" who find advertising uninformative, see few economic benefits flowing from it, and regard it as misleading, manipulative, and corrupting. Among adults, 38 percent were contented consumers and 39 percent were critical cynics. For each group, however, many people fell into other attitudinal segments. Richard W. Pollay and Banwari Mittal, "Here's the Beef: Factors, Determinants, and Segments in Consumer Criticism of Advertising," *Journal of Marketing* 57 (July 1993): 99–114.

In addition, some scattered evidence suggests that attitudes toward advertising correlate with more general attitudes. For example, another survey of adults found that criticism of advertising tends to rise along with alienation. It defined alienation as involving powerlessness, normlessness, meaninglessness, isolation, and self-estrangement. Richard M. Durand and Zarrel V. Lambert, "Alienation and Criticisms of Advertising," *Journal of Advertising* 14, no. 3 (1985): 9–17.

3. Jerry Kirkpatrick, *In Defense of Advertising: Arguments from Reason, Ethical Egoism, and Laissez-Faire Capitalism* (Westport, Conn.: Quo-

rum Books, 1994), 19. For more on the paternalism of advertising's critics, see John O'Toole, *The Trouble with Advertising* (New York: Times Books, 1985), 17, 20–21.

4. David A. Reisman, *Galbraith and Market Capitalism* (New York: New York University Press, 1980), 100.

5. F. A. Hayek, "The *Non Sequitur* of the 'Dependence Effect'," *Southern Economic Journal* 27 (1961): 348.

6. Ibid.

7. The assumption that there is a human nature whose dictates we should obey coexists uneasily with most notions of autonomy. It puts both moral and practical constraints on the inner freedom often seen as essential to autonomy. This assumption seems especially inconsistent with Kant's conception of autonomy—and with his ethics in general. Kant identified autonomy with adherence to the rational law embodied in the categorical imperative; this excluded its motivation by "heterono-mous" influences such as the inclinations resulting from some tangible conception of human nature. See Immanuel Kant, *Groundwork of the Metaphysic of Morals*, trans. and ed. H. J. Paton (New York: Harper Torchbooks, 1964), 108, 114. For a discussion of Kant's "transcendental self," its relation to his ethics, and the difficulties that notion creates, see Roger Scruton, *Kant* (Oxford, England: Oxford University Press, 1982; paperback reprint, 1989), chap. 5.

8. Michael Lewis, "The Normal Person of Tomorrow," *The New Republic* 214, no. 21, 20 May 1996, 20.

9. Another possible way to unify the critics' vision, one this book does not explore, is the idea that, owing to its command of the physical and social sciences and its devotion to the public interest, an elite corps of knowers is entitled to direct the organization of society. On the intellectual roots of this notion, which has been a recurrent feature of the post–seventeenth century Western world, see Thomas A. Spragens, Jr., *The Irony of Liberal Reason* (Chicago: University of Chicago Press, 1981), chaps. 3–5.

10. As we saw in chapter 5, however, advertisers should escape Kantian censure on those (perhaps infrequent) occasions when *informative* advertising stimulates the propensity to consume.

11. Kant, *Groundwork*, 62.

12. See, for example, James Rachels, *The Elements of Moral Philoso-phy*. 2d ed. (New York: McGraw-Hill, 1993), 129–30.

13. This is mainly because those portions of the agenda involve definite notions of the good life. Kant's philosophy and his ethics argu-ably reject such notions. See Kant, *Groundwork*, 108, 114. See also Scruton, *Kant*, chap. 5 (discussing Kant's "transcendental self," its impli-cations for his ethics, and the problems that conception creates).

14. Rachels, *The Elements of Moral Philosphy*, 117, 122–23. Rachels's discussion is based on Kant's "On a Supposed Right to Lie from Altruistic Motives," in Lewis White Beck, trans., *Critique of Practical Reason and Other Writings in Moral Philosophy* (Chicago: University of Chicago Press, 1949). Because I have been unable to locate this volume, I follow Rachels's account.

15. Something like the views expressed in the last two sentences, I think, is contained in the essays "The Tower of Babel" and "Political Education" in Michael Oakeshott, *Rationalism in Politics and Other Essays* (New York: Basic Books, 1962).

16. However, this argument cannot apply to the proposals made by Richard Lippke, who urges various social changes through which people might be rendered more autonomous and less susceptible to advertising. See chapter 1. Lippke's proposals, I think, fail for a different reason. If manipulative advertising is a relatively weak force, who needs them? In addition, Lippke's whole argument rests on empirical premises that are very controversial and that he does little or nothing to substantiate.

17. The FTC's authority to regulate "unfair" acts or practices was briefly discussed in chapter 1.

18. However, although such studies probably do not predominate, it is worth noting that some researchers doubt whether cigarette advertising significantly influences teens' decision to smoke. See, for example, Colin McDonald, "Children, Smoking, and Advertising: What Does the Research Really Tell Us?," *International Journal of Advertising* 12 (1993): 279–87; George P. Moschis, "Point of View: Cigarette Advertising and Young Smokers," *Journal of Advertising Research* 29, no. 2 (April-May 1989): 51–60. Also, even those who believe the contrary admit that there are many other reasons why teens smoke; see, for example, "Hooked on Tobacco: The Teen Epidemic," *Consumer Reports* 60, no. 3, March 1995, 142–47.

19. John Kenneth Galbraith, "Economics and Advertising: Exercise in Denial," *Advertising Age*, 9 November 1988, 81.

20. Ibid.

21. Ibid. Galbraith had made the same point in *The Affluent Society*, where he said that "[advertising] outlays must be integrated with the theory of consumer demand. They are too big to be ignored." John Kenneth Galbraith, *The Affluent Society* (Boston: Houghton Mifflin, 1958), 156.

22. See, for example, Michael Schudson, *Advertising, the Uneasy Persuasion: Its Dubious Impact on American Society* (n.p.: Basic Books, 1986), xiii–xiv. See also the quotations from Schudson in chapter 4.

23. Ibid., chap. 7.

24. Ibid., 232.

25. See, for example, Daniel Little, *Varieties of Social Explanation: An Introduction to the Philosophy of Social Science* (Boulder, Colo.: Westview Press, 1991), chap. 9; Alexander Rosenberg, *Philosophy of Social Science*, 2d ed. (Boulder, Colo.: Westview Press, 1995), chaps. 5–6. Here, holism is the view that "social facts," such as groups and societies, really exist as entities in themselves. Holism sometimes is allied with functionalist views in which society's major institutions (such as advertising, perhaps) fulfill certain functions within the entity which is the social whole. Methodological individualism, on the other hand, asserts that individual human beings are the primary units of social explanation, and that a group or a society is the aggregate of the individuals who form it and nothing more. To holists, by contrast, groups are real entities with attributes not present among the people who make up the group.

26. Julian L. Simon, *Issues in the Economics of Advertising* (Urbana: University of Illinois Press, 1970), 284.

SELECTED BIBLIOGRAPHY

"Advertising and the Corrupting of America." *Business and Society Review* 41 (Spring 1982): 64–69.

Albion, Mark S., and Paul W. Farris. *The Advertising Controversy: Evidence on the Economic Effects of Advertising.* Boston: Auburn House, 1981.

Alexander, M. Wayne, and Ben Judd, Jr. "Do Nudes in Ads Enhance Brand Recall?" *Journal of Advertising Research* 18, no. 1 (1979): 47–50.

Arrington, Robert L. "Advertising and Behavior Control." *Journal of Business Ethics* 1 (1982): 3–12.

Baker, Michael J., and Gilbert A. Churchill, Jr. "The Impact of Physically Attractive Models on Advertising Evaluations." *Journal of Marketing Research* 14 (November 1977): 538–55.

Baran, Paul A., and Paul M. Sweezy. "Theses on Advertising." *Science and Society* 28 (Winter 1964): 20–30.

Barry, Thomas E., and Daniel J. Howard. "A Review and Critique of the Hierarchy of Effects in Advertising." *International Journal of Advertising* 9 (1990): 121–35.

Beatty, Sharon E., and Del I. Hawkins. "Subliminal Stimulation: Some New Data and Interpretation." *Journal of Advertising* 18, no. 3 (1989): 4–8.

Beauchamp, Tom L. "Manipulative Advertising." *Business and Professional Ethics Journal* 3 (1984): 1–22.

Belch, Michael A., Barbro E. Holgerson, George E. Belch, and Jerry Koppman. "Psychophysical and Cognitive Responses to Sex in Advertising." *Advances in Consumer Research* 9 (1981): 424–27.

Belk, Russell W., and Richard W. Pollay. "Images of Ourselves: The Good Life in Twentieth Century Advertising." *Journal of Consumer Research* 11 (March 1985): 887–97.

Benn, Stanley I. "Freedom and Persuasion." *Australasian Journal of Philosophy* 45 (1967): 259–75.

Borden, Neil H. *The Economic Effects of Advertising*. Chicago: Richard D. Irwin, 1942.

Braybrooke, David. "Skepticism of Wants, and Certain Subversive Effects of Corporations on American Values." In *Ethical Theory and Business*, edited by Tom L. Beauchamp and Norman E. Bowie, 502–8. Englewood Cliffs, N.J.: Prentice-Hall, 1979.

Buttle, Francis. "What Do People Do with Advertising?" *International Journal of Advertising* 10 (1991): 95–110.

Caballero, Marjorie J., James R. Lumpkin, and Charles S. Madden. "Using Physical Attractiveness as an Advertising Tool: An Empirical Test of the Attraction Phenomenon." *Journal of Advertising Research* 29, no. 4 (August-September 1989): 16–22.

Capps, Pamela Marsden. "Rock on Trial: Subliminal Message Liability." *Columbia Business Law Review* 1 (1991): 27–50.

Chestnut, Robert W., Charles C. LaChance, and Amy Lubitz. "The 'Decorative' Female Model: Sexual Stimuli and the Recognition of Advertisements." *Journal of Advertising* 6 (Fall 1977): 11–14.

Christman, John. "Autonomy and Personal History." *Canadian Journal of Philosophy* 21, no. 1 (March 1991): 1–24.

———. "Constructing the Inner Citadel: Recent Work on the Concept of Autonomy." *Ethics* 99 (October 1988): 109–24.

———, ed. *The Inner Citadel: Essays on Individual Autonomy*. New York: Oxford University Press, 1989.

Clark, Eric. *The Want Makers. The World of Advertising: How They Make You Buy*. New York: Viking Penguin, 1988.

Crisp, Roger. "Persuasive Advertising, Autonomy, and the Creation of Desire." *Journal of Business Ethics* 6 (1987): 413–18.

Cuperfain, Ronnie, and T. K. Clarke. "A New Perspective of Subliminal Perception." *Journal of Advertising* 14, no. 1 (1985): 36–41.

Davis, Robert H, and John A. Welsch. "A New Viewpoint on Nudes in Advertising and Brand Recall." *International Journal of Advertising* 2 (1983): 141–46.

De Fleur, Melvin L., and Robert M. Petranoff. "A Televised Test of Subliminal Persuasion." *Public Opinion Quarterly* 23 (Summer 1959): 168–80.

Doyle, Peter. "Economic Aspects of Advertising: A Survey." *Economic Journal* 78 (1968): 570–602.

Dudley, Sid C. "Subliminal Advertising: What Is the Controversy About?" *Akron Business and Economic Review* 18, no. 2 (Summer 1987): 6–18.

Durand, Richard M., and Zarrel V. Lambert. "Alienation and Criticisms of Advertising." *Journal of Advertising* 14, no. 3 (1985): 9–17.

Dworkin, Gerald. "The Concept of Autonomy." In *The Inner Citadel: Essays on Individual Autonomy*, edited by John Christman, 54–62. New York: Oxford University Press, 1989.

Ekelund, Robert B., Jr., and David S. Saurman. *Advertising and the Market Process: A Modern Economic View*. San Francisco: Pacific Research Institute for Public Policy, 1988.

Ewen, Stuart. *Captains of Consciousness: Advertising and the Social Roots of the Consumer Culture*. New York: McGraw-Hill, 1976. First paperback reprint, 1977.

Flandin, M. P., E. Martin, and L. P. Simkin. "Advertising Effectiveness Research: A Survey of Agencies, Clients, and Conflicts." *International Journal of Advertising* 11 (1992): 203–14.

Frankfurt, Harry G. "Freedom of Will and the Concept of a Person." In *The Inner Citadel: Essays on Individual Autonomy*, edited by John Christman, 63–76. New York: Oxford University Press, 1989.

Gable, Myron, Henry T. Wilkens, Lynn Harris, and Richard Feinberg. "An Evaluation of Subliminally Embedded Sexual Stimuli in Graphics." *Journal of Advertising* 16, no. 1 (1987): 26–30.

Galbraith, John Kenneth. *The Affluent Society*. Boston: Houghton Mifflin, 1957.

———. "Economics and Advertising: Exercise in Denial." *Advertising Age*, 9 November 1988, 81.

———. *The New Industrial State*. Boston: Houghton Mifflin, 1967.

———. "A Review of a Review." *Public Interest* 9 (Fall 1967): 109–18.

Gold, Philip. *Advertising, Politics, and American Culture: From Salesmanship to Therapy*. New York: Paragon House, 1987.

Goldman, Alan H. *The Moral Foundations of Professional Ethics*. Totowa, N.J.: Rowman & Littlefield, 1980; 2d printing, 1982.

Greyser, Stephen A., and Raymond A. Bauer. "Americans and Advertising: Thirty Years of Public Opinion." *Public Opinion Quarterly* 30 (Spring 1966): 69–77.

Haber, Ralph Norman. "Public Attitudes regarding Subliminal Advertising." *Public Opinion Quarterly* 23 (Summer 1959): 291–93.

Haberstroh, Jack. "Can't Ignore Subliminal Ad Charges: Adfolk Laugh, but Students Listen." *Advertising Age*, 17 September 1984, 3, 42–43.

Hare, R. M. "Commentary." *Business and Professional Ethics Journal* 3 (1984): 23–28.

Hawkins, Del. "The Effects of Subliminal Stimulation on Drive Level and Brand Performance." *Journal of Marketing Research* 7 (August 1970): 322–26.

Hayek, F. A. "The *Non Sequitur* of the 'Dependence Effect.'" *Southern Economic Journal* 27 (1961): 346–48.

Heilbroner, Robert L. "The Demand for the Supply Side." *New York Review of Books*, 11 June 1981, 37–41.

Helgesen, Thorolf. "The Rationality of Advertising Decisions: Conceptual Issues and Some Empirical Findings from a Norwegian Study." *Journal of Advertising Research* 32, no. 6 (November/December 1992): 22–30.

Hill, Thomas E., Jr. "The Kantian Conception of Autonomy." In *The Inner Citadel: Essays on Individual Autonomy*, edited by John Christman, 91–105. New York: Oxford University Press, 1989.

Hung, C. L., and Douglas C. West. "Advertising Budgeting Methods in Canada, the UK and the USA." *International Journal of Advertising* 10 (1991): 239–50.

Jacobson, Robert, and Franco M. Nicosia. "Advertising and Public Policy: The Macroeconomic Effects of Advertising." *Journal of Marketing Research* 18 (February 1981): 29–38.

Jones, John P. "Advertising: Strong Force or Weak Force? Two Views an Ocean Apart." *International Journal of Advertising* 9 (1990): 233–46.

Kant, Immanuel. *Groundwork of the Metaphysic of Morals*. Translated and edited by H. J. Paton. New York: Harper Torchbooks, 1964.

Kelly, J. Steven. "Subliminal Embeds in Print Advertising: A Challenge to Advertising Ethics." *Journal of Advertising* 8 (1979): 20–24.

Key, Wilson Bryan. *Subliminal Seduction: Ad Media's Manipulation of a Not So Innocent America*. Englewood Cliffs, N.J.: Prentice-Hall, 1973. New York: Penguin Group paperback reprint, 1981.

Kiesel, Diane. "Subliminal Seduction: Old Ideas, New Worries." *American Bar Association Journal* 70 (July 1984): 25–27.

Kilbourne, William E., Scott Painton, and Danny Ridley. "The Effect of Sexual Embedding on Responses to Magazine Advertisements." *Journal of Advertising* 14, no. 2 (1985): 48–56.

Kirkpatrick, Jerry. *In Defense of Advertising: Arguments from Reason, Ethical Egoism, and Laissez-Faire Capitalism*. Westport, Conn.: Quorum Books, 1994.

———. "A Philosophic Defense of Advertising." *Journal of Advertising* 15, no. 2 (1986): 42–48, 64.

Krutch, Joseph Wood. *Human Nature and the Human Condition*. New York: Random House, 1959.

Lantos, Geoffrey P. "Advertising: Looking Glass or Molder of the Masses?" *Journal of Public Policy and Marketing* 6 (1987): 104–28.

Levitt, Theodore. "The Morality (?) of Advertising." *Harvard Business Review* (July-August 1970): 84–92.

Lippke, Richard L. "Advertising and the Social Conditions of Autonomy." *Business and Professional Ethics Journal* 8, no. 4 (1990): 35–58.

————. *Radical Business Ethics*. Lanham, Md: Rowman & Littlefield, 1995.

MacIntyre, Alasdair. *After Virtue: A Study in Moral Theory*. Notre Dame, Ind.: University of Notre Dame Press, 1981; 2d ed., 1984.

————. *A Short History of Ethics*. New York: Macmillan Co., 1966. Paperback reprint, Collier Books, 1966.

Marris, Robin. "Galbraith, Solow, and the Truth about Corporations." *Public Interest* 11 (Spring 1968): 37–46.

Mixon, Franklin G., Jr. "The Role of Advertising in the Market Process: A Survey." *International Journal of Advertising* 13 (1994): 15–23.

Moore, Timothy E. "Subliminal Advertising: What You See Is What You Get." *Journal of Marketing* 46 (Spring 1982): 38–47.

Murray, Hugh. "Advertising's Effect on Sales—Proven or Just Assumed?" *International Journal of Advertising* 5 (1986): 15–36.

Norris, Vincent P. "The Economic Effects of Advertising: A Review of the Literature." *Current Issues and Research in Advertising* 2 (1984): 39–134.

Ogilvy, David. *Confessions of an Advertising Man*. New York: Macmillan Co., 1963. Atheneum paperback reprint, 1987.

————. *Ogilvy on Advertising*. New York: Random House, 1983. Vintage Books paperback reprint, 1985.

O'Toole, John. *The Trouble with Advertising*. New York: Times Books, 1985.

Packard, Vance. *The Hidden Persuaders*. New York: David McKay, 1957.

Phillips, Michael J. "The Inconclusive Ethical Case against Manipulative Advertising." *Business & Professional Ethics Journal* 13, no. 4 (1994): 31–64.

Poiesz, Theo B. C., and Henry S. J. Robben. "Individual Reactions to Advertising: Theoretical and Methodological Developments." *International Journal of Advertising* 13 (1994): 25–53.

Pollay, Richard W., and Banwari Mittal. "Here's the Beef: Factors, Determinants, and Segments in Consumer Criticism of Advertising." *Journal of Marketing* 57 (July 1993): 99–114.

Preston, Ivan L. *The Tangled Web They Weave: Truth, Falsity, and Advertisers*. Madison: University of Wisconsin Press, 1994.

Quarles, Rebecca Colwell, and Leo W. Jeffres. "Advertising and National Consumption: A Path Analytic Re-Examination of the Galbraithian Argument." *Journal of Advertising* 12, no. 2 (1983): 4–13, 33.

Rachels, James. *The Elements of Moral Philosophy*. New York: McGraw-Hill, 1986: 2d ed., 1993.

Reid, Leonard N., and Lawrence C. Soley. "Another Look at the 'Decorative' Female Model: The Recognition of Visual and Verbal Ad Components." *Current Issues and Research in Advertising 1981*, 123–33.

———. "Decorative Models and the Readership of Magazine Ads." *Journal of Advertising Research* 23 (April-May 1983): 27–32.

———. "Generalized and Personalized Attitudes toward Advertising's Social and Economic Effects." *Journal of Advertising* 11, no. 3 (1982): 3–7.

Reisman, David A. *Galbraith and Market Capitalism*. New York: New York University Press, 1980.

Rogers, Martha, and Christine A. Seiler. "The Answer Is No: A National Survey of Advertising Industry Practitioners and Their Clients about Whether They Use Subliminal Advertising." *Journal of Advertising Research* 34, no. 2 (March-April 1984): 36–45.

Rose, Alvin W. "Motivation Research and Subliminal Advertising." *Social Research* 25 (Fall 1958): 271–84.

Ross, W. D. *The Right and the Good*. Oxford, England: Oxford University Press, 1930. Paperback reprint. Indianapolis: Hackett Publishing, 1988.

Saegert, Joel. "Another Look at Subliminal Perception." *Journal of Advertising Research* 19, no. 1 (1979): 55–57.

Santilli, Paul C. "The Informative and Persuasive Functions of Advertising: A Moral Appraisal." *Journal of Business Ethics* 2 (1983): 27–33.

Schudson, Michael. *Advertising, the Uneasy Persuasion: Its Dubious Impact on American Society*. N.p.: Basic Books, 1984; paperback reprint, 1986.

Sciglimpaglia, Donald, Michael A. Belch, and Richard F. Cain. "Demographic and Cognitive Factors Influencing Viewers' Evaluations of 'Sexy' Advertisements." *Advances in Consumer Research* 6 (1979): 62–65.

Severn, Jessica, George E. Belch, and Michael A. Belch. "The Effects of Sexual and Non-Sexual Advertising Appeals and Information Level on Cognitive Processing and Communication Effectiveness." *Journal of Advertising* 19, no. 1 (1990): 14–22.

Silverglate, Scot. "Subliminal Perception and the First Amendment: Yelling Fire in a Crowded Mind?" *University of Miami Law Review* 44 (1990): 1243–81.

Simon, Julian L. *Issues in the Economics of Advertising.* Urbana: University of Illinois Press, 1970.

Soley, Lawrence, and Gary Kurzbard. "Sex in Advertising: A Comparison of 1964 and 1984 Magazine Advertisements." *Journal of Advertising* 15, no. 3 (1986): 46–54, 64.

Solow, Robert M. "The New Industrial State *or* Son of Affluence." *Public Interest* 9 (Fall 1967): 100–108.

——— . "A Rejoinder." *Public Interest* 9 (Fall 1967): 118–19.

——— . "The Truth Further Refined: A Comment on Marris." *Public Interest* 11 (Spring 1968): 47–52.

Sturgess, Brian T. "Dispelling the Myth: The Effects of Total Advertising Expenditure on Aggregate Consumption." *Journal of Advertising* 1 (1982): 201–12. This journal was later renamed the *International Journal of Advertising.*

Thalberg, Irving. "Hierarchical Analyses of Unfree Action." In *The Inner Citadel: Essays on Individual Autonomy,* edited by John Christman, 123–36. New York: Oxford University Press, 1989.

Waide, John. "The Making of Self and World in Advertising." *Journal of Business Ethics* 6 (1987): 73–79.

Zanot, Eric J., J. David Pincus, and E. Joseph Lamp. "Public Perceptions of Subliminal Advertising." *Journal of Advertising* 12, no. 1 (1983): 39–45.

INDEX

About the Author

MICHAEL J. PHILLIPS is Professor of Business Law at Indiana University's School of Business. He holds a J.D. degree from Columbia University, and LL.M. and S.J.D. degrees from George Washington University. A former editor-in-chief of the *American Business Law Journal*, he has authored more than 40 scholarly articles and coauthored two business law texts. He is also author of *The Dilemmas of Individualism: Status, Liberty, and American Constitutional Law* (Greenwood, 1983).